SPC SIMPLIFIED

Practical Steps to Quality

SECOND EDITION

SPC SIMPLIFIED

Practical Steps to Quality

SECOND EDITION

ROBERT T. AMSDEN

HOWARD E. BUTLER

DAVIDA M. AMSDEN

PRODUCTIVITY

Productivity, Inc.
P.O. Box 13390
Portland, Oregon 97213-0390
United States of America
Telephone: 503-235-0600
Telefax: 503-235-0909
E-mail: info@productivityinc.com

Printed in the United States of America

Library of Congress Cataloging-in-Publication Data

Amsden, Robert T.
    SPC simplified : practical steps to quality / Robert T. Amsden, Howard E. Butler, Davida M. Amsden – 2nd ed.
        p.   cm.
    Included index.
    ISBN 0-527-76340-3 (alk. paper)
    1. Quality control—Statistical methods.   I. Butler, Howard E.   II. Amsden, Davida M.
III. Title.
TS156.A47   1998
658.5′62—dc21   97-47363
                                                                                              CIP

05 04 03 02   7 6 5 4

Contents

Preface

Statistical process control, a set of procedures using statistical techniques, has been used in industry for decades. However, widespread use of statistical process control declined throughout the 1950s, 1960s, and 1970s. The emphasis of most manufacturing organizations during this period was typically on the quantity of production and not on the quality of the products or services being produced. In many cases, the demand for products was greater than the ability to produce. Few managers felt the need to use any techniques designed to improve quality or even maintain a high level of quality in the products they manufactured. Statistical process control techniques were used mainly to help solve severe production problems. Quality engineers were ready with statistical problem-solving techniques, but by and large, production managers neither wanted nor needed the techniques.

Then, in the late 1970s a serious problem entered the American industrial scene. Markets were becoming global. Companies encountered competition from manufacturers located all over the world. This globalization created a drive for increased efficiency in the manufacture of products. The United States had long been the world's largest producer of manufactured goods. Previously, there was very little competition from other countries. It became apparent however, that other countries had now acquired the ability to produce many products at a lower cost and at better quality than similar products being produced in the United States.

Many manufacturing operations were studied in various companies around the world. Visitors to manufacturing plants in Japan reported that the competition outperformed the United States by working harder for less money. Others reported that the Japanese used something they called quality circles to get the people who worked in the same area on the production floor to work more effectively and produce better quality products. Neither of these answered the problem.

One thing learned was that in Japan many people on the production floor were making decisions concerning their operations as a normal part of their daily tasks. By contrast, workers in the United States had very little control and were seldom allowed to make decisions concerning their operations. In theory, management took all responsibility for the quality of the product. On rare occasions operators or line supervisors were asked to collect information or data and record it on a chart, but a quality engineer held the "secrets" of statistical process control. Even in such a situation, when the product did not meet standards, managers generally blamed the poor quality on lack of care on the part of the production operators.

Starting in the 1970s and especially during the 1980s, the production of goods and services has undergone drastic changes in the United States. In light of the global competition, international standards have been established stressing the importance of the customer. These standards are organizational guidelines for companies who expect to compete not only in their traditional marketing areas but in world markets. Market areas sometimes are very local, but more and more companies are expanding their area of business interests. Companies are finding that they are required to be certified as meeting the international standard. These standards are known as the ISO 9000 series of guidelines. They require, among other activities, the use of statistical process control in the manufacturing processes. Certification to the standard is a legal requirement to do business in many countries around the world. It is rapidly becoming a requirement of original equipment manufacturers in the United States. In fact, the three large automotive manufacturers in the United States have published their own standard, QS-9000, which adds specific requirements to the ISO 9001 standard. Certification of conformance to QS-9000 will be mandatory in the near future if a company wants to be a supplier to any of the three large manufacturers.

Good managers have learned over the years that everyone is responsible for maintaining quality. Associates on the production floor are encouraged to monitor their operations and take corrective action when necessary. Managers have realized that if so much is expected of the production floor workers, they must be provided with the training, tools, and environment to do their jobs well. Companies have learned that the best way to become efficient and competitive is to prevent defects. In turn, production associates are expected to take responsibility for their operations. If the people who "make it happen" on the production floor are to be successful, they must be supplied with the necessary tools and know-how to do their job.

After many years of working to solve quality problems in all kinds of processes and in companies of every size, we were convinced that a book was needed for everyone who has a responsibility to produce a product or service that meets the customer's wants, needs, and expectations. We have written this book mainly for production associates, set-up people, inspectors, and first line supervisors. Manufacturing managers and newcomers to quality engineering and quality improvement will also find it useful.

In this book you will learn how to develop and use the statistical techniques that are used most often to improve quality. These tools of quality are based on a number of mathematical principles. You don't need to know or understand the principles to use the techniques any more than you need to know how a television set works to enjoy your favorite program. The techniques you will use most often, whether it be in group problem solving activities or in monitoring and improving the quality of a production operation, are very simple and require only a little arithmetic. You can usually find the numbers you need in a specially prepared table, or you can make simple calculations with pencil and paper or a pocket calculator.

SPC Simplified has grown out of the experiences we have shared with many people over the years. The insights we gained working with production associates, inspectors, supervisors, engineers, managers, and customers made this book possible. We developed the book from a practical point of view, using examples based on real situations and working with people who have had the same problems that you face every day on the production floor. We thank all those people for their contributions.

We also wish to acknowledge the following: in Module 2 the bucket of plastic-coated chips is based on the work of the late Dr. Walter Shewhart; in Module 3 the late Harold Dodge told the story of the munitions factory; the late Dr. W. Edwards Deming gave the account of the paper coating process. Thanks to Mr. Stewart Schofe for the data for the individual and range chart in Module 3. We thank the American Society for Quality for allowing us to use the forms for the charts discussed in Module 3. Our thanks also go to Sid Rubinstein for allowing us to use the shaft movement data in Module 2.

The following people read portions of the manuscript: Joan and Garth Borton, Phyllis Cole, Bob Coon, Rick Eggers, Craig Kottke, Janice Losiert, Dave Loudner, Bob Morrison, Stephanie and Bill Paris, Drifty Miller, Stew Schofe, and Bernie Williams. Our thanks to them for their helpful suggestions and encouragement.

We give grateful acknowledgement to my wife, Jean, for her useful comments and suggestions.

Finally, we thank the editor, Karen Feinberg, who so skillfully shaped the ideas of three technical-minded authors into a very readable book.

H.E.B.
R.T.A.
D.M.A.

Introduction

This is a "how-to" book. In it you will learn how to use statistical techniques to monitor the quality of parts produced in manufacturing operations. These techniques can also be used in other ways, but in this book we will concentrate on manufacturing operations.

If you are involved in a manufacturing operation, you are trying constantly to make parts that meet the customer's requirements. You are also trying to make each part as much like the others as possible. To do these things you must gain and keep control of your operation.

To control the conditions of your operation you must be able to measure them. Over 100 years ago Lord Kelvin, an English scientist, said:

> "When you can measure what you are speaking about, and express it in numbers, you know something about it; but when you cannot express it in numbers, your knowledge is . . . unsatisfactory."

You can use calipers, gauges, or thermometers to measure a dimension, but statistical process control techniques will give you the tools to measure the performance of an operation and express it in numbers. By looking at the numbers you will know whether your operation is running smoothly or whether it needs to be adjusted. More important, you will learn to predict how well the operation will run in the future.

With the use of the simple statistical techniques discussed in this book, you will be able to measure the performance of operations both before and after corrective actions have been taken. This is true whether you are trying to bring an operation into control or to break through to a new, improved level of performance.

This book is divided into seven modules. At the beginning of each module you will find a list of the new terms used in that module. These terms will be explained as you read. For your convenience, all the new terms are listed and explained again in a glossary at the end of the book.

Module 1 gives the basic ideas or principles behind statistical control techniques. These principles are based on mathematics, but we will not ask you to get involved in mathematics. All you need to do is accept the basic principles and learn how to apply them in your job.

Module 2 deals with frequency histograms and checksheets. These are the simplest of the statistical techniques you will use. In fact, you may already be familiar with them. Histograms are a popular, easy way of picturing the variations you find when you measure a dimension of a part. You will find that many quality problems can be solved by using frequency histograms. Checksheets are useful in analyzing data that can not be measured.

Variables charts are covered in Module 3. These charts use the same type of measurements that are used in frequency histograms, but in a different way. The statistical techniques used to monitor and control these measurements are the most powerful and useful techniques you will learn here. They can tell you the most about the variation in a product with the smallest sample.

Module 4 deals with attributes, a different kind of quality measurement. In the language of quality control, an attribute is a measure of quality that can be stated as "good" or "bad." A part is defective or it is not. It is accepted or rejected by a "go/no-go" gauge. This type of inspection result is not usually regarded as a dimension, but the statistical techniques discussed in Module 4 will show you how to assign numbers to the results of attribute inspections. Once you can assign a number to your information, you can use control charts to maintain control of the quality.

Module 5 discusses capability analysis. If you intend to control the quality of your products, you should know the capability of your processes and operations—that is, how well they can meet the customer's requirements. Some of the same techniques you use to control your operations can also be used to measure capability.

The "tools of quality" are useful not only to improve the quality of products and processes, but also to identify the causes of problems in your work area and solve them. Module 6 shows some problem-solving techniques. Even though they may not fall under the heading of statistical quality control, these techniques are becoming more and more important in modern quality control systems.

Module 7 explains the concepts of total quality management and continuous improvement, and discusses how the SPC and problem-solving tools may be used to help a TQM program.

At the end of Modules 2, 3, 4, 5, and 6 you will find practice problems. These problems are typical applications of the "tools of quality" and will give you a chance to use your statistical techniques. The solutions to the problems will be found in a separate section at the end of the book. We suggest that you pay special attention to the solutions—they will confirm what you learned in the modules and explain the ideas behind the problems.

1 Basic Principles

NEW TERMS IN MODULE 1
(in order of appearance)

frequency distribution	*average and range chart*
normal distribution curve	*average*
fishbone diagram	$\overline{X}$
chance causes or system causes	*range*
assignable causes or special causes	*R*
stable process	*upper control limit*
histogram	*lower control limit*
process spread	*out of control*
standard deviation	*in control*
sigma (σ)	*percent defective chart*
control limits	*management team solvable problem*
variables chart	*floor solvable problem*
attribute chart	

Have you ever been sick enough to be confined to a hospital bed, with a nurse coming around and taking your temperature, your pulse, and your blood pressure? If you have, you already know something about statistical process control. The readings that the nurse records on a chart are like the readings you will record on charts on your job. When you're sick, the doctor wants to know what is normal about you and what is not. With this information he will take the right steps to make you well.

Jobs can get sick, just like people. Like the doctor, you need a picture of how the job is performing. You need a running record of what is happening on your job to tell when it is sick and when you must take action to make it well.

Just as the doctor uses temperature and pulse charts to keep track of your condition, you will use control charts to monitor the condition of your job. When properly used, control charts will tell you three things:

1. When you're doing something you shouldn't.
2. When you're not doing something you should.
3. When you're doing things right.

In short, control charts will indicate how "well" your job is. They'll show you:

1. When the job is running satisfactorily.

or

2. When something has gone wrong which needs correcting.

Control charts will provide you with "stop" and "go" signals. They'll enable you to "point with pride" or "view with alarm" (and look for the cause of the trouble!).

To use these statistical tools effectively and profitably, you must understand some of the basic principles underlying statistical process control techniques. You may be one of the many people who feel uncomfortable when the word "statistics" is mentioned, but in using statistical process control techniques, you don't need to get deeply involved in mathematics. All you need to do is learn a few basic principles. An understanding of these principles will make it easier for you to understand and use the control chart techniques presented in this book.

All the ideas and techniques in this book are based on six principles. The first principle is:

1. No two things are exactly alike.

Experience has shown that things are never exactly alike. When two things seem to be alike, we often say that they're "like two peas in a pod." But when we open a pea pod and take a close look at the peas, we see slight differences. The peas are different in size, shape, or freedom from blemish. If you're concerned with manufacturing parts, you know that no two manufactured parts are exactly alike either. In one way or another, the parts will be slightly different in size, shape, or finish.

We often want to make parts interchangeable. To do this, we want to make them identical, but no two things are exactly alike. Therefore, we want to keep the variation between parts as small as possible. To help ourselves do this, we use a second basic principle:

2. Variation in a product or process can be measured.

Some variation is normal to your job, and this variation tends to increase. If you make no effort to measure or monitor the variation normally expected in your job, you could find yourself in a lot of trouble. That is, all processes that are not monitored "go downhill." Therefore, it's necessary to measure the output of any process or operation to know when trouble is brewing.

When you check the output of a process or operation, you will quickly notice one feature. This feature provides a basis for the third principle:

3. Things vary according to a definite pattern.

If you want to see this pattern take shape, all you need to do is record the measurements of a dimension on parts from one of your operations on

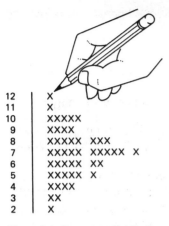

```
12 |  X
11 |  X
10 |  XXXXX
 9 |  XXXX
 8 |  XXXXX  XXX
 7 |  XXXXX  XXXXX  X
 6 |  XXXXX  XX
 5 |  XXXXX  X
 4 |  XXXX
 3 |  XX
 2 |  X
```

Figure 1-1. Frequency distribution.

```
12 |  X
11 |  X
10 |  XXXXX
 9 |  XXXX
 8 |  XXXXX  XXX
 7 |  XXXX  XXXXX  X
 6 |  XXXXX  XX
 5 |  XXXXX  X
 4 |  XXXX
 3 |  XX
 2 |  X
```

Figure 1-2. Bell-shaped curve.

Figure 1-3. Approximate percentages of different measurements within the normal distribution curve.

your job. If you record them in tally form, you will see a pattern begin to form after you have measured and recorded several parts.

An easy way to demonstrate this principle is to roll a pair of dice fifty or more times and record the total number of spots that come up on each throw. After a while you will see a pattern begin to form. This pattern is sometimes called a *frequency distribution*, and is shown in Figure 1-1.

A frequency distribution curve is formed by enclosing the tally marks in a curved line. This curve shows that there are more measurements or numbers in the middle and fewer as you go away from the middle. As you can see, the curve is shaped like a bell. (See Figure 1-2.)

A frequency distribution curve will repeat itself whenever you take groups of measurements. This fact leads to the fourth basic principle:

4. Whenever things of the same kind are measured, a large group of the measurements will tend to cluster around the middle.

Most measurements fall close to the middle. In fact, mathematicians can make a fairly accurate prediction of the percentage of measurements in various sections of the frequency distribution curve. This prediction is shown in Figure 1-3.

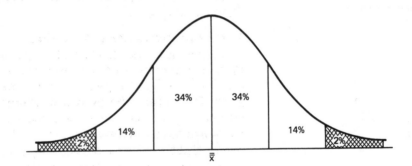

How can we understand this curve in a practical way?

- If we measure each piece that comes from a machine or operation and make a tally of the measurements, we will eventually have a curve similar to the one in Figure 1-3.
- If we don't measure each piece, but merely reach into a tote pan, grab a handful of pieces, and measure them, the chances are that 68 out of 100 measurements (34% + 34%) will fall within the two middle sections of the graph in Figure 1-3.
- The chances are that 28 out of 100 pieces (14% + 14%) will fall into the next two sections, one on each side of the middle sections.
- Finally, the chances are that 4 out of 100 of the pieces (2% + 2%) will fall into the two outside sections.

This may sound a little complicated, but don't worry about it. Just remember that measurements *do* tend to cluster around the middle, as shown by the bell shape of the curve. This particular curve is known as the *normal distribution curve.*

All of this brings us to the fifth basic principle:

5. It's possible to determine the shape of the distribution curve for parts produced by any process.

By making a tally or frequency distribution of the pieces produced by a process, we can compare it to the blueprint specification for that dimension. In this way we can learn what the process *is doing*, as compared to what we *want* it to do. If we don't like the comparison, we may have to change the process or the blueprint.

CAUSES OF VARIATION

The source of variation in a process can be found in one or more of five areas. These are the materials, the machines, the methods, the environment, and the people.

All variation in a product is caused by variation in these five areas, as illustrated in Figure 1-4.

Figure 1-4. Fishbone diagram.

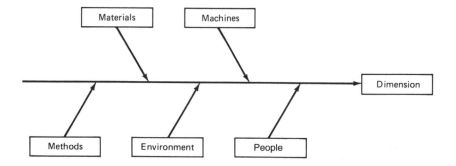

The diagram in Figure 1-4 is sometimes called a *fishbone diagram*, which is very useful for searching out causes of trouble in a process. This will be discussed in detail in a later module.

The variation seen when measuring pieces from a process is the result of two types of causes. In this book we will call them *chance causes* and *assignable causes.* (Some people call them *system causes* and *special causes.*) Chance causes are those that are continuously active in the process and are built in as part of the process. Assignable causes are those we *can* more easily do something about. They can be detected because they are not always active in the process.

If the variations in the product (caused by materials, machines, methods, environment, and people) are due to chance causes alone, the product will vary in a normal, predictable manner. The process is said to be *stable.* We want to know how the product varies under normal, stable conditions—that is, when only chance causes are contributing to the variations. Then, if any unusual change occurs, we can see this change in our normal distribution curve. We can say that it's the result of an assignable cause and not due to chance causes alone.

When assignable causes are present, the curve will be distorted and lose its normal bell shape. Figure 1-5 shows some typical distortions to the normal distribution curve.

Figure 1-5. Distortions of the normal curve.

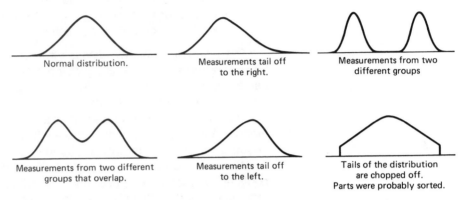

Normal distribution.

Measurements tail off to the right.

Measurements from two different groups

Measurements from two different groups that overlap.

Measurements tail off to the left.

Tails of the distribution are chopped off. Parts were probably sorted.

This brings us to the sixth basic principle:

6. Variations due to assignable causes tend to distort the normal distribution curve.

A frequency distribution is a tally of measurements that shows the number of times each measurement is included in the tally. The tally you saw in Figure 1-1, which was made by rolling dice, is a frequency distribution.

A frequency distribution helps us determine whether chance causes alone exist in a process or whether an assignable cause is also present. (We have statistical techniques that can detect when an assignable cause is present, and we will cover this subject later in the book.) Frequency distributions are a very good quality control tool because of their simplicity, and they are a very good way to illustrate the six basic principles.

These basic principles are the foundation for the tools of process control found in this book. Let's take another look at them before we move on.

1. NO TWO THINGS ARE EXACTLY ALIKE.

2. VARIATION IN A PRODUCT OR PROCESS CAN BE MEASURED.

3. THINGS VARY ACCORDING TO A DEFINITE PATTERN.

4. WHENEVER MANY THINGS OF THE SAME KIND ARE MEASURED, A LARGE GROUP OF THE MEASUREMENTS WILL TEND TO CLUSTER AROUND THE MIDDLE.

5. IT'S POSSIBLE TO DETERMINE THE SHAPE OF THE DISTRIBUTION CURVE FOR PARTS PRODUCED BY ANY PROCESS.

6. VARIATIONS DUE TO ASSIGNABLE CAUSES TEND TO DISTORT THE NORMAL DISTRIBUTION CURVE.

Figure 1-6. The six basic principles of statistical process control.

TOOLS OF QUALITY

To improve the quality of your products or to maintain current quality, you must have stable processes. The six basic principles we have discussed are the foundation for the statistical techniques you will use to answer these questions:

- Are we doing something we shouldn't?
- Are we failing to do something we should?
- Is the process operating satisfactorily, or has something gone wrong which needs correction?

The techniques we will discuss in this book can be used on a one-time basis to solve specific quality problems, but their greatest value comes from using them every day to continuously improve quality. They must become a way of life in your workplace.

Your goal should be to demonstrate that your job is operating in a stable manner. When the assignable causes have all been corrected, the variation in your products is due only to chance causes.

When your operation is stable, then—and *only* then—can you know with confidence what your quality level is. When your operation is stable, your productivity and quality are the best they can be with your process, until you reduce chance causes.

Statistical methods of process control give you a way to depict and improve quality through the use of these "tools of quality":

1. The histogram or frequency distribution.
2. The control chart.

THE HISTOGRAM OR FREQUENCY DISTRIBUTION

In many families it is a custom to have a picture taken each year. Just as a family picture is a snapshot of a group of people, the *histogram* is a "snapshot" of a group of parts from a manufacturing operation. It shows how a process is operating at a given time.

A histogram is simple to construct. It is nothing more than a frequency distribution put into block form. We will discuss this in more detail in the next module, but for now, let's just say we want a picture of the diameters of 100 bushings being machined on a lathe.

By the end of our check, the frequency distribution might be as it is shown in Figure 1-7. Putting this distribution into graphic form produces the histogram shown in Figure 1-8. Like the family picture, each histogram has a story to tell.

Three questions can be answered by a quick look at the pattern of the histogram:

1. Is the process producing parts to the bell-shaped curve?
2. Where is the process centered?
3. Is the process capable of meeting the engineering specification?

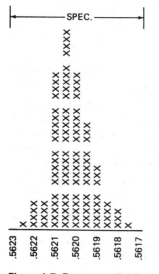

Figure 1-7. Frequency distribution.

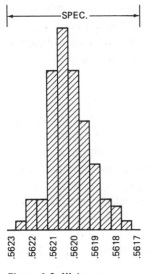

Figure 1-8. Histogram.

Let's review each of these questions in terms of the histogram in Figure 1-8.

1. Is the process producing parts to the bell-shaped curve?

   Because the histogram is roughly bell-shaped, then for practical applications we may say:
   a. The process appears "normal" and stable.
   b. Variations are generally due to chance causes.
   However, when the histogram is *not* roughly bell-shaped:
   a. The process is *not* "normal."
   b. Assignable causes are influencing the variations. In special cases a frequency distribution or histogram of measurements from a stable process will not match the normal curve, but in most manufacturing operations, measurements from a stable process will make a good match to the normal curve.

2. Where is the process centered?

   The average of the histogram and the specification midpoint are close together; therefore, the process is well centered.
   When the average of the histogram and the specification midpoint are far apart, then the process setting needs some adjustment.

3. Is the process capable of meeting the engineering specification?

   The spread of the process falls within the specification limits; therefore, the process is estimated to be capable of meeting the engineering specification.

Remember, the histogram is merely a snapshot of the process. If we take another set of data at another time, the picture may be different. However, the information we have on this process tells us that it is capable of meeting the engineering specification.

People in manufacturing often form opinions about the quality of the parts they are making based on far less information than we had in the example above. It is much wiser and safer to use a statistical technique, as we did, to see what the job is doing before we decide how good or how bad the parts are. Remember the old saying, "One picture is worth a thousand words." Few people can look at a set of jumbled-up data and see the same things they can see after the data have been organized in pictorial form.

Once you begin to think statistically about your job, you will find that you naturally want to get factual data and plot it in the appropriate form. With this method, you will make good decisions based on facts instead of giving opinions based on measurements from only a few pieces.

The *process spread* is determined by the curve it forms. When this curve is compared to the specification, we can tell when the process is making parts outside the specification. When the spread of the curve is wider than the specification, or when one tail of the curve goes outside the specification, we can estimate the number of pieces that fall outside the specification.

We will discuss this subject later in more detail, but a quick glance at the normal curve in Figure 1-9 will show that such a spread is possible. You will see this curve again later with the percentages stated more precisely than in this figure.

The curve in Figure 1-9 also shows *standard deviations.* The sections of the curve are labeled here with the symbol σ (*sigma*). This is the symbol for the standard deviation of the normal curve. The standard deviation is calculated mathematically and can be estimated in graphic form, but for now let's just say that it is a number that describes how the measurements cluster around the middle of the normal curve.

In Figure 1-9 a normal curve is compared to the specification; 2% of the pieces at each end, or 4%, will fall outside the specification. These sections of the curve are shaded in Figure 1-9.

Figure 1-9. Normal curve.

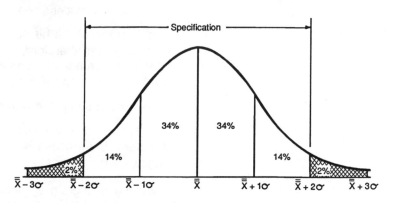

The frequency distribution and the histogram are used for such purposes as:

- Evaluating or checking processes.
- Indicating the need to take corrective action.
- Measuring the effects of corrective actions.
- Comparing machine performances.
- Comparing materials.
- Comparing vendors.

The frequency distribution and histogram are like a snapshot or a picture of a process at a particular time. Because of the time required to gather and record measurements for a frequency distribution, it is not practical to make more than a few distributions per day. Between distributions the process may change and many defective parts may be produced. Any action to correct the process after the defective parts have been produced is like locking the barn after the horse has been stolen.

For this reason frequency distributions or histograms are a good statistical tool for the purposes listed above, but they are not very good for monitoring the quality level of an ongoing manufacturing process. To monitor an ongoing process we have another useful tool—the control chart.

THE CONTROL CHART

If the frequency distribution is like a snapshot of a process, then a control chart is like a movie—a continuous series of smaller pictures. A control chart is a record of the results of periodic small inspections.

The control chart is a running record of the job—it tells us when the process is running smoothly and when it needs attention. You will find the control chart a very good tool to show when you have a problem and when you have corrected the problem successfully.

Some people think they can tell if a job is okay by looking at one or two pieces or by using some sort of mystical powers. Most of us find that we don't need mystical powers, but we do need *control limits* for our control charts.

Control limits are the boundaries on a control chart within which we can operate safely. These limits are based on past performance, and they show what we can expect from the process as long as nothing is changed. Each time we check the job, we compare the results to the control limits. If the results are within the limits—no problem. But if some of the points on a control chart fall outside the control limits, we know something has happened and the job is no longer operating normally. When this happens, we should take action to correct the situation.

In other words, control limits are warning signs that tell us:

1. When to take action.
2. When to leave the job alone. This doesn't necessarily mean you don't have a problem. It just means you must take a different tack to identify the problem.

There are two general types of control charts.

1. *Variables chart:*
   This type of chart is used where a dimension or characteristic is measured and the result is a number.
2. *Attribute chart:*
   This type of chart is used where a dimension or characteristic is not measured in numbers, but is considered either "good" or "bad."

VARIABLES CHARTS:
Average and Range Chart

The *average and range chart* is the most commonly used of the variables charts. Several other variables charts can be used, but we will use the average and range chart for illustration.

The example shown here is taken from a bushing grinding operation. The diameter has been measured and the results of the measurements have been recorded on the control chart. (See Figure 1-10.) The specified diameter for this bushing is .6250 inches ± .0003 inch. The chart shows that parts were measured and recorded hourly. The performance of this job is shown for an eight-hour period. Let's see how this chart was developed.

A production associate checked the job hourly by taking five pieces in a row from the operation and measuring the diameter of each.

On the chart, where it says "sample measurements," you will note that small numbers have been recorded. Obviously these small numbers are not the whole measurement the operator read from the gauge. This job is a precision grinding operation, requiring measurements to one-tenth of a thousandth of an inch.

Figure 1-10. Average and range chart.

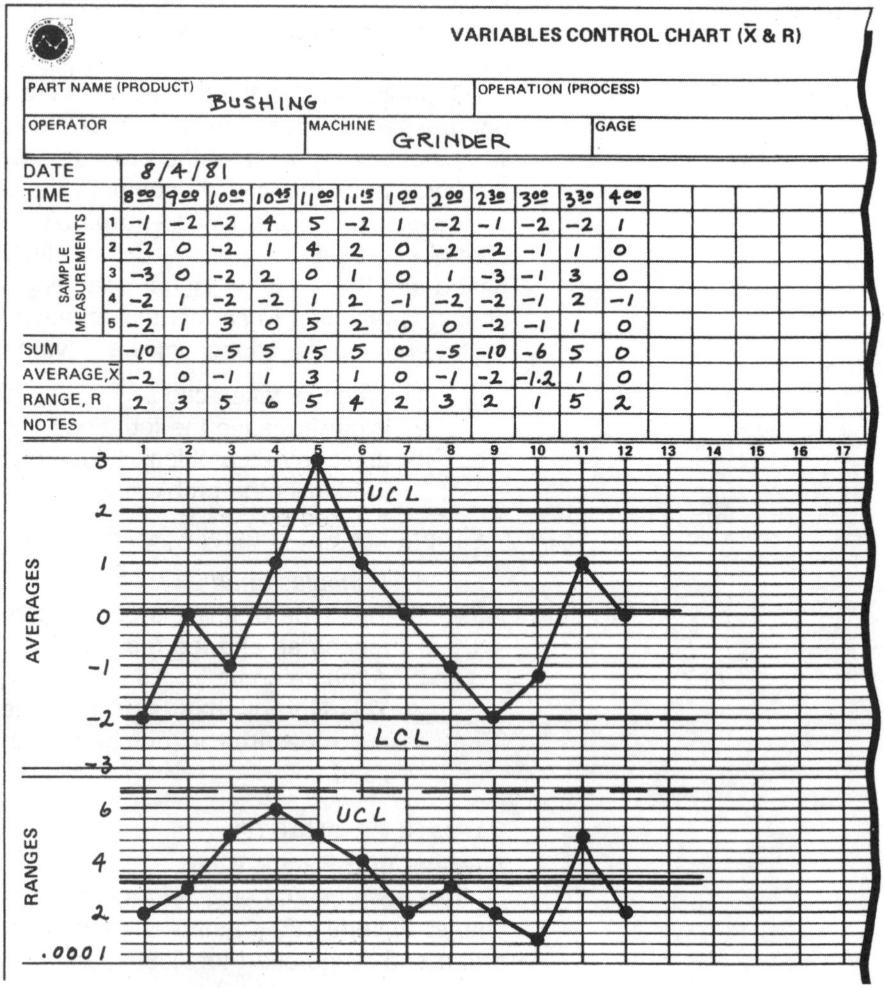

VARIABLES CONTROL CHART ($\bar{X}$ & R)

PART NAME (PRODUCT): BUSHING | OPERATION (PROCESS):

OPERATOR: | MACHINE: GRINDER | GAGE:

DATE	8/4/81																
TIME	8:00	9:00	10:00	10:45	11:00	11:15	1:00	2:00	2:30	3:00	3:30	4:00					
SAMPLE MEASUREMENTS 1	-1	-2	-2	4	5	-2	1	-2	-1	-2	-2	1					
2	-2	0	-2	1	4	2	0	-2	-2	-1	1	0					
3	-3	0	-2	2	0	1	0	1	-3	-1	3	0					
4	-2	1	-2	-2	1	2	-1	-2	-2	-1	2	-1					
5	-2	1	3	0	5	2	0	0	-2	-1	1	0					
SUM	-10	0	-5	5	15	5	0	-5	-10	-6	5	0					
AVERAGE, $\bar{X}$	-2	0	-1	1	3	1	0	-1	-2	-1.2	1	0					
RANGE, R	2	3	5	6	5	4	2	3	2	1	5	2					
NOTES																	

The numbers are small because it isn't easy to write the full reading in the space allotted on the control chart. It would be a nuisance to have to add and divide the full measurement numbers. Instead, the associate has used a technique of coding the measurements. The first piece measured and recorded at 8:00 was .6249 inches. This is .0001 inch less than the specified diameter of .6250, and so it was recorded as -1. The measurements recorded on this control chart are all coded to show the bushing diameter in tenths of thousandths of an inch. When the measured diameter is .6250, a zero is recorded. When the measured diameter is .6251, a plus 1 ($+1$ or 1) is recorded. When the measured diameter is .6248, a minus 2 (-2) is recorded. This method greatly simplifies the arithmetic needed to use this chart.

This chart makes use of a five-piece sample each hour. After the five measurements are recorded, they are added together and this total is recorded in the "sum" line. Next, figure the *average* of the five measurements by dividing the total, or sum, of the measurements by the number of parts measured (five, in this case), and enter it in the "average" line. The average is plotted as one point on the chart. It also is called $\overline{X}$ (pronounced "X bar").

Another point to be plotted on the chart is the *range*. We find the range (or *R*, as it is called) by subtracting the smallest of the five readings from the largest of the readings. This number is recorded on the "range" line of the chart and plotted as one point on the range chart.

As you can see, the average and range chart is actually two charts. We use the average to monitor how well the operation is centered on the specified dimension, and we use the range to monitor the spread of the dimension around the average.

You can see lines on the chart that are marked UCL and LCL. These letters stand for *upper control limit* and *lower control limit*. The upper control limit (UCL) and the lower control limit (LCL) are the limits within which we expect the plotted points to stay. If a point falls outside one of these limits, the job is said to be *"out of control."*

In our example we can see that an average point fell outside the upper control limit at 11:00. This is a signal that something was distorting the normal distribution of the diameter of the bushing. A grinding wheel adjustment was made, and the job was back *in control* again.

ATTRIBUTE CHARTS

We use attribute charts with "go/no go" or "good/bad" inspection results and we do this by finding ways to assign numbers to these results. When we can assign numbers to our information, we can use a statistical technique to monitor and control those numbers.

Several different attribute charts are available, and these will be discussed in detail in Module 4. Now, for a simple illustration, let's look at an attribute chart that was used to monitor an earlier operation on the bushing described above.

This job was a rough grinding operation, which prepared the bushing for the precision grinding operation. The diameter specified for the bushing at this operation was .625 inches ± .003 inch, a much larger tolerance than the one allowed for the precision operation. It is not unusual in such an operation to use a "go" and "no-go" snap gauge. Such a gauge tells when the part is within the limits established for gauging and when it is not. It gives no actual dimensional readings.

An average and range chart cannot be used when this type of information is available. Instead we use an attribute chart. One commonly used type of attribute chart is the *percent defective chart*, which is shown in simplified form in Figure 1-11.

Figure 1-11. Percent defective chart.

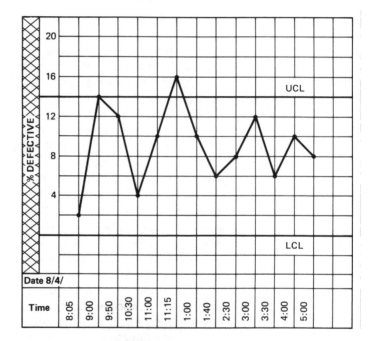

The points plotted on this chart were obtained by checking a sample of 50 pieces each time an inspection was called for. A production associate gauged the pieces, counted the number rejected by the gauge, and calculated the percent defective of the 50-piece sample. The percentage value was then plotted on the percent defective chart.

Here again, the points within the control limits indicate that everything is satisfactory, while the point outside the upper control limit (UCL) shows that something needs to be corrected.

SUMMARY

Later in this book you will learn how to develop these control charts and their control limits and how to interpret them, but for now you can see that they are statistical tools, which are based on a few easy-to-understand basic principles.

The greatest use of control charts is to demonstrate that the process is operating in statistical control (that is, all points on the chart fall between the upper and lower control limits), but is still producing parts that are out of specification. When this happens, it is a waste of time to try to find a solution to the problem by adjusting the process. You can make this type of adjustment or take this kind of corrective action only when assignable causes are present.

When a process is in statistical control, the only variation seen in the process is due to *chance* causes. Even those parts that fall outside the specification limits are made as a result of chance. You will not find an assignable cause for that variation. The only way to solve such a problem effectively is to make a basic change in the process. This is often called a *management team solvable problem.*

On the other hand, if the control chart indicates that the process is out of statistical control, it means that an *assignable* cause is present, and it can be found and corrected. This is often called a *floor solvable problem,* and it's the type of problem most of you face each day on the job.

It is often said that 85% of all quality problems are management solvable and 15% are floor solvable. Statistical methods of process control will help you detect the existence of assignable or floor solvable causes, which you must identify and correct.

Those who are uninformed in the use of statistical methods of quality control might say, "This is all well and good, but can I use it in my work area?" The answer can be given in one word: yes! A control chart can be used on anything that can be assigned a number.

If you intend to use control charts to help maintain and ensure the quality of your work and your products, you must learn to think statistically. All the statistical techniques you will encounter in this book have their foundation in the basic principles, and an understanding of these principles will help you understand and use statistical control charts.

2 Frequency Histograms and Checksheets

```
NEW TERMS IN MODULE 2
(in order of appearance)

frequency histogram                frequency histogram checksheet
intervals or class intervals       checklist checksheet
boundaries                         item checksheet
midpoints                          location checksheet
underlying frequency distribution  matrix checksheet
checksheets
```

WHAT IS VARIATION?

Suppose you and a friend go to the rifle range. Your friend loads, aims, fires, and hits the bull's-eye. Would you conclude, on the basis of this one shot, that your friend is a sharpshooter, perhaps even Olympic material? Or would you ask to see more shots?

Suppose you ask a travel agent for the temperature at a resort area where you want to spend your vacation. The agent says, "75 degrees." Does that one figure tell you enough, or would you ask for a series of temperature readings over a period of time?

Suppose you want to know the burst strength of one day's production of brake hoses. Would you be satisfied with a single number, such as 1200 pounds per square inch?

We think you will say "no" to each of these questions. The rifle marksman may have happened to hit the bull's-eye on the very first shot, and might not hit another in the next hour of shooting. For the resort, you need to know whether 75 degrees is the temperature for summer or winter, night or day. You may need to know the lowest and the highest strengths on the brake hoses. A single measurement is not enough.

Why not? Because, as we said before, no two items are exactly the same. They vary. We need a number of examples so that we can tell how good the marksman is; what the temperatures are at the resort area; how consistent the burst strengths are.

Variation is natural. It is found in many, if not all, processes. Even the best marksman sometimes misses the bull's-eye; temperatures vary, even at a resort; brake hose burst strengths are not all the same. Variation is common and is to be expected.

FREQUENCY HISTOGRAMS

The *frequency histogram* is one tool that helps us keep track of variation. As we mentioned in Module 1, a frequency histogram is a "snapshot" of a process that shows (1) the spread of measurements and (2) how many of each measurement there are. Figure 2-1 illustrates these points.

Figure 2-1. Frequency histogram.

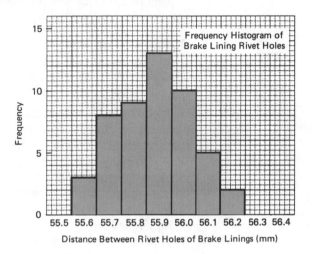

In Figure 2-1, which is a frequency histogram, the lower edge of the chart, called the horizontal scale, records the distances between the centers of two rivet holes on thirty minutes' production of brake linings. Notice that the measurements are listed in order from left to right. In this example, each measurement really represents a group or class of measurements: the 55.6 represents all measurements or readings from 55.55 millimeters to 55.64 millimeters, the 55.7 represents measurements from 55.65 millimeters to 55.74 millimeters, and so on.

The vertical scale along the left-hand edge records how often each measurement occurred. As you can see, there are no measurements in the 55.5-mm. category (55.45 to 55.54); three in the 55.6-mm. category (55.55 to 55.64); eight in the 55.7-mm. category (55.65 to 55.74); and so on.

Figure 2-1 tells us a great deal about variation. The measurements vary from about 55.6 mm. for the shortest distance between the rivet holes to about 56.2 mm. for the longest. The most frequent distance is 55.9 mm. The center, or average, measurement is about 55.9 mm. This frequency histogram shows you all these things quickly and easily without formulas or tables.

Still, frequency histograms don't tell you everything about variation. The histogram in Figure 2-1, for example, does not tell you whether the variations were caused by just one machine or by more than one. Also, it does not show you any patterns over time. That is, you can't tell from Figure 2-1 whether the first brake lining measured was in the 56.2-mm. category, the next one in the 56.1-mm. category, and so on all the way to 55.6-mm., which would indicate that the machine was drifting down. Could the machine have been drifting in the opposite direction? Was it drifting at all? The frequency histogram does not give information about patterns over time. (See Module 3 for a chart that does show patterns through time.)

Before we discuss what frequency histograms can or cannot do, we will see how to construct one.

CONSTRUCTING A FREQUENCY HISTOGRAM

In this section we will go through the steps for constructing a frequency histogram. At each step we will describe the step and give you an example.

Step 1. Collect the measurements.

If you're lucky, the measurements have already been recorded by a production associate. If not, you may have to collect them yourself. Divide the measurements into fairly small groups to make them easy to work with.

A company builds small electric motors. Coming out of the center of the motor is the rotor shaft, the part that delivers the power. The shaft has to have endplay; that is, it must be free to move back and forth. If there is no endplay, the motor will burn out. Too much endplay will keep the motor from doing its job.

A production associate has taken 50 measurements to see how well the motors are meeting the specification. (See Table 2-1.)

		TABLE 2-1 Shaft endplay (.001 inch).		
32	44	44	42	57
26	51	23	33	27
42	46	43	45	44
53	37	25	38	44
36	40	36	48	55
47	40	58	45	38
32	39	43	31	45
41	37	31	39	33
20	50	33	50	51
28	51	40	52	43

As you recall from Module 1, variation in a product or process can be measured. Table 2-1 is a list of measurements that shows the variations in the endplay. Think of the five columns in this table as five groups of data. There are only ten numbers in each group, so the numbers will be easy to work on.

Step 2. Find and mark the largest and smallest number in each group.

Circle the largest numbers and draw boxes around the smallest. Check your work.

TABLE 2-2
Shaft endplay. Largest and smallest numbers in each column have been marked.

32	44	44	42	(57)
26	(51)	[23]	33	[27]
42	46	43	45	44
(53)	[37]	25	38	44
36	40	36	48	55
47	40	(58)	45	38
32	39	43	[31]	45
41	37	31	39	33
[20]	50	33	50	51
28	51	40	(52)	43

In Table 2-2 we circled the largest number in each column and drew a box around the smallest. Then we checked each column.

Step 3. Find the largest and the smallest numbers in the whole set.

Double circle the very largest and draw a double box around the very smallest. Check your work.

In Step 2 you worked on small groups of measurements, and it was easy to find the largest and the smallest in each group. Now, in Step 3, look only at the numbers with circles and boxes around them. In Table 2-3, 58 is the largest of all the circled numbers. Put a second circle around it. The 20 is the very smallest of the numbers in boxes. Draw a second box around it. Now check to make sure you did it correctly.

You may feel that this procedure takes you through too much detail, but keep two things in mind. First, we are writing this book with the expectation

TABLE 2-3

Shaft endplay. Largest and smallest numbers in the set have been marked.

32	44	44	42	(57)
26	(51)	[23]	33	[27]
42	46	43	45	44
(53)	[37]	25	38	44
36	40	36	48	55
47	40	((58))	45	38
32	39	43	[31]	45
41	37	31	39	33
[[20]]	50	33	50	51
28	51	40	(52)	43

that you are learning this technique for the first time. Once you have learned and practiced it you will be able to zip through the steps. Second, we are giving you details that will make it easy to use the technique and prevent you from making mistakes. Breaking this set of measurements into small groups makes it simple to find the largest and the smallest measurement in each group. Then it is easy to locate the very largest and the very smallest. Because you broke the measurements down into small groups, you can check your work easily and reduce the chance of making errors.

Step 4. Calculate the range of the measurements.

Subtract the very smallest number from the very largest number. The very largest number is 58 and the very smallest is 20, so the range is 38.

Very largest minus very smallest equals range.

$$58 - 20 = 38$$

Step 5. Determine the intervals (also known as class intervals) for your frequency histogram.

From previous steps, you know that the measurements cover an *interval* from 20 to 58. Now divide this large interval into a number of smaller intervals of equal width. One rule of thumb is to use about ten intervals, but this number of intervals doesn't always work. See Table 2-4 for guidelines.

It is important to choose the right number of intervals for the number of readings. Too few intervals sometimes hide valuable information. Too many intervals may give such a flat histogram that you miss something important. You need to be skillful in picking the right number of intervals so that the

TABLE 2-4
Guidelines for determining the number of intervals.

NUMBER OF READINGS	NUMBER OF INTERVALS
Fewer than 50	5 to 7
50 to 100	6 to 10
101 to 150	7 to 12
more than 150	10 to 12

information in the data will show up in the histogram. This skill comes with practice.

Let's try eight class intervals for our data because Table 2-4 recommends six to ten intervals for 50 readings.

Step 6. Determine intervals, boundaries, and midpoints.

First, divide the range of the data by the desired number of intervals. Round off this result for convenience. This gives the width of each interval.

The range of the set of 50 observations is 38. When you divide this range by 8 (the desired number of intervals), the result is 4.75.

$$38/8 = 4.75$$

If you round off 4.75 to 5.0, which will be much easier to work with, you can group your data into eight intervals, each 5.0 units wide.

Next, set up *boundaries* for the intervals. Every reading must fall between two boundaries, for reasons we will discuss below.

Since the smallest reading is 20, you may want to make the first interval go from a lower endpoint of 20 to an upper endpoint of 25, the second from 25 to 30, and so on because you decided to make the intervals 5.0 units wide. But if you should have a measurement of exactly 25, you will have the problem of deciding whether to put the 25 into the first interval (20 to 25) or the second (25 to 30).

Boundaries solve this problem. Set up boundaries between the intervals and make the boundaries such that no readings can fall on them. The easy way to do this is to add or subtract one decimal place from an endpoint. Since the data in Table 2-3 have no decimal places, subtract .5 from the endpoint of each interval. This changes the 20 endpoint to 19.5, the 25 endpoint is 24.5, and so on. In this case you have subtracted, but you could just as easily have added .5 to the endpoints of the intervals.

Now no observation can fall on the boundaries, and the problem is solved. The first interval runs from 19.5 to 24.5, the second from 24.5 to 29.5, and so on. Table 2-5 has eight intervals, each 5.0 units in width.

Finally, set a *midpoint* at the center of each interval. (A little rounding off is all right.) The first interval runs from 19.5 to 24.5, a width of 5.0 units. Half this width is 2.5. Add 2.5 to the lower boundary, 19.5. The result is 22, the midpoint of the first interval. Set all the other midpoints in the same way to obtain midpoints of 27, 32, and so on as shown in Table 2-5.

TABLE 2-5		
Midpoints, intervals, and boundaries for shaft endplay measurements.		
MIDPOINT	INTERVAL	BOUNDARIES
22	20–24	19.5–24.5
27	25–29	24.5–29.5
32	30–34	29.5–34.5
37	35–39	34.5–39.5
42	40–44	39.5–44.5
47	45–49	44.5–49.5
52	50–54	49.5–54.5
57	55–59	54.5–59.5

Step 7. Determine the frequencies.

Tally the data in each class interval. Then check the tallies, add them, and list the totals under "Frequency." As a final check, add all the numbers in the "Frequency" column. This final total should equal the total number of readings.

Using the setup in Table 2-5, read a number from Table 2-3 and make a tally mark beside the interval where that number fits. The first number from Table 2-3 is 32, so make a tally mark beside the "29.5 to 34.5" interval. (See Table 2-6.)

When you look at the completed Table 2-6, you will see that there are two tally marks in the first interval of 19.5 to 24.5. In the third interval, 29.5 to 34.5, we made four tally marks as / / / / and drew a fifth horizontally through them: ̸H̷L̷. Later we added two more tally marks to make a total of 7 for this interval: ̸H̷L̷ / / . This method makes it easy to count the tallies, and reduces errors.

Once all the tallies are done, check by doing them again. Then total the tallies for each interval under the "Frequency" column.

You can check the total in two ways. First, count the tally and the tally check to make sure each gives the same result. Then add up the entries in

TABLE 2-6
Tally and frequency of readings in each interval.

MIDPOINT	INTERVAL	BOUNDARIES	TALLY	TALLY CHECK	FREQUENCY
22	20–24	19.5–24.5	II	II	2
27	25–29	24.5–29.5	IIII	IIII	4
32	30–34	29.5–34.5	HHt II	HHt II	7
37	35–39	34.5–39.5	HHt III	HHt III	8
42	40–44	39.5–44.5	HHt HHt III	HHt HHt III	13
47	45–49	44.5–49.5	HHt I	HHt I	6
52	50–54	49.5–54.5	HHt II	HHt II	7
57	55–59	54.5–59.5	III	III	3
					50

the "Frequency" column. The sum is 50, which you already know is the total number of readings in Table 2-3.

Step 8. Prepare the frequency histogram.

There are two main principles to follow in preparing the frequency histogram. It should:

— Tell the story of the data, no more and no less.
— Be neat and easy to read.

In drawing the frequency histogram you must:

— Mark and label the vertical scale.
— Mark and label the horizontal scale.
— Draw in the bars according to the tallies.
— Label the histogram.

Figure 2-2 shows the tallies in the form of a frequency histogram.

The vertical scale is labeled "Frequency" and the horizontal scale is labeled "Shaft Endplay." The intervals are identified by their midpoints. (The 19.5-24.5 interval is labeled 22, and so on.) The tally for the 22 midpoint is two units high, the tally for the 27 midpoint is four units high, and so on. Each bar has a width of five units: the first goes from 19.5 to 24.5, the second from 24.5 to 29.5, and so forth. Finally, the label in the upper left-hand corner "Frequency Histogram of Shaft Endplay," identifies the histogram.

Figure 2-2. Frequency histogram, shaft endplay.

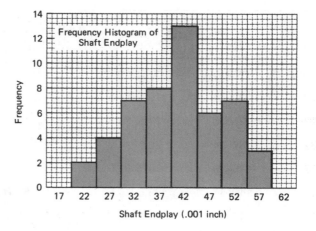

Does the histogram tell the story of the data? Let's see. First, there are eight bars in the histogram. Table 2-4 recommended six to ten intervals for a set of 50 readings, so eight intervals are O.K. As far as we know, there is nothing unusual about this data that doesn't show up on the histogram, so we think this histogram tells the story of the data.

Is this histogram neat and easy to read? You can gain eye appeal in several ways, as we did here: paste graph paper onto a white background and write on the background; make the frequencies and midpoints easy to read; don't make the histogram too tall, too short, too wide, or too narrow. Above all, keep the histogram simple. Don't include extra information or superimpose another histogram on this one.

SOME CAUTIONS

In preparing a frequency histogram you must be careful about several things so that the histogram will tell the story of the data it represents. The following guidelines will help you to accomplish this.

1. *Use equal width intervals.* Unequal width intervals tend to be confusing. Figure 2-3 is poor because the reader may miss the fact that the ship-

Figure 2-3. Unequal width intervals.

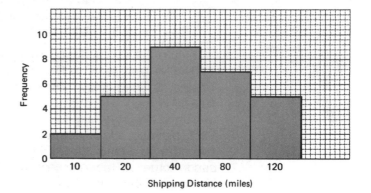

ping distances do *not* go up by ten units from one interval to the next. Figure 2-4 is just as bad. Which interval has more readings, the 35-midpoint interval or the 65-midpoint interval? Which is bigger, the 10- or the 95-midpoint interval? The reader may not get the information that was intended.

Figure 2-4. Unequal width intervals.

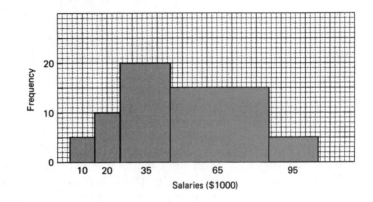

2. *Do not use open intervals.* That is, make sure every interval has definite boundaries. Figure 2-5 is an example of a histogram with open intervals. What is the proper midpoint of the 40+ interval? How large is the largest number in the 40+ interval? It could be in the millions, for all the histogram tells us.

Figure 2-5. Open interval.

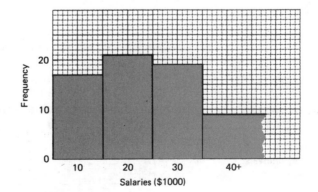

3. *Do not make any breaks in the vertical or horizontal scales.* If you do, they may be overlooked. In Figure 2-6, did you see that the first interval is seven times as tall as the second one? And did you notice that the two intervals on the end, 90 and 100, are far away from the others?

Figure 2-6. Breaks in horizontal and vertical scales.

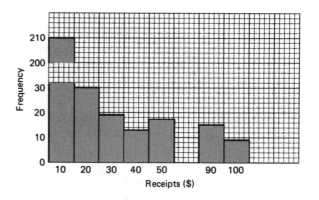

4. *Do not have too few or too many intervals.* Figure 2-7 shows data for gasoline miles per gallon, but the figure has only two intervals. By using so few intervals, the histogram hides the fact that there is one high reading of 25.21 mpg, which is much different from all the others. The first interval runs from 7.00 to 16.99, but there's no way to tell from this histogram that most of the readings are at one end of the interval.

Figure 2-7. Too few intervals.

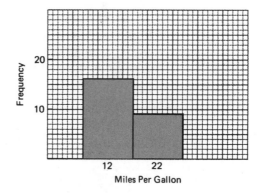

Figure 2-8 shows the other extreme. There are so many intervals in this histogram that the horizontal axis goes on and on. It is so flat that it is hard to see the true pattern of the frequencies. Figure 2-2, which is based on the

Figure 2-8. Too many intervals.

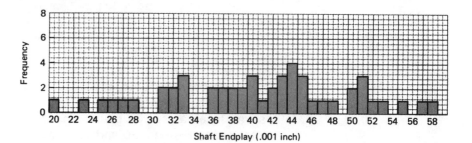

same data, shows the pattern much more clearly. We will talk more about these patterns a little later.

5. *Do not put too much information on one histogram.* It can be confusing.

Figure 2-9 combines two frequency histograms in one chart. One shows miles per gallon for an Oldsmobile and the other for a Dodge Colt. This figure is a mess. It may be interesting to study it carefully to see what is there, but most people would look at it quickly, blink, and go on, hoping to find something easier to understand. Since the two histograms overlap and we have used two crosshatching methods, one for each histogram, it is hard to see where one ends and the other begins. We might be able to show the two histograms by using two different colors, but not in black and white, as it's done here.

Figure 2-9. Too much information.

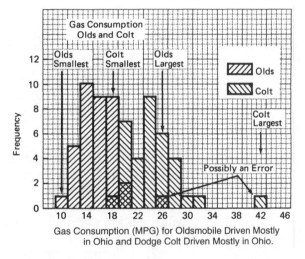

Gas Consumption (MPG) for Oldsmobile Driven Mostly in Ohio and Dodge Colt Driven Mostly in Ohio.

6. *Give everything needed to identify all the information completely and to make the graph understandable.* Figure 2-10 suffers from a lack of necessary information.

What does the vertical scale represent? Dollars? Something else? Does the horizontal scale show gallons, bales of hay, or something else? What is a "Colt"? An automobile? A young horse? While you don't want too much information on a histogram, this figure goes to the other extreme.

WHAT FREQUENCY HISTOGRAMS TELL YOU ABOUT UNDERLYING FREQUENCY DISTRIBUTIONS

We learned at the beginning of this module that there are variations between individual units, such as rifle target shots, temperatures at a resort, and burst strengths of brake hoses. We learned that a good way to describe these variations is to build a frequency histogram.

The frequency histograms that you develop at work will usually be based on samples. Even though they may come from the same process, your histograms will look different because the samples are different.

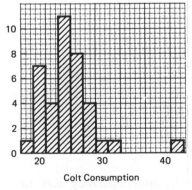

Colt Consumption

Figure 2-10. Too little information.

Suppose we fill a bucket with 1000 small metal disks coated with plastic and stir them thoroughly. We draw out a sample of ten disks and measure the thickness of the coating on each one. We put the sample back, stir the bucket, and take another sample of ten. The frequency histograms for these two samples are shown in Figures 2-11 and 2-12.

Figure 2-11. Coating thickness, sample #1.

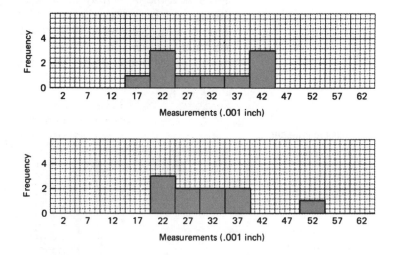

Figure 2-12. Coating thickness, sample #2.

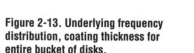

The histogram in Figure 2-13 shows what happens when we measure all 1000 disks. The pattern created by taking all 1000 disks as our sample is called the *underlying frequency distribution.* The underlying frequency distribution will always create the same pattern because it includes *all* the disks, which are the same every time.

Figure 2-13. Underlying frequency distribution, coating thickness for entire bucket of disks.

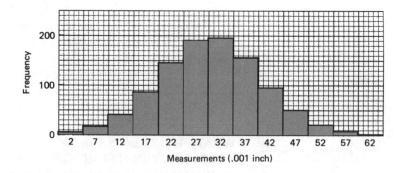

By contrast, the two ten-disk samples are so small that they don't give a clear idea of the underlying distribution. In addition, the samples are so small that the two histograms are different from each other. (Compare Figures 2-11 and 2-12). Histograms based on small samples like this will usually be different from each other because it is not likely that you will pick the same ten disks twice.

The bigger the sample, the more the histogram will look like the underlying distribution and show what is really "in the bucket." For this reason we recommend that you take samples of at least 50 pieces. A sample of 100 is even better.

Frequency histograms that are based on small samples will tell you something about the averages, even though they don't show the underlying frequency distributions. When you compare the histograms in Figures 2-11 and 2-12 to the underlying frequency distribution of Figure 2-13, you can see that the averages of both histograms for the smaller samples are about 30; so is the average of the underlying frequency distribution.

FREQUENCY HISTOGRAMS IN PRODUCTION SITUATIONS

A frequency histogram can show different production situations, some good and some not so good. Figure 2-14 shows a good situation. The amount of variation is so small that all units in the histogram have been produced inside the specifications. In addition, the process is centered at the midpoint between the specifications.

Figure 2-14. A good situation: process spread is narrow and is centered between specifications.

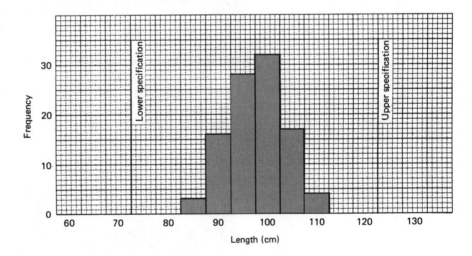

Figure 2-14 shows a good situation, but we must give you a word of warning. Even though all the units pictured in this histogram fall inside the specifications, it is still possible that a very small percentage of the production falls outside. You can't tell one way or the other unless you use another technique, which you will learn in Module 5.

Also, remember that a histogram is a "snapshot" of your process. It doesn't tell you anything about the process over time. To see what your process is doing over time, you need a "moving picture." In Module 3 you'll learn to construct control charts, which will give you that type of information.

Figure 2-15 shows a process in trouble. The tensile strengths of some units are too low, and others are too high. Moving the center of the process won't help. In fact, it will probably put a larger portion of the process outside the specifications. There's just too much variation in this process for the given specifications.

Figure 2-15. Inherent variation is too large for specifications.

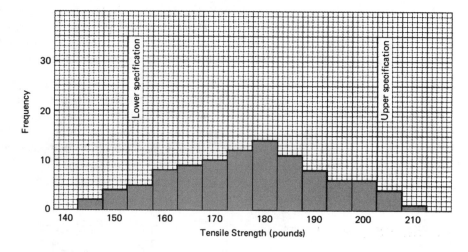

A production associate alone probably can't solve this problem. It will be decided based on a management team discussion. They might overhaul the process to reduce the variation and make it look more like the process shown in Figure 2-14. They could widen the specifications. They might even decide that everybody will just have to live with the situation.

Sometimes the frequency histogram shows a process off center, as in Figure 2-16. You, as the production associate, can often correct this problem. You might need no more than a simple adjustment to center the

Figure 2-16. Process is off center.

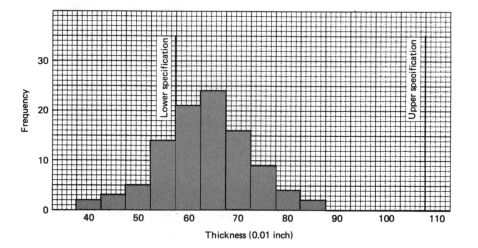

process halfway between the lower and upper specifications. You might have to adjust the temperature for a chemical batch, the time for plastic molding, or the pressure for die casting. The histogram will tell you whether an adjustment is needed and how much of an adjustment to make.

Even if you can center the process perfectly, a small portion of units may still fall outside the specifications. Even when centered, the process shown in Figure 2-16 is not as good as the process in Figure 2-14.

Figure 2-17 is actually *two* histograms. Much of the product is outside the specifications on both the high and the low sides. This pattern suggests that there may be two underlying frequency distributions, not one. There are many possible reasons for two distributions, such as two machines feeding the same bin of parts, two heads on one machine, two batches of material, or two shifts performing differently.

Figure 2-17. Two distributions present in one sample.

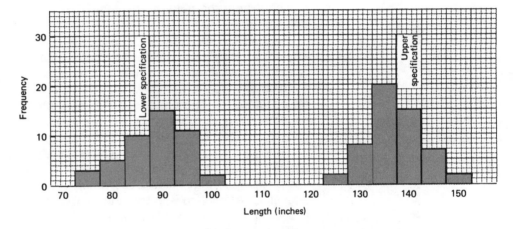

To correct the situation shown in Figure 2-17 you must understand what is going on. You may be able to adjust one process upward and the other down, and so bring the two histograms into focus. For example, you may be able to make simple adjustments of the two heads on the machine. If two machines are feeding parts into one bin or if two shifts are producing the parts, you need to identify which histogram comes from which machine or which shift before you can make any adjustments.

There are many other patterns in frequency histograms, and each pattern will tell you something about what's going on in production. For further information see some of the books in the "Recommended Readings" section.

CHECKSHEETS

Variable data comes from things you can measure, such as weight, time, or distance. Frequency histograms are useful for analyzing such data. However, many times the data you need to work with are not variable—that is, the data are not measurable. For instance, you may want to know whether or not a series of tasks has been completed. Or you may need to determine how many of each of several categories occur, such as kinds of errors or defects. In a continuous improvement project, the location of external defects, such as gouges or oil spots, is important. Or, in a manufacturing process, you may need to track the performance of several machines over two shifts.

The *checksheet* helps collect nonvariable data and analyze them. It is simply a form on which you can record data in an organized manner, making the job of collecting and analyzing data easier. There are many kinds of checksheets. Five of the most common ones are described in the following sections.

The frequency histogram checksheet.

The *frequency histogram checksheet* is a special type of frequency histogram. Like the histogram, this checksheet presents a great deal of information: where the data are centered, the amount of variation, and the distribution of the data.

Figure 2-18 is a frequency histogram checksheet. Measurements of the amount of endplay in an electric motor shaft have been recorded directly onto the checksheet. By using the checksheet, data are handled only once; each observation is written as an "X" directly on the checksheet—they are not recorded on one piece of paper and then organized and plotted on a separate histogram. This means fewer opportunities for errors in transferring the data. It may also mean less time spent compiling data.

The frequency histogram checksheet method should be used when you already have some familiarity with the data. You need to know the approximate value of the smallest observation you are likely to get, as well as the largest. One problem with this checksheet is the difficulty in setting it up so that all observations will fit on it. As you can see in Figure 2-18, one of the points falls outside the chart, below the 50/54 range. You also need to know what the intervals are for the bottom horizontal axis of your frequency histogram checksheet. If you do not know these things, then you probably will have to construct a frequency histogram as described earlier in this module. If you are familiar with the process, you can plot a range of possible results along the horizontal axis with reasonable intervals. As you take each measurement, mark an "X" in the range in which the measurement falls. After all measurements have been marked on the grid, you will have a graphical representation of the variation in your process.

This type of checksheet will not work if the order in which you record your data depicts trends through time. If this is the case, you must record the data in a way that preserves the time factor of your observations. By plotting them directly onto the histogram checksheet as in Figure 2-18, you lose the time component, or order, of the data. If the order or time factor of the data is not important, then you can use this kind of checksheet. Be sure to label your checksheet, indicating when the data were collected and who collected them. Make a note of anything interesting or unusual that you notice—later it could give you a clue how to improve your process.

Figure 2-18. Frequency histogram checksheet for measurements of the amount of endplay in an electric motor shaft. One mark is outside the graph.

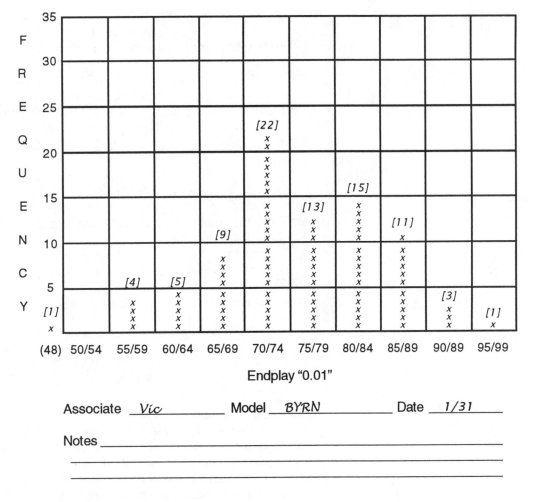

Associate __*Vic*__ Model __*BYRN*__ Date __*1/31*__

Notes _____

_____

_____

The checklist checksheet.

When you think of a checksheet, you probably think of a *checklist* such as an airline pilot uses. When boarding a commercial airliner you may have noticed the pilot holding a clipboard with a checklist on it. The pilot checks off each task as it is finished. This checklist is a type of checksheet because it is a form for recording data in an organized way as the data are collected. Figure 2-19 is a checklist for the associate who prepares a batch of instant pudding. As each ingredient is added, the associate checks off that ingredient.

There are many situations in which you can use this type of checksheet. You could use one to make certain that all your materials will be available at an assembly station. Associates can use this type of checksheet to ensure that all the preventive maintenance procedures for an injection mold have been carried out at shift change. An engineering department might

Figure 2-19. Ingredients checklist for "Yummo Instant" pudding.

Batch Number __022027__   Date __2/20__

Associate ____EM____   Shift ____1____

Ingredients   **Yummo Instant**

Sugar   ✓

Food starch   ✓

Thickening agent   ✓

Salt   ✓

Anti-foaming agents   ✓

Dry skim milk   ✓

Color   ✓

Flavor   ✓

Preservative   ✓

keep a checklist of required procedures for certain types of design work. In problem solving you could develop a checklist of procedures to follow in identifying and solving problems.

The item checksheet.

Another kind of checksheet is the *item checksheet.* This tool is used to count the number of times an item occurs in a process. To construct an item checksheet, either list each item as you come to it and then count it each time it recurs, or prepare a list ahead of time with all the items already listed. Such a checksheet, when completed, is a partial analysis of the data, for it shows at a glance the amount in each category of items. We can take the data from this checksheet and easily construct a Pareto diagram. (See Module 6 for an explanation of a Pareto diagram.)

Problem-solving teams have used the item checksheet to record how many and what kinds of adjustments and/or corrective actions are needed at final test of light trucks. An item checksheet could also be used by a training department to keep track of the types of skill development classes available for associates, such as advanced computer-aided manufacturing, and the number of associates participating in these classes. Or, an item checksheet can be used to track types and amounts of waste from a cutting operation.

An example of an item checksheet is shown in Figure 2-20. As associates in a work cell inspect blower motors after manual soldering, they record defects directly onto the checksheet.

Figure 2-20. Item checksheet for defects in manual solder operation on blower motor.

Types of Defects	No. of Occurrences
Short circuit	ЖЖ III
Soldering	ЖЖ ЖЖ ЖЖ
Dirt	ЖЖ I
Wire breaks	ЖЖ ЖЖ II
Wrong solder	ЖЖ
Too much resistance	IIII
Lead wire nipped too short	ЖЖ ЖЖЖЖ ЖЖ ЖЖ IIII

Date _3/26_____   Model # _RV7_____

Associate _TA_____

Notes _____

_____

The location checksheet.

With a *location checksheet* you can indicate the physical location of whatever data you are collecting. Figure 2-21 is a diagram of the cabinet top of an electric clothes dryer, showing the location of deformities caused during metal forming.

Other uses of the location checksheet include location of defects in a grinding operation, for instance. Production workers can use this type of checksheet to determine where breaks in paper webbing are occurring most often during a print job, which could help them in the scheduling of maintenance. A just-in-time facility could use a map as a location checksheet to see where suppliers are located. A quality improvement team trying to improve the layout of a work area might plot the flow of parts on a location checksheet to identify major patterns.

The matrix checksheet.

The *matrix checksheet* is a powerful tool for many situations, because it conveys more than one type of data. For example, we can set up a matrix checksheet showing kinds of errors along with the names of associates. This provides valuable information on both the kinds of errors being made and where they are happening. In solving problems and pursuing continuous improvement, the people component cannot be ignored. However, you should be very careful in using names in any analysis. You want to solve

Figure 2-21. Location checksheet for deformations in clothes dryer top. "Xs" indicate the location of deformations.

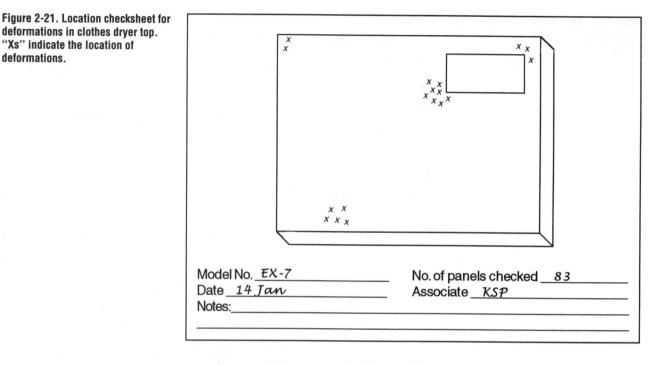

Model No. _EX-7_   No. of panels checked _83_

Date _14 Jan_   Associate _KSP_

Notes:_____

problems, *not* blame people. Be sure that your checksheet is seen as a help to your associates and not a threat. Otherwise you may win the battle while losing the war.

Figure 2-22 is an example of a matrix checksheet. In this figure, three types of assemblies appear along the top of the checksheet. Along the left-hand margin is a list of part numbers for seven components used in these assemblies. An associate tallies each component by part number during an inspection audit of the kits used for the three assemblies. This grid-type of arrangement is called a matrix.

SUMMARY

Variation is a familiar part of our lives. No two things are exactly the same. Variation is found everywhere: in bowling scores, parts made on a single machine, temperatures at a favorite vacation spot.

The frequency histogram is a tool to help you deal with variation. It is a snapshot of your process, which shows the range of measurements in a sample at one point in time and tells how many measurements there are of each.

Frequency histograms have different patterns, which can reveal important information about your process. One pattern may tell you that the variation in your process is small enough so that you can produce all your parts within specifications. Another pattern may show that your process is in trouble and cannot help producing defective parts.

Figure 2-22. Matrix checksheet for widget assemblies.

Part No.	Assembly A	Assembly B	Assembly C
1017d	////	ℍ	ℍ //
2938r	ℍ ///	ℍ ℍ //	ℍ ℍ
315at	ℍ ℍ		////
487z	ℍ //	ℍ	
51066n	ℍ //		
6217j			////
721e90		///	ℍ ///

Date of Audit Inspection __6/8__

Associate _AK_

Notes: _6217j short in Assembly C; missing in Assembly A_

The frequency histogram can tell you about the underlying frequency distribution of your process, but it does not tell you anything about what happens over time. Other techniques, which we will discuss in later modules, will help you control and monitor your process over time.

Although frequency histograms are useful for analyzing such variable data as time, weight, or distance, you will encounter nonvariable data as well. Checksheets are tools to help you handle data that cannot be measured.

The frequency histogram checksheet is a quick way of constructing a frequency histogram. However, you must already know approximately where the largest and smallest observations will be; you must know the intervals; and the time component of the data must not be important. The checklist checksheet allows you to check off whether each of a series of tasks is completed. By using the item checksheet, you can easily tally the items as they occur. The location checksheet gives you a way to record locations where problems occur, such as the position of oil spots around or under a machine. The matrix checksheet sets up a grid on which you can record two or more attributes of each observation.

In continuous improvement and solving problems, you need to focus on all five sources of assignable causes: equipment, method, materials, environment, and people. While the people component cannot be left out, be careful that you do not alienate others. Don't blame people; rather, draw them into the problem-solving process to find the causes of, and solutions to, problems.

PRACTICE PROBLEMS: FREQUENCY HISTOGRAMS

To practice using the statistical techniques you learned in Module 2, work through the following problems. The solutions can be found in the "Solutions" section beginning on page 194.

You will find that a frequency histogram worksheet form is helpful in developing your histograms. An example of such a worksheet is shown in Figure 2-23.

Problem 2-1a.

The inspection records of a hose assembly operation indicated a high rate of rejection. An analysis of the records showed that "leaks" were a major cause of the problem. A review of the assembly operations led to the decision to investigate the hose clamping operation.

The hose clamping force, or torque, was measured on twenty-five hose assemblies. The torque was recorded in foot-pounds (ft-lbs.) as follows:

7 ft-lbs.	15 ft-lbs.	13 ft-lbs.	19 ft-lbs.
10 ″	12 ″	9 ″	12 ″
14 ″	13 ″	13 ″	16 ″
11 ″	14 ″	14 ″	14 ″
13 ″	10 ″	16 ″	
12 ″	11 ″	17 ″	
13 ″	15 ″	15 ″	

The clamping torque specification is 12 to 24 ft-lbs. How does this process compare to the specification? Should any corrective action be taken? If so, what?

Problem 2-1b.

In the problem above, the air pressure in the torque wrench was reduced to allow the torque wrench to stall out at a torque of 18 ft-lbs. Before this corrective action was taken, the air pressure was not regulated. This meant that the production associate had to "feel" when the clamp was tight enough.

Twenty-five more torque readings were taken after the corrective action, with the following results:

17 ft-lbs.	17 ft-lbs.	19 ft-lbs.
19 ″	20 ″	18 ″
19 ″	21 ″	19 ″
20 ″	20 ″	19 ″
21 ″	19 ″	18 ″
17 ″	18 ″	
18 ″	18 ″	
20 ″	19 ″	
19 ″	20 ″	
20 ″	19 ″	

Was the corrective action effective?

Problem 2-2.

A hole location dimension was measured on fifty pieces taken from an operation. The readings were as follows:

1. 40.4	14. 41.0	27. 40.4	40. 40.7
2. 40.8	15. 40.4	28. 40.8	41. 40.4
3. 40.3	16. 40.8	29. 40.5	42. 41.0
4. 40.6	17. 40.5	30. 40.9	43. 40.4
5. 40.4	18. 40.9	31. 40.4	44. 40.8
6. 40.8	19. 40.4	32. 40.8	45. 40.3
7. 40.5	20. 40.9	33. 40.4	46. 40.8
8. 40.7	21. 40.3	34. 40.8	47. 40.3
9. 40.4	22. 40.6	35. 40.4	48. 40.6
10. 40.8	23. 40.4	36. 40.7	49. 40.4
11. 40.4	24. 40.7	37. 40.4	50. 40.8
12. 40.8	25. 40.3	38. 40.8	
13. 40.4	26. 40.8	39. 40.2	

Plot the frequency histogram of the measurements. Is there anything wrong with this data?

Problem 2-3.

The accompanying shaft movement data gives measurements of the endplay in an electric motor shaft. The data are given in the order of production so that column A (reading down) shows that the first unit produced had an endplay of 61, the second had 61, the third had 57, and so forth.

Plot frequency histograms for the data in the following columns:

1. A,B,C, and D.   4. M,N,O, and P.
2. E,F,G, and H.   5. A,E,I, and M.
3. I,J,K, and L.

Compare the five histograms.

(a) Do you see any differences among the averages of the first four histograms?
(b) Do you see any differences among the spreads of the first four histograms?
(c) How does the fifth histogram compare to the other four? Is the spread more or less? Why or why not?

Figure 2-23. Frequency histogram worksheet.

FREQUENCY HISTOGRAMS — WORKSHEET

Title _____

● Tally the data

Midpoint	Interval	Boundaries	Tally	Tally Check	Frequency

● Prepare the graph

Shaft movement data in .001 inch

A	B	C	D	E	F	G	H
61	56	62	59	56	68	56	60
61	55	61	63	56	62	56	55
57	62	59	57	61	55	60	61
56	61	61	53	67	57	56	62
60	59	55	49	58	60	62	65
52	57	52	60	63	61	63	57
62	61	59	54	56	57	60	62
59	52	52	56	60	63	63	67
62	60	53	42	55	59	62	65
67	51	54	62	46	64	62	62
55	52	52	53	62	63	64	63
56	64	43	58	65	55	65	65
52	58	62	42	63	60	55	65
60	41	59	62	59	65	60	55
59	56	55	59	60	66	62	60
59	56	52	60	60	68	63	58
60	65	52	53	59	53	63	59
59	53	56	43	60	62	67	65
49	55	60	50	65	62	58	64
42	56	59	59	65	67	60	55
55	60	45	63	62	59	65	55
67	52	60	53	51	63	68	62
53	61	59	60	62	56	60	59
66	41	57	63	52	65	61	55
60	55	51	60	58	62	64	57

I	J	K	L	M	N	O	P
65	54	67	61	65	79	65	70
62	61	57	68	70	70	78	50
59	66	65	63	73	65	65	68
62	60	67	64	70	72	66	69
63	65	68	68	69	64	66	66
68	67	65	67	64	65	65	66
64	62	65	64	68	69	63	68
67	56	62	64	65	78	70	69
60	64	59	62	72	69	73	70
59	63	69	59	73	68	63	73
59	63	66	61	75	66	65	71
61	62	65	60	72	69	66	72
58	68	63	65	75	65	67	69
65	69	61	65	64	62	71	74
64	63	60	52	69	67	72	64
70	60	65	62	60	72	63	70
63	66	63	68	68	65	66	66
68	62	58	60	66	70	75	72
62	64	72	62	69	68	59	69
61	69	65	61	72	62	64	70

Problem 2-4.

One measure of quality in a radio is called the signal-to-noise ratio. This is measured in decibels (db) at a very low voltage. Five consecutive radios were taken from the production line and measured for this quality characteristic. This was done once each day for 24 hours during a period of a month and a half.

The specification calls for a minimum reading of 15db for each radio. Make a histogram of the measurements listed below. The readings are shown in the order of production for the time period.

What is your estimate of the quality of the radios made during this period?

db		db		db		db	
1.	21	5.	26	9.	25	13.	25
2.	20	6.	27	10.	28	14.	25
3.	30	7.	27	11.	32	15.	28
4.	27	8.	29	12.	24	16.	29

I	J	K	L	M	N	O	P
62	63	62	59	70	67	70	73
62	69	62	62	70	63	70	70
72	62	60	52	50	70	73	79
63	61	61	68	68	70	70	66
51	56	69	65	71	78	62	64

db	db	db	db
17. 28	43. 23	69. 26	95. 36
18. 28	44. 29	70. 25	96. 31
19. 25	45. 30	71. 29	97. 26
20. 25	46. 27	72. 31	98. 25
21. 25	47. 24	73. 27	99. 22
22. 27	48. 26	74. 24	100. 27
23. 25	49. 22	75. 22	101. 25
24. 25	50. 25	76. 24	102. 27
25. 18	51. 24	77. 26	103. 27
26. 24	52. 23	78. 27	104. 28
27. 26	53. 27	79. 28	105. 26
28. 25	54. 22	80. 24	106. 26
29. 26	55. 25	81. 25	107. 24
30. 22	56. 23	82. 27	108. 28
31. 27	57. 25	83. 25	109. 24
32. 26	58. 26	84. 28	110. 25
33. 23	29. 26	85. 25	111. 31
34. 25	60. 21	86. 26	112. 33
35. 27	61. 32	87. 29	113. 22
36. 27	62. 28	88. 20	114. 24
37. 30	63. 25	89. 21	115. 28
38. 24	64. 23	90. 26	116. 28
39. 31	65. 25	91. 27	117. 23
40. 23	66. 30	92. 31	118. 26
41. 27	67. 23	93. 30	119. 28
42. 27	68. 25	94. 26	120. 28

PRACTICE PROBLEMS: CHECKSHEETS

Problem 2-5.

Suppose you are planning to buy a personal computer for business use at home. What characteristics would you look for? Prepare a checklist checksheet for this purchase.

Problem 2-6.

Set up an item checksheet for defects or problems with a PC.

Problem 2-7.

Construct a location checksheet for recording defects, such as leaks in the seal of a windshield. How will you label your location checksheet?

Problem 2-8.

Prepare a frequency histogram checksheet representing the oil temperature of a stamping press. What kind of information will you include in your label?

Problem 2-9.

Make up a matrix checksheet for six envelope-making machines over two shifts. You will be recording the number of unscheduled shutdowns this week. What information will be important to include in the label?

MODULE 3

Variable Control Charts

NEW TERMS IN MODULE 3
(in order of appearance)

$\bar{X}$-R chart	median
mean $(\bar{X})$	median of medians $(\widetilde{\widetilde{X}})$
inherent variation	median of ranges $(\widetilde{R})$
overall mean $(\bar{\bar{X}})$	$\widetilde{A}_2$
average range $(\bar{R})$	$\widetilde{D}_4$
decision chart or flow chart	individual and range (X-R) chart
median and range $(\widetilde{X}$-R) chart	

Why use control charts? The following story will help answer this question.

In a munitions factory during World War II, many of the line people were young women with boyfriends or family overseas on the front lines. These operators were determined to make the best product possible for their men to use in battle. At the end of the line someone would weigh an artillery shell for the powder content. If it was above the standard, she would yell back to the beginning of the line and they would reduce the amount of powder. If it was below, they would increase it. The correcting went on like this all day long, up or down.

Then the company put in control charts. The charts told the operator when to correct the process *and* when to leave it alone. The result was fewer corrections to the process and a more consistent product. The line people didn't work as hard but they made a better product!

We will begin this module by looking at one of the best known and most widely used control charts, the average and range or $\bar{X}$-R ("X bar, R") control chart. The average and range chart will help you to see whether or not you have done your work correctly.

First you will learn how to use average and range charts that are already set up. That is, someone else has figured out the control limits, the sample size, and how often to sample. You will put the charts to work in order to tell whether or not your process is running well.

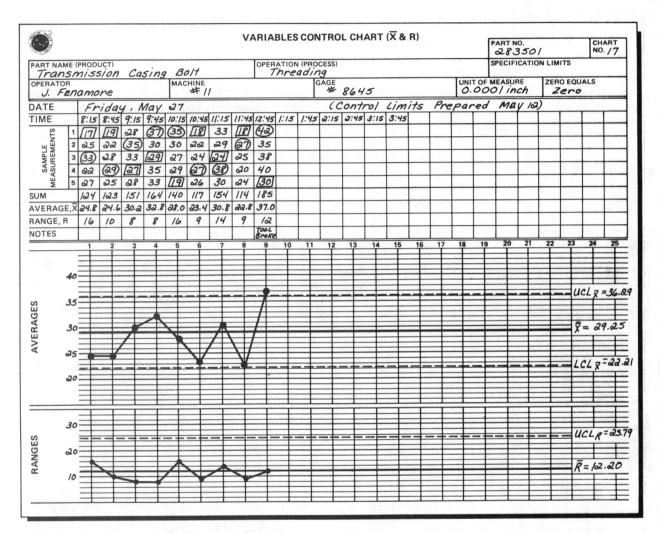

Figure 3-1. Average and range (X̄-R) chart.

Next you'll learn how to interpret average and range charts. What are the charts telling you if a range (R) or an average (X̄) is close to the control chart limits? What if one point falls just outside the limits, or several points in a row fall on one side of the center line?

Finally, you will have an opportunity to set up average and range charts. This is detailed work, with more arithmetic than you've used so far, but some people like to set up charts because new charts can reveal surprises about the process.

USING AVERAGE AND RANGE CHARTS THAT ARE ALREADY SET UP

Suppose you are a production associate in a factory. You manually place a small wheel on the end of the shaft of a small electric motor. It's important to push the wheel far enough onto the shaft, but not too far. You have been asked to select five of your motors every half hour and measure the endplay of the wheel; that is, how far back and forth you can move the motor shaft once you have put on the wheel. You have a measuring device that makes it easy and quick to measure the endplay.

Someone else, maybe an engineering technician, set up the control charts yesterday. The technician has done the first two samples for today. Figure 3-2 shows the control chart.

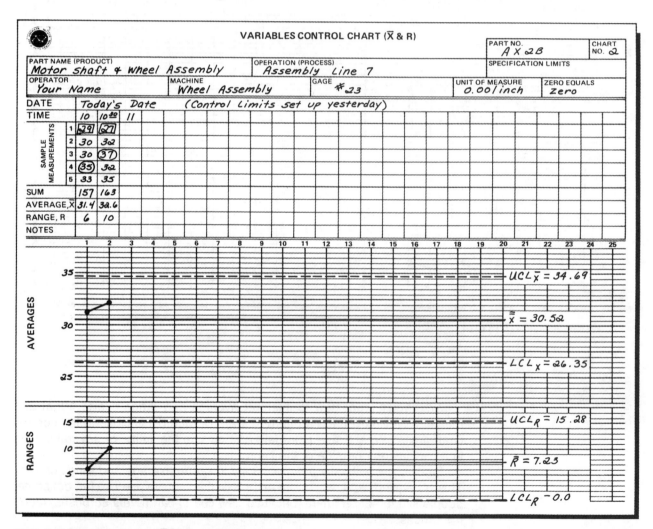

Figure 3-2. Average and range (X̄-R) chart with two samples.

It's 11:00 and the technician is off on a break. Now it's your turn. Take the next five motors you assemble, put them to the side, and measure the endplay for each one. The first measures 26 thousandths of an inch, so write 26 on the chart just under "11:00." The next also reads 26 thousandths of an inch, so write 26 on the chart again. Continue in this way for the other three pieces, which measure 30, 27, and 31. If anything seems out of the ordinary, write it down in the "NOTES" row under "11:00."

Figure 3-3. Portion of $\overline{X}$-R chart with new measurements.

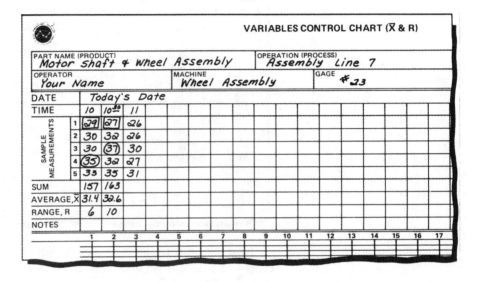

Now add up the five measurements and write the result, 140, in the "11:00" column in the "SUM" row. (See Figure 3-4.) Next, figure out the average, which is sometimes called the *mean* or $\overline{X}$. (You have already seen the symbol $\overline{X}$ in Module 1.) The average is simply the total, or sum, of the measurements divided by the number of measurements.

Average equals total divided by number of measurements.

$$\overline{X} = 140/5$$

Since your sum was 140 and you made five measurements, simply divide 140 by 5. A calculator makes it easy, or if you're good with figures, do it in your head. (A trick that works only with *five* numbers is (a) multiply the sum, 140, by 2 for a total of 280 and (b) move the decimal point *one* place to the left.) The result should be 28.0, which you enter in the "AVERAGE, $\overline{X}$" row. (See Figure 3-4.)

Finally, figure the range of the sample data. Find and mark with a circle the largest measurement in your 11:00 sample, 31. Draw a box around the smallest, 26. Find the range as follows:

Range equals largest measurement minus smallest measurement.

$$R = 31 - 26$$
$$R = 5$$

Write 5 on your chart in the "RANGE, R" row. The top part of your chart now looks like Figure 3-4.

Figure 3-4. Portion of $\overline{X}$-R chart with sum, average, and range.

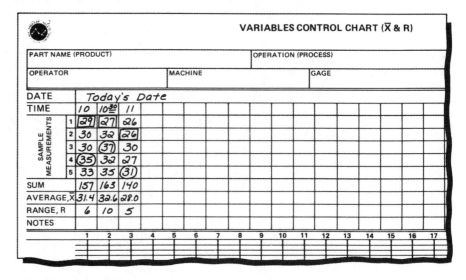

Next plot the range and the average as small dots on the graph and draw a line to connect each new dot with the previous dot. Your chart should look like Figure 3-5.

Figure 3-5. Portion of $\overline{X}$-R chart with new average and range plotted.

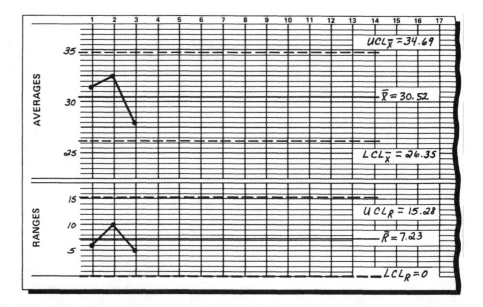

As you learned in Module 1, averages and ranges have control limits marked by UCL (upper control limit) and LCL (lower control limit). Keep that fact in mind as you look at what you plotted. First, is the range where it's supposed to be? The range is 5, and that falls between the lower control limit of zero and the upper control limit of 15.28, so the range is O.K. Second, is the average where it is supposed to be? Yes—it's 28.0, which falls between the lower control limit of 26.35 and the upper control limit of 34.69.

What do these plots tell you? When the range *and* the average are inside the control limits, your process is O.K. It's "in statistical control." Don't make any adjustments—just keep on producing.

INTERPRETING AVERAGE AND RANGE CHARTS

Now that you know how to figure averages and ranges and how to plot the points, take a few more samples and plot their ranges and averages. Then you can go on to interpret average and range charts.

Figure 3-6. All points are inside control limits.

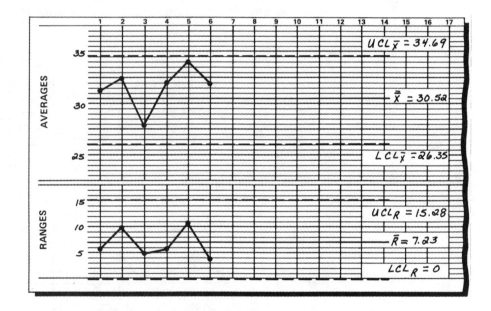

On your control chart (Figure 3-6), every point is inside the control limits. This tells you to keep running the process. No changes or corrections are required because all points are inside the limits.

You may ask, "What about the fifth average, 34.2, which is very close to the upper control limit of 34.69?" The rule is clear-cut: if the point is inside, make no corrections and keep on producing. If the point is outside, find the assignable cause and correct it.

Why do the points move up and down inside the limits? What you see in Figure 3-6 is most likely natural variation in the process. This is called *inherent variation* and is due to chance causes. Usually the production associate cannot get rid of it because it is a part of the process itself. For example, if you're working with motors, there's variation in the widths of the wheels, variation in the inside diameters of the wheels, variation in the diameters of the shafts, and so on. All these variations are natural, and all are beyond your control. But these inherent variations pull the ranges and averages up and down *within* the control limits. (This is true *only* for inherent variation. We are not including variations due to assignable causes, such as a new batch of motor shafts that have larger diameters.)

AVERAGES OUTSIDE CONTROL LIMITS

When an average is outside the control limits, what does the chart tell you to do? It tells you to adjust the process, to correct it. For some reason the process has shifted up and needs to be corrected downward. How do you make the correction? There is no simple answer. In the case of motor endplay, you might have to adjust the jig. For another process you might have to change the setting on a tool or adjust the temperature of a plastic extrusion die. Some corrections are easy to make, some are not.

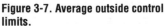

Figure 3-7. Average outside control limits.

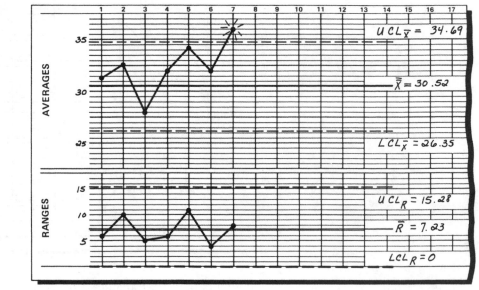

How do we interpret the average outside the limits in Figure 3-7? Because it is outside, the process is now out of statistical control. This one average shows that simple inherent variation is no longer at work. Inherent variation is now combined with something more—an assignable cause. The assignable cause changes the overall average of the process. Once that happens, the averages begin to fall outside the control limits. That is why our seventh average, 36.0, is outside the limits.

Usually an assignable cause points to a problem that you can handle yourself at the floor level, such as the need to adjust the tool setting. At other times you will have to notify your team leader because of the nature of the problem, such as a change in raw material. We are not talking here about *who* is responsible. Instead, we want you to see that *something, somewhere,* has changed. The point outside the control limits tells you just that.

What's special or assignable about this point outside the limits? It's not natural to the process, it doesn't happen all the time, and, most important, you may be able to identify the cause—that's why it's called an assignable cause. In the case of the motors, your sample average may have gone outside the limits just when a new batch of wheels came in; careful checking of the wheels might show that the new ones are slightly thicker than usual. In this case, a few measurements can identify the assignable cause. Note that the control chart only tells *when* the assignable cause occurred, not *why*.

OTHER SIGNS OF A PROCESS OUT OF CONTROL

From time to time, the points you plot may form a pattern. One particular pattern to look for is seven points in a row above or below the line marked $\overline{\overline{X}}$ in the "AVERAGES" section or the line marked $\overline{R}$ in the "RANGES" section. What is such a pattern telling you? This is another signal—a weaker one—that the process is out of control, even though all the points are still inside the control limits.

There are other patterns of longer runs of points, as well as too many or too few points close to the process average. To interpret these patterns we suggest that you look them up in Ishikawa's *Guide to Quality Control* and in Ellis Ott's *Process Quality Control* or Grant and Leavenworth's *Statistical Quality Control*. If you don't own any of these books, somebody in the company probably has a copy, or you can look for them at your public library.

SOURCES OF ASSIGNABLE CAUSES

The sources of assignable causes often come from one of several main categories, which you can find on the fishbone diagram in Module 1 (see Figure 1-4). These include the following:

(1) *Machine.* By *machine* we mean that the machine itself has changed somehow, and that's why the sample average went outside the limits. The device that puts the wheel on the motor shaft may have slipped or worn down.

(2) *Materials.* The assignable cause of *materials* means that something has changed in the materials themselves. The wheels for the motors may have come from a new batch and for some reason are thicker than usual. This change has caused the average to go outside the control limits.

(3) *Method* is the way we do things. We may yank the lever that pushes the wheel onto the shaft, or we may give it a steady pull. Switching from one method to another may cause the average to go outside the control limits.

(4) *Environment* may also be a source of variation. In an automobile tire manufacturing company, summer humidity affects the cure rate of the rubber. Temperature fluctuations in a plastic injection mold, dust in the atmosphere of a laser disc production facility, or atmospheric pressure changes in producing polyurethane foam can send the average outside the control limits.

(5) You, the production associate. We listed you last because in our opinion, it's usually not the person that is the cause. Most of the time it turns out to be one of the other four. Too often people have been blamed when the machine, method, materials, or environment is the real source of the problem. When the production associate *is* the assignable cause, it may be because a relief associate has just come on, or maybe one of the associates is not adequately trained.

RANGES OUTSIDE CONTROL LIMITS

In Figure 3-8, range number 8 is out of control. In this situation it is helpful to ask first, "Is the inherent variation under the associate's control?" In our opinion, a production associate does not usually have control over the inherent variation of the process. Therefore, a range outside the limits probably means that the process itself has gone haywire. Examples of this are wear in a machine used to fabricate a part, or fluctuations in the thickness

Figure 3-8. Range outside control limits.

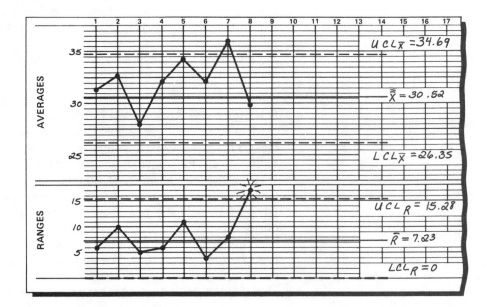

of sheet steel used in forming soup cans. In those cases an associate would probably have no control over the inherent variation, but the control chart shows that there is a problem. It is your job to notify your team leader so that the cause of the change in the inherent variation can be determined and corrections can be made.

One word of caution—check your arithmetic and (if possible) your measurements to be sure you didn't make a mistake in arithmetic or in measuring. Such a mistake can easily send the range outside the control limits, so avoid possible embarrassment by checking it out. *You* could be an assignable cause!

In rare cases, though, the variation is due to something you *can* control, at least partially. If this is so, you may be able to make a correction that will bring the ranges back into statistical control. These cases might include hand assembling parts or weighing chemicals before a mixing operation. In these situations the range might have gone out of control because of momentary lack of attention, fatigue, or a change in your method.

SETTING UP AVERAGE AND RANGE CHARTS

Now that you know how to use average and range charts, you can try setting up your own. Control charts serve several purposes. (1) They can be used for control. That is, the charts can be used to tell you whether to continue the operation or to find and correct assignable causes. (2) Charts can be used for analysis. You might be looking for the amount of inherent variation in the process, or you might want to find the differences between days, materials, or even operating techniques. (3) Charts can also be used for education, communication, or documentation. They may help you, as the associate, to focus attention on consistent quality.

In the case of the electric motor, both production and staff have agreed that ongoing control is required in the assembly of a small wheel on an electric motor. Average and range charts should help you and your work group in controlling your process. Even though control is the primary purpose, the charts will also provide some extras. They will help show your customers, staff, and other work groups how well the process is doing. Then, at some later time, an improvement team may use the charts as documents in reviewing the process for possible improvement.

Step 1. Choose what to measure.

Many different things about a process can be measured, so you must choose what you want to measure. There are two things to remember. First, select something important in the process and control that one thing. Don't make control charts for every characteristic in the process. Second, you may not be able to measure directly the characteristic that you choose. If you can't, you must find something *measurable* that will allow the important characteristic to be controlled with charts. An example is the hardness of rubber; you can control the amount of time for curing, which in turn controls the hardness.

In the case of the electric motors, it is important that the wheel not be pushed too far onto the shaft so that the motor binds up and does not turn. On the other hand, the wheel must be pushed on far enough. If it is not, it may stick out too far and may rub the part of the final assembly on which the motor is eventually mounted.

What measurable characteristic will allow you to control how far the wheel goes onto the shaft? Endplay: that is, how far back and forth the motor shaft can move easily. This is the important characteristic, and it can be measured easily and quickly in thousandths of an inch. Thousandths of an inch are expressed in numbers, and numbers can be entered on control charts. In other words, you can control endplay through the use of average and range control charts. Because you can control endplay, you can keep the wheel from being pushed on too far or not far enough.

Step 2. Take the samples.

In setting up average and range charts, you will need a series of samples. Each sample will consist of several measurements of pieces, often four or five. You will use the information from these measurements in several ways on the control chart, such as determining the average of each sample.

How you choose the sample is very important. Remember that the sample is to be taken in such a way that *only* inherent variation is seen within the sample. If there is an assignable cause, you want it to act on every piece in the sample. Then the variation between the sample pieces will be only inherent variation.

One way to do this is to choose your samples so that the individual pieces within each sample are as much alike as possible. Two things will help you do this. First, take each sample over a very short period of time. Second, take each sample (and all the samples for your initial control charts) from a single source of data. That is, take the sample from *one* machine, *one* machine head, *one* production associate, *one* batch of materials, and so forth. (Sometimes there are so many different sources of data that it is not worthwhile to make separate control charts on each source. In that case, how many charts should you make? That depends on how many charts you need and how many charts your company is willing to pay for.)

In setting up control charts for endplay, let's suppose that you took samples of your work every 15 minutes. The five motors in each sample were produced one right after another, and you noted the order of production. This means that each sample came from a very short period of time, there was only one production associate, and the pieces came from only one machine. Also, chances are that you drew parts from one batch of motors and from one batch of wheels. As a result, each sample of five motors will be as much alike as possible. Therefore any differences or variations within a sample should be no more than the inherent variation.

To give another example of gathering data for the initial control charts, an engineer set up control charts for a paper coating process. The engineer did not let the production associate adjust the thickness of the coating for 48 hours. Samples taken through this 48-hour period showed variations in thickness, but these were inherent variations due to chance causes. They were not production associate-caused because he had made no corrections.

Before using control charts the associate had worked hard to keep the coating thickness just right. He measured the thickness each time. If one measurement was too thick, he adjusted the coating to be thinner. If one was too thin, he adjusted it to be thicker. All through his shift he was constantly adjusting the process to make the best possible product. However, once he began to use control charts, he adjusted less often yet made a more consistent product. He was working smarter, not harder.

Step 3. Set up forms for data and graphs.

Once you have decided on your important characteristics and your sample, it's time to think about the forms. Good forms can make the calculations easy. They have boxes for necessary background information such as date, product, part, service, what is being measured (hour, minute, inch, centimeter), and production associate.

The excellent chart in Figure 3-9 is available from the American Society for Quality (ASQ). This chart shows boxes filled in with the name of the part, the date, and other information.

Step 4. Collect the samples and record the measurements.

Take the samples according to your plan. Measure them in the way that you have determined, and record the measurements on the form. Be sure to put the measurements on the form *in the order of production.* Record the time of each sample. (See Figure 3-10.)

Step 5. Calculate the averages.

Now that you have collected the data for the initial control charts, the first thing to do is to calculate the averages ($\overline{X}$'s). For each sample add up the measurements and record the total on the form in the row marked "SUM." (See Figure 3-11.) Then divide this total by the number of observations in your sample and write the answer in the row marked "AVERAGE, $\overline{X}$," as you have already learned to do. Finally, check your arithmetic. (One of the best ways to check is to do it all over again.)

Your calculations for the first two samples will look like this.

First sample:	Second sample:
32	47
26	32
42	41
53	20
36	28
Total = 189	Total = 168

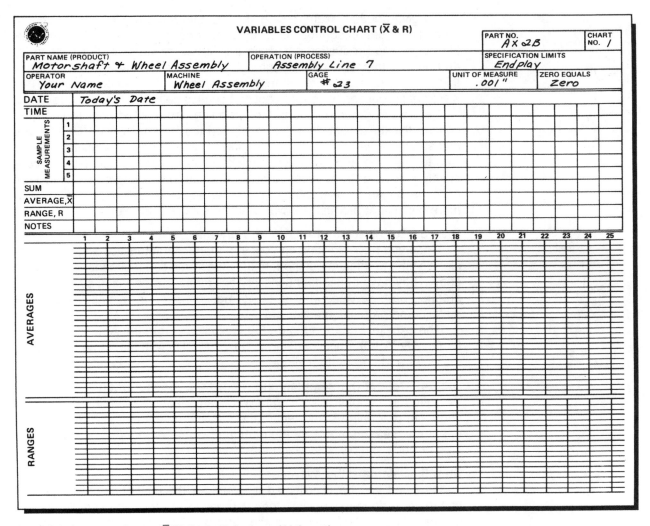

Figure 3-9. Average and range (X̄-R) chart with background information.

Average = Total/number in sample
           189/5
      = 37.8
      = $\overline{X}$

Average = Total/number in sample
           168/5
      = 33.6
      = $\overline{X}$

Step 6. Calculate the overall average $(\overline{\overline{X}})$.

The overall average, or *overall mean $\overline{\overline{X}}$), is the average of all your sample averages. First add up all the averages ($\overline{X}$'s). Then divide this total by the *number* of averages. Check your arithmetic by repeating the calculations. (Another way to check your arithmetic is to add up all the individual measurements on your chart. Count the individual measurements. Then divide the total of all the measurements by the number of measurements.)

VARIABLES CONTROL CHART (X̄ & R)																				PART NO. Ax 2B		CHART NO. 1

PART NAME (PRODUCT) Motorshaft & Wheel Assembly **OPERATION (PROCESS)** Assembly Line 7 **SPECIFICATION LIMITS** Endplay

OPERATOR Your Name **MACHINE** Wheel Assembly **GAGE** #23 **UNIT OF MEASURE** .001" **ZERO EQUALS** zero

DATE Today's Date

TIME	10	10¹⁵	10³⁰	10⁴⁵	11	11¹⁵	11³⁰	11⁴⁵	12	12¹⁵	12³⁰	12⁴⁵	1	1¹⁵	1³⁰	1⁴⁵	2	2¹⁵	2³⁰	2⁴⁵
1	32	47	44	40	44	58	42	45	57	38	32	46	47	46	50	40	34	46	36	30
2	26	32	51	39	23	43	33	31	27	45	31	41	49	47	57	28	45	51	38	45
3	42	41	46	37	43	31	45	39	44	33	39	47	29	53	41	43	53	49	50	37
4	53	20	37	50	25	33	38	50	44	51	32	44	40	36	41	44	51	30	48	31
5	36	28	40	51	36	40	48	52	55	43	44	45	44	40	49	50	45	40	30	34

SAMPLE MEASUREMENTS

SUM

AVERAGE, X̄

RANGE, R

NOTES

AVERAGES

RANGES

Figure 3-10. Average and range chart with measurements.

The endplay for the electric motors gives the following data (See Figure 3-11):

Averages, X̄'s: 37.8, 33.6, 43.6, 43.4, 34.2, 41.0, 41.2, 43.4, 45.4, 42.0, 35.6, 44.6, 41.8, 44.4, 47.6, 41.0, 45.6, 43.2, 40.4, 35.4

Total of X̄'s: 825.2
Number of X̄'s: 20
Overall mean, X̄̄: 825.2/20 = 41.26

Don't enter the X̄̄ on your chart yet. Just make a note of it. You will need it later.

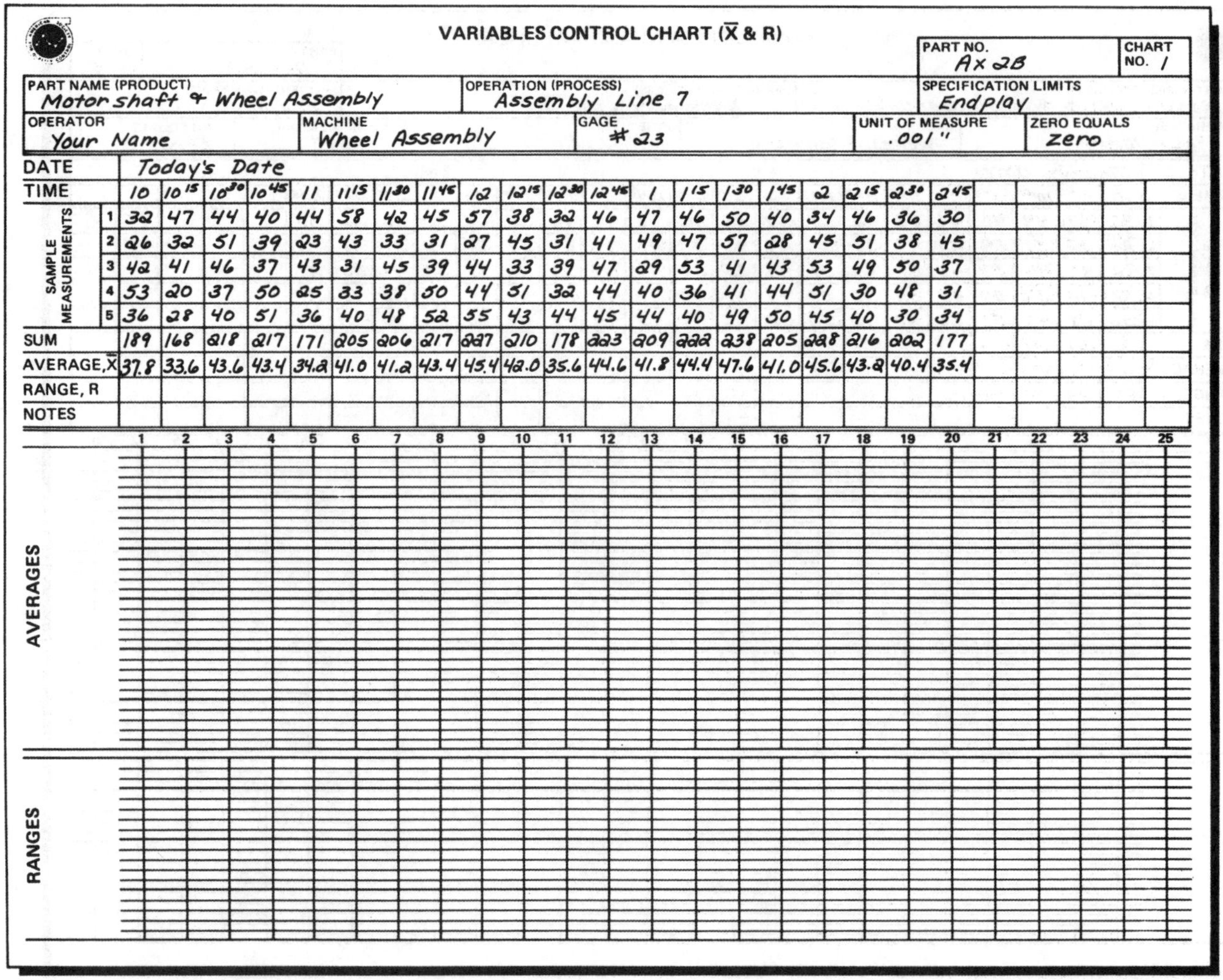

VARIABLES CONTROL CHART (X̄ & R)

	PART NO. Ax 2B	CHART NO. 1

PART NAME (PRODUCT) Motor shaft & Wheel Assembly **OPERATION (PROCESS)** Assembly Line 7 **SPECIFICATION LIMITS** Endplay

OPERATOR Your Name **MACHINE** Wheel Assembly **GAGE** #23 **UNIT OF MEASURE** .001" **ZERO EQUALS** zero

DATE Today's Date

TIME	10	10¹⁵	10³⁰	10⁴⁵	11	11¹⁵	11³⁰	11⁴⁵	12	12¹⁵	12³⁰	12⁴⁵	1	1¹⁵	1³⁰	1⁴⁵	2	2¹⁵	2³⁰	2⁴⁵
SAMPLE MEASUREMENTS 1	32	47	44	40	44	58	42	45	57	38	32	46	47	46	50	40	34	46	36	30
2	26	32	51	39	23	43	33	31	27	45	31	41	49	47	57	28	45	51	38	45
3	42	41	46	37	43	31	45	39	44	33	39	47	29	53	41	43	53	49	50	37
4	53	20	37	50	25	33	38	50	44	51	32	44	40	36	41	44	51	30	48	31
5	36	28	40	51	36	40	48	52	55	43	44	45	44	40	49	50	45	40	30	34
SUM	189	168	218	217	171	205	206	217	227	210	178	223	209	222	238	205	228	216	202	177
AVERAGE, X̄	37.8	33.6	43.6	43.4	34.2	41.0	41.2	43.4	45.4	42.0	35.6	44.6	41.8	44.4	47.6	41.0	45.6	43.2	40.4	35.4
RANGE, R																				
NOTES																				

AVERAGES

RANGES

Figure 3-11. Average and range chart with sums and averages.

Step 7. Determine the ranges for the samples.

Find and circle the largest number in each sample. Find and draw a box around the smallest. Then calculate the range for each sample as follows:

Range = Largest observation less smallest observation.

(Subtract the smallest from the largest.)

Record the ranges in the row marked "RANGE, R". Check your arithmetic.

The chart for the electric motors shows the following (see Figure 3-12):

VARIABLES CONTROL CHART (X̄ & R)

PART NO. *Ax2B* CHART NO. *1*

PART NAME (PRODUCT): *Motor shaft & Wheel Assembly*
OPERATION (PROCESS): *Assembly Line 7*
SPECIFICATION LIMITS: *Endplay*

OPERATOR: *Your Name*
MACHINE: *Wheel Assembly*
GAGE: *#23*
UNIT OF MEASURE: *.001"*
ZERO EQUALS: *Zero*

DATE: *Today's Date*

TIME	10	10¹⁵	10³⁰	10⁴⁵	11	11¹⁵	11³⁰	11⁴⁵	12	12¹⁵	12³⁰	12⁴⁵	1	1¹⁵	1³⁰	1⁴⁵	2	2¹⁵	2³⁰	2⁴⁵					
1	32	(47)	44	40	(44)	(58)	42	45	(57)	38	32	46	47	46	50	40	[34]	46	36	[30]					
2	[26]	32	(51)	39	[23]	43	[33]	[31]	[27]	45	[31]	[41]	(49)	47	(57)	[28]	45	[51]	38	(45)					
3	42	41	46	[37]	43	[31]	45	39	44	[33]	39	(47)	[29]	(53)	41	43	(53)	49	(50)	37					
4	(53)	[20]	[37]	50	25	33	38	50	44	(51)	32	44	40	[36]	[41]	44	51	[30]	48	31					
5	36	28	40	(51)	36	40	(48)	(53)	55	43	(44)	45	44	40	49	(50)	45	40	[30]	34					
SUM	189	168	218	217	171	205	206	217	227	210	178	223	209	222	238	205	228	216	202	177					
AVERAGE, X̄	37.8	33.6	43.6	43.4	34.2	41.0	41.8	43.4	45.4	42.0	35.6	44.6	41.8	44.4	47.6	41.0	45.6	43.2	40.4	35.4					
RANGE, R	27	27	14	14	21	27	15	21	30	18	13	6	20	17	16	22	19	21	20	15					
NOTES																									

(SAMPLE MEASUREMENTS)

AVERAGES

RANGES

Figure 3-12. Average and range chart with ranges.

First Sample
32
26
42
53
36
Range = 53 minus 26
R = 27

Second sample:
47
32
41
20
28
Range = 47 minus 20
R = 27

Step 8. Calculate the average range.

Add up all the ranges; then count them. Then divide the total of all the ranges by the number of ranges. The result is the *average range, ($\overline{R}$)*. Finally, check your arithmetic carefully. (You can't check $\overline{R}$ by calculating the range of all the data. It won't work.)

Ranges, R:	27, 27, 14, 14, 21, 27, 15, 21, 30, 18, 13, 6, 20, 17, 16, 22, 19, 21, 20, 15
Total of R's:	383
Number of R's:	20
Average Range, $\overline{R}$ = 383/20 = 19.15	

Don't write the $\overline{R}$ on the chart yet. Save it for later.

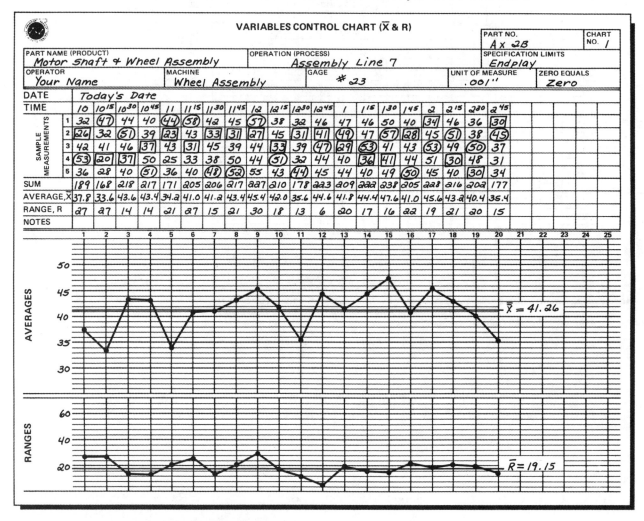

Figure 3-13. Average and range chart with data plotted on graph. Lines are drawn for $\overline{\overline{X}}$ and $\overline{R}$.

Step 9. Determine scales for the graphs and plot the data.

First, find the largest and smallest averages ($\overline{X}$'s). Find the largest and the smallest ranges (R's) and check to make sure they *are* the largest and the smallest. Then set the scale for the graph in such a way that the largest and the smallest values will fit comfortably inside the ends of the scales. (The lower end of the graph for ranges is usually set at zero.) Pick scales that make it easy for you to plot the data and leave extra room on the graphs for the statistical control limits. Now plot the data and draw a line for the overall mean ($\overline{\overline{X}}$) and a line for the average range ($\overline{R}$).

Largest average ($\overline{X}$): 47.6 Largest range (R): 30
Smallest average ($\overline{X}$): 33.6 Smallest range (R): use 0.0

For averages you can run your scales from 30.0 to 50.0. All the averages will fit comfortably but will leave room for the control limits. On your form there will be five lines between 45.0 and 50.0, so each line will represent 1.0 unit. (See Figure 3-13.)

For the ranges, run the scale up to 60 at the highest heavy line. All the ranges will fit and some room will be left for control limits. Each line represents 4.0 units, which makes it easy to plot the ranges. You may be tempted to mark the three dark lines as 10, 20, and 30, but that arrangement won't leave much room for the upper control limit for ranges.

Finally, plot the averages and ranges as dots and connect the dots with straight lines. Draw a heavy, solid line for the overall mean ($\overline{\overline{X}}$) and mark its value at the far end. Do the same for the average range ($\overline{R}$). (See Figure 3-13.)

Step 10. Determine control limits for ranges.

Calculate control limits for ranges *before* you calculate the limits for averages so you will know whether the inherent variation is stable. If it is not, there is no sense in checking whether the averages are in control.

On the back of the average and range chart form, which is available from the American Society for Quality (ASQ), is a box marked "FACTORS FOR CONTROL LIMITS." (See Figure 3-14.) From the table of average and range chart factors choose the D_4 factor that corresponds to the sample size you are using. Circle the 5 under the **n** column because 5

Figure 3-14. Factors for control limits. D_4 is circled for a sample of five measurements.

n	A_2	D_4	d_2	$\dfrac{3}{d_2}$	A_M
2	1.880	3.268	1.128	2.659	0.779
3	1.023	2.574	1.693	1.772	0.749
4	0.729	2.282	2.059	1.457	0.728
⑤	0.577	2.114	2.326	1.290	0.713
6	0.483	2.004	2.534	1.184	0.701

FACTORS FOR CONTROL LIMITS

is the size of your sample. Circle the 2.114 because that D_4 factor corresponds to a sample size of 5.

To find the upper control limit for ranges, use this formula:

Upper control limit for ranges (UCL_R) equals D_4 times $\overline{R}$.

$$UCL_R = 2.114 \times 19.15$$
$$UCL_R = 40.48$$

Because our sample size is 5, our lower control limit will be zero.

$$LCL_R = 0.0$$

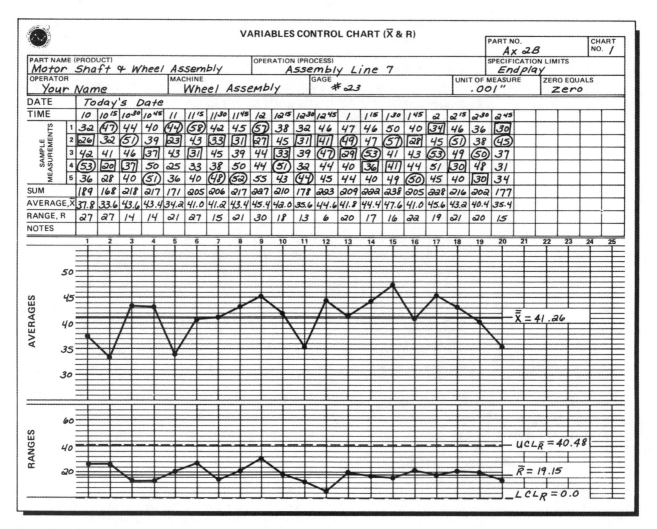

Figure 3-15. Average and range charts with control limits for ranges.

For samples of six measurements or less, the lower control limit for ranges is always zero. Be sure to check your sample size, the D_4 factor, and your arithmetic. Then draw the control limits on your range chart and label them UCL_R and LCL_R. We recommend that you draw the limits as dashed lines or colored lines so that they will be easy to see. (See Figure 3-15.)

Step 11. Are the ranges in statistical control?

There are three possible answers to this question: (1) *all* the ranges (R's) fall *inside* the control limits; (2) *one or two* ranges fall *outside* the limits; (3) *three or more* ranges fall *outside* the limits.

(1) If all the ranges are inside the control limits—that is, if no ranges fall above the upper control limit (UCL_R) or below the lower limit (LCL_R)—the ranges are in statistical control. Now you may go ahead and figure out control limits for the averages. If a range falls exactly on the control limit, don't worry about it; it counts as inside. When we say that the ranges are in control, we are really saying that the inherent variation is stable and there are *no* assignable causes disturbing the ranges.

(2) Sometimes one or two ranges will fall outside the control limits. When this happens, it is common practice to throw out those ranges, the samples from which they came, and the sample averages. (We don't like to throw out data because even wild or extreme data can tell us something.) Then completely refigure the overall mean ($\bar{\bar{X}}$), the average range ($\bar{R}$), and the control limits for the ranges without those out-of-control ranges.

After you refigure the upper and lower control limits for the ranges, one of two things may happen. First, one or more of the remaining ranges may still fall outside the new control limits. If that happens, the ranges are out of statistical control. In that case do *not* figure control limits for averages. Find and remove the assignable causes that are upsetting the ranges. Then set up new average and range charts with new data.

On the other hand, you may find that all the ranges are now inside the new control limits. In that case you may go on to develop control limits for the averages. But be careful! There may still be some assignable causes which can give you trouble until you find and remove them.

(3) If three or more ranges are outside the original control limits, the ranges are out of statistical control and the inherent variation is not stable. Do *not* bother to figure out control limits for the averages. Find and remove the assignable causes that are upsetting the ranges. Then start over again—collect new data and set up new control charts.

To help you keep track of all these possibilities, a *decision chart* or *flow chart* may be helpful. Figure 3-16 is a decision chart for working with the ranges.

The ranges for the electric motor data were shown in Figure 3-15. When you look at the range chart, you can see that all the ranges fall between the lower control limit of 0.0 and the upper control limit of 40.48. Therefore the

Figure 3-16. Decision chart for working with ranges.

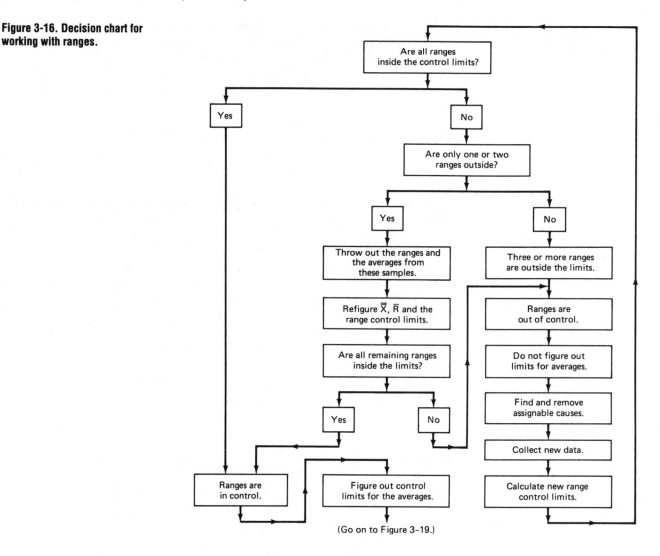

(Go on to Figure 3–19.)

ranges are in statistical control. Now you can go ahead to work out the control limits for the averages chart.

Step 12. Determine control limits for averages.

Once you have found the ranges to be in statistical control, then and *only* then can you work on the control limits for averages.

On the back of the ASQ form look under "FACTORS FOR CONTROL LIMITS" to find the A_2 factor that corresponds to the sample size you have been using. (See Figure 3-17.)

Circle the 5 under the **n** column because your samples consist of five electric motors. Then circle 0.577 in the A_2 column because this is the A_2

Figure 3-17. Factors for control limits. A_2 is circled for a sample of five measurements.

FACTORS FOR CONTROL LIMITS

n	A_2	D_4	d_2	$\dfrac{3}{d_2}$	A_M
2	1.880	3.268	1.128	2.659	0.779
3	1.023	2.574	1.693	1.772	0.749
4	0.729	2.282	2.059	1.457	0.728
⑤	0.577	2.114	2.326	1.290	0.713
6	0.483	2.004	2.534	1.184	0.701

factor to be used with samples of five. Next, multiply this A_2 factor by 19.15, the average range you found earlier.

$$A_2 \text{ times } \overline{R} \text{ equals } 0.577 \text{ times } 19.15$$
$$= 11.05$$

To find the upper control limit, add this figure, 11.05, to the overall average, 41.26, which you found in Step 6.

Upper control limit for averages equals $\overline{\overline{X}}$ plus (A_2 times $\overline{R}$).

$$= 41.26 + (0.577 \times 19.15)$$
$$= 41.26 + 11.05$$
$$= 52.31$$

To find the lower control limit, subtract 11.05 from the overall average:

Lower control limit for averages equals $\overline{\overline{X}}$ minus (A_2 times $\overline{R}$).

$$= 41.26 - 11.05$$
$$= 30.21$$

In summary, these are the formulas for upper and lower control limits for averages ($\overline{X}$):

Upper control limit for averages $= UCL_{\overline{x}}$
$$= \overline{\overline{X}} + (A_2 \text{ times } \overline{R})$$
Lower control limit for averages $= LCL_{\overline{x}}$
$$= \overline{\overline{X}} - (A_2 \text{ times } \overline{R})$$

After checking your arithmetic, draw the control limits on the "AVERAGES" portion of the chart and label them $UCL_{\overline{x}}$ and $LCL_{\overline{x}}$. We recommend dashed or colored lines. (See Figure 3-18.)

Step 13. Are the averages in statistical control?

Make the same kind of check for the averages as you did for the ranges. As with the ranges, there are three possible situations: (1) *all* the averages fall inside the control limits; (2) *one or two* averages fall outside the limits; or (3) *three or more* averages fall outside the limits.

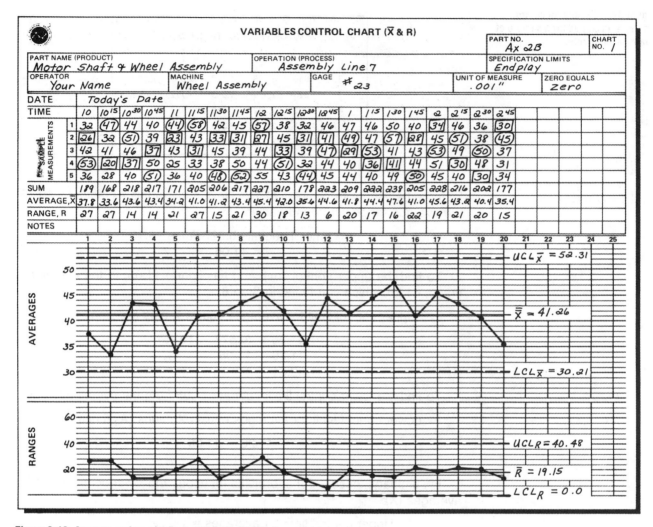

Figure 3-18. Average and range chart with control limits for averages.

(1) If *all* the averages fall inside the control limits—that is, if no averages fall above the upper control limit (UCL$_{\bar{x}}$) or below the lower control limit (LCL$_{\bar{x}}$)—the averages are in statistical control. Apparently *no* assignable causes are disturbing the averages. If the averages and ranges are in control, then you may use your average and range charts to control ongoing production.

(2) If one or two averages fall outside the control limits, it is common practice to throw out those averages for the time being. Then refigure the overall mean ($\bar{\bar{X}}$) and the control limits for the averages without the one or two averages you discarded. If any averages fall outside the new control

limits, the averages are out of statistical control. Find and remove the assignable causes. Then, when you think the process is cleaned up, collect new data. You will need to set up *both* the range and the average control charts again.

However, if you refigure the overall mean $(\overline{\overline{X}})$ and the control limits for the averages and find that all the averages are now inside the new control limits, you can use the average and range control charts to control ongoing production. But be careful—the one or two averages that you threw out could be a signal that some assignable causes are still at work.

Figure 3-19. Decision chart for working with averages.

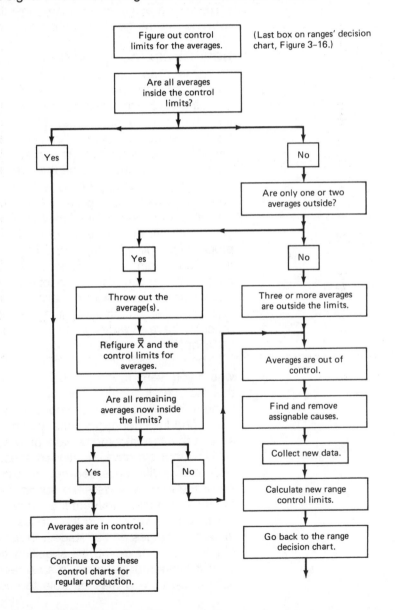

(3) If three or more averages are outside the initial control limits, the averages are out of control. This situation shows something more than inherent variation. Some assignable cause or causes are at work. Find and remove the assignable causes, start again with new data, and set up new range and average control charts.

Figure 3-19 is a decision chart that shows all the possible situations in picture form.

In the chart for electric motors, all the averages fall inside the upper and lower control limits, so you know the averages are in control. Apparently there are no assignable causes upsetting the averages. You may use this average and range control chart for regular production.

HOW TO USE CONTROL CHARTS IN CONTINUED PRODUCTION

As soon as you find that both the ranges and averages are in control, you can say that the process is in statistical control. This means that, as far as you can tell from the charts, only inherent variation is at work, and that the inherent variation is present because of chance causes. There seem to be no assignable causes. The stable inherent variation results in a range chart that is in control. As far as you can tell, the overall process average ($\overline{\overline{X}}$) is also constant because the average chart is also in control.

Just because the process is in control, it is not necessarily doing what you want it to do. Being in control simply means that it is humming along smoothly and turning out *consistent* products. Once the process is in control, you must determine whether or not it is *capable*. (You will learn more about process capability in Module 5.) The ranges may be in control, showing that the inherent variation is stable, but the amount of inherent variation may be so large that much of the product falls outside the specifications. In this case you would be faced with a management/team solvable problem. That is, a problem-solving team of production associates, managers, and others would probably have to redesign the process to decrease the amount of inherent variation, or they might decide to relax the specifications.

You must also determine whether the overall average ($\overline{\overline{X}}$) is adjusted to where you want it. The process may be in control, but that is no guarantee that the overall average is where it belongs. The overall average may need to be adjusted so that the product is within specifications. If you have both upper and lower specifications, you may even decide to adjust the process so that the overall average falls halfway between the specifications.

Now that we have mentioned specifications, we cannot emphasize too strongly the difference between control limits and specifications. *Specifications and control limits have nothing to do with each other.* Specifications are the designer's requirements for individual units. Control limits are based strictly on the variation in the process. They describe the inherent variation in *sample* ranges and averages. In the electric motor problem you will note that we never gave you the specifications.

If the inherent variation is small enough so that the process can meet specifications, you may be able to continue the process while using your control charts. If not, then you may have to take the problem to a problem-solving team. How do you know whether the inherent variation is small enough? You will probably have to run a process capability test, which we will describe in Module 5. You may also have to adjust the process so that the overall average ($\overline{\overline{X}}$) is where you want it. This adjustment should not affect the control limits for the ranges, but it will change the limits for the averages.

We recommend that once you have made this adjustment, you check it out by looking at the next few averages. Take ten new samples as close together as possible. Calculate the overall average of these samples and draw it in on your control chart for averages. Figure out new upper and lower control limits by using the new overall average, but keep the old average range:

$$\text{new UCL}_{\overline{x}} \text{ equals new } \overline{\overline{X}} \text{ plus } (A_2 \text{ times old } \overline{R})$$
$$\text{new LCL}_{\overline{x}} \text{ equals new } \overline{\overline{X}} \text{ minus } (A_2 \text{ times old } \overline{R})$$

Now you should be ready to use the control charts, as discussed in the first section of this module.

MEDIAN AND RANGE CHARTS

Now that you have learned how to make and use average and range charts, let's take a look at another type of control chart, which you can sometimes use in place of an average and range chart. This is the *median and range* ($\widetilde{X}$-R) *chart.* (Figure 3-20).

The median and range chart is easier to use than an average and range chart, but is not suitable for all operations. It is a good chart to use in operations that (1) are known to be distributed normally, (2) are not very often disturbed by assignable causes, and (3) are easily adjusted by the production associate. If the operation does not meet these requirements, you should use an average and range chart.

The development of the median and range chart is like that of the average and range chart. It is easy to use, once you have established the control limits. For a median and range chart, you can use a sample size of two to ten pieces, but a sample of three or five is the easiest to work with.

The form for this chart looks very much like the average and range chart form. In fact, you can use the average and range chart form but label it as a median and range chart.

DEVELOPING A MEDIAN AND RANGE CHART

The chart shown in Figure 3-21 is based on a three-piece sample. The procedure for developing the chart is as follows.

Step 1. Collect samples.

Take samples that were made as close to the same time as practical.

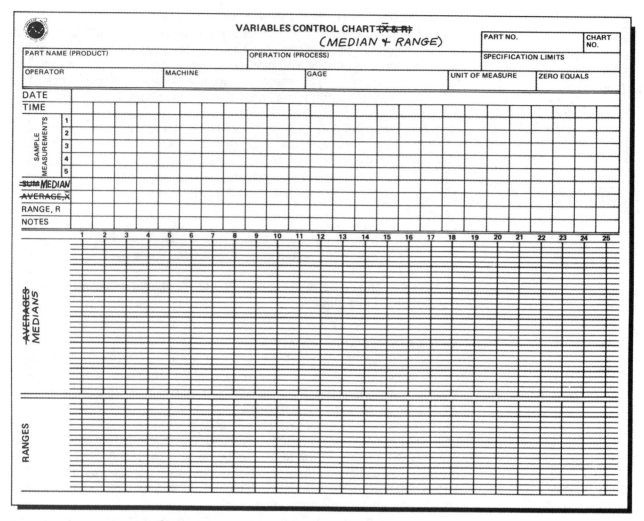

Figure 3-20. Median and range ($\tilde{X}$-R) chart.

Step 2. Measure the dimension to be charted.

Take your measurements and record the results in the "SAMPLE MEASUREMENTS" columns.

Step 3. Determine the median measurement.

Find the *median* measurement of the sample and record it in the "MEDIAN" row on the chart. A median is always in the *middle* of a group of measurements when you count from the smallest to the largest measurement. Half the measurements will be smaller than the median and half will be larger.

VARIABLES CONTROL CHART ~~(X̄ & R)~~
(MEDIAN + RANGE)

PART NO.	CHART NO.
128865	1

PART NAME (PRODUCT)	OPERATION (PROCESS)	SPECIFICATION LIMITS
Brake hose fitting	Brake hose fitting - grinding	—

OPERATOR	MACHINE	GAGE	UNIT OF MEASURE	ZERO EQUALS
Your Name	#6	12A	0.001 inch	0.0

DATE: Today's Date

TIME	8:30	8:45	9:00	9:15	9:30	9:45	10:00	10:15	10:30	10:45	11:00	11:15	11:30	11:45	12:00
SAMPLE MEASUREMENTS 1	32	47	44	40	44	58	42	45	57	38	32	46	47	46	50
2	26	32	51	39	23	43	33	31	29	45	31	41	49	47	57
3	42	41	46	37	43	31	45	39	44	33	39	47	29	53	41
4															
5 $\tilde{\tilde{X}}$															
~~SUM~~ MEDIAN	32	41	46	39	43	43	42	39	44	38	32	46	47	47	50
~~AVERAGE, X̄~~	①	⑥		⑤		⑧	⑦	④		③	②				
RANGE, R	16	15	7	3	21	27	12	14	28	12	8	6	20	7	16
NOTES			③	①			⑦	$\tilde{R}$		⑥	⑤	②		④	

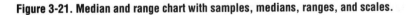

Figure 3-21. Median and range chart with samples, medians, ranges, and scales.

In this chart you are using a three-piece sample, so the median is the measurement between the largest and smallest measurements. (We suggest that you draw a circle around the largest number in the sample and a box around the smallest.) If you had chosen to use a five-piece sample, the median would be the third measurement, which falls between the two largest and the two smallest measurements. When you use an even-numbered sample size, the median is the number halfway between the two middle measurements in the sample (for example, between the third and fourth pieces of a six-piece sample). An easy way to figure the median in a sample with an even number of pieces is to add the two middle measurements in the sample and divide by two. This result is the median and will be halfway between these two measurements.

Do not confuse the *median* of a group of measurements with the *mean* of that group. The mean is the average value of the measurements and the median is the middle measurement of the group. In a group of five measurements, 9, 3, 2, 8, 10, for example, the average is 6.4 (9 + 3 + 2 + 8 + 10 = 32 divided by 5, which equals 6.4). To find the median, first rank the numbers by size: 2, 3, 8, 9, 10. There are two numbers below the 8 and two numbers above the 8, so 8 is the middle number or the median.

Step 4. Determine the ranges for the samples.

Figure the range, as you have already learned to do, by subtracting the smallest measurement from the largest. Record the range readings in the "RANGE" row on the chart.

In this example, the first three-piece sample contains the measurements 32, 26, and 42. When you rank them 26, 32, 42, you can see that 42 is the largest and 26 is the smallest, so the median is 32, the number between these two measurements.

To figure the range of the first sample, subtract the smallest measurement (26) from the largest (42). The result, 16, is the range.

As you can see on the chart, the second sample is:

> 47 (largest)
> 32 (smallest)
> 41 (median)

47 (largest) minus 32 (smallest) equals 15 (range).

Step 5. Determine the median of medians ($\widetilde{\widetilde{X}}$) and the median of ranges ($\widetilde{R}$).

When you have measured and recorded fifteen samples, you figure the *median of medians ($\widetilde{\widetilde{X}}$)* and the *median of ranges ($\widetilde{R}$)*.

To find the median of medians, count up from the smallest median to find the middle value of the fifteen medians. The middle value in the group of fifteen is the eighth median from the bottom (or the top) of the values. On the chart in Figure 3-21 we have ranked the eight smallest medians to help you count up from the smallest to the eighth in the group of fifteen. The first and smallest median is 32; the next smallest is also 32, and is numbered 2; the next is 38 and is numbered 3; the next is 39 and numbered 4; number 5 is another 39; number 6 is 41; number 7 is 42; and number 8 is 43. This number, 43, is the median of the medians ($\widetilde{\widetilde{X}}$). For the time being, write $\widetilde{\widetilde{X}}$ over this value.

Find the median of ranges or median range in the same way as you found $\widetilde{\widetilde{X}}$. Count the fifteen range values from the smallest to find the eighth or middle value. The chart in Figure 3-21 shows that the median range value ($\widetilde{R}$) is 14. An $\widetilde{R}$ is written underneath the 14 in the "RANGE" row.

Step 6. Set the scale for the median ($\widetilde{X}$) chart.

Select a scale for the median ($\widetilde{X}$) chart such that the spread between the largest and smallest of all the individual measurements will take up about one-half to three-fourths the available chart space on the median chart.

Because the median of the medians ($\widetilde{\widetilde{X}}$) is 43 in this example, set the value 40 at the middle of the scale. Then each major division will be worth 10 units on the scale. The scale we have selected runs from 10 to 70. Write these numbers on the chart in the area marked "MEDIANS."

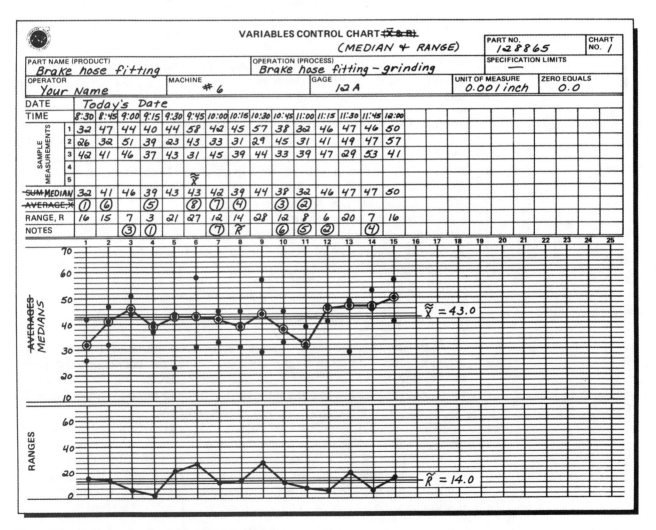

Figure 3-22. Median and range chart with points plotted.

Step 7. Set the scale for the range.

Do this the same way as you set the median chart scale.

Each major division on the range chart scale is worth 20 units. (The divisions have been marked along the side of the range chart.) This arrangement allows room for the upper control limit on the chart.

Step 8. Plot the measurements on the control chart.

All the measurements in the sample are plotted on the median and range chart. For the first sample place small dots on the first vertical line at the appropriate place on the scale. Place the first measurement at 32, the second at 26, and the third at 42. Identify the dot representing the median, which is 32, by placing a small circle around that dot. Plot the rest of the measurements in the same way. (See Figure 3-22.) Connect the medians with straight lines to help you spot trends. Draw in a line for $\widetilde{X}$, the median of medians, and label it.

Plot the ranges on the median and range chart just as you did on the average and range chart. Draw in a line for $\widetilde{R}$, the median of ranges, and label it.

Step 9. Determine the control limits for medians and ranges.

Calculate the control limits for the medians ($\widetilde{X}$) and the ranges (R) by using formulas and factors that are similar to the ones for average and range charts. The factors are shown in Figure 3-23. Note that the $\widetilde{A}_2$ and $\widetilde{D}_4$ factors for the median and range chart are *not* the same as the A_2 and D_4 factors for the average and range charts.

To figure the upper control limit (UCL$_R$) for the ranges, multiply the median range (14) by the $\widetilde{D}_4$ factor from the chart in Figure 3-23. This value is 2.75 for a sample size of three. The calculation is as follows:

$$\text{UCL}_R \text{ equals } \widetilde{D}_4 \text{ times } \widetilde{R}$$
$$\text{UCL}_R = 2.75 \times 14 = 38.5$$

The lower control limit for ranges (LCL$_R$) is zero.

At this point, check all the range numbers on the chart to see whether any are larger than 38.5. If no more than two ranges fall outside the upper control limit, throw out those ranges *and* their medians. Find the new median range and refigure the upper control limit. If three or more ranges fall outside the control limit, start over with new measurements.

In the example, no ranges fall outside the upper control limit, so now you can figure the control limits for the medians.

The $\widetilde{A}_2$ factor for a sample size of three is 1.26. (See Figure 3-23.) Multiply this number by the median range ($\widetilde{R}$) and add the result to the median of the sample medians ($\widetilde{X}$) to find the upper control limit for medians (UCL$_{\widetilde{x}}$).

$$\text{UCL}_{\widetilde{x}} \text{ equals } \widetilde{X} \text{ plus } (\widetilde{A}_2 \text{ times } \widetilde{R}).$$

Sample size, n	$\widetilde{A}_2$	$\widetilde{D}_4$
2	2.22	3.87
3	1.26	2.75
4	0.83	2.38
5	0.71	2.18

Figure 3-23. Control limit factors for median and range charts.

First multiply $\widetilde{A}_2$ by $\widetilde{R}$. Then add that to $\widetilde{\widetilde{X}}$, which is 43.

$$UCL_{\widetilde{x}} = 43 + (1.26 \times 14)$$
$$= 43 + 17.64$$
$$= 60.64$$

The lower control limit for medians ($LCL_{\widetilde{x}}$) is as follows:

$$LCL_{\widetilde{x}} \text{ equals } \widetilde{\widetilde{X}} \text{ minus } (\widetilde{A}_2 \text{ times } \widetilde{R})$$

First multiply $\widetilde{A}_2$ by $\widetilde{R}$. Then subtract the result from $\widetilde{\widetilde{X}}$, which is 43.

$$LCL_{\widetilde{x}} = 43 - (1.26 \times 14)$$
$$= 43 - 17.64$$
$$= 25.36$$

Again, compare the medians to the control limits to see whether any medians fall outside the upper or lower control limits. If one or two fall outside, throw them out, refigure the median of the medians, and then calculate new control limits. If *any* medians fall outside the new control limits, throw out the chart and start over with new measurements. If three or more medians fall outside the original control limits, throw out all the measurements and start over, just as you did with the average and range charts.

Draw control limits using broken or dashed lines as shown on the chart. (See Figure 3-24.) It's good practice to identify the lines with their values as shown on the chart.

The median and range chart is plotted with individual measurements. For this reason you can compare the plotted points to the specification, but remember that corrective action is needed when the median or range values are outside the control limits. Individual points (not medians) can appear outside the control limits even when the job is running normally. Individual points outside the specification do *not* indicate that the job is out of control. It is not a symptom of an assignable cause. Remember, the process needs to be adjusted *only* when medians ($\widetilde{X}$) or ranges (R) lie outside the control limits.

INDIVIDUAL AND RANGE CHARTS

An *individual and range (X-R) chart* can be useful in special situations. This control chart is based on individual measurements rather than small samples.

The individual and range chart does not detect changes in the process as quickly as an average and range chart. Like the median and range chart, it is best to use the individual and range chart when the frequency distribution of the measurements from the process or operation is already known to match the bell-shaped (normal) curve.

A good use for this chart is in the manufacture of products that are made in batches, such as chemical solutions, coatings on parts, or products made

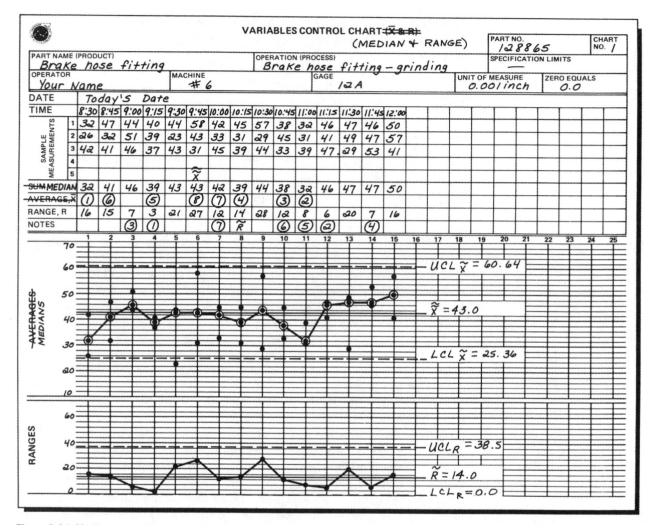

Figure 3-24. Median and range chart with control limits.

up of compounds that are a mixture of several ingredients. To give an example, several ingredients may be mixed together in large batches and those batches used later to make many units of product. In such a situation, the measurement would be about the same no matter where you took the sample from the batch. It is also likely that a long time would elapse between batches. For these reasons you need to plot only one measurement from each batch on the chart.

To monitor chemical solutions used to plate metal parts, you can use an individual and range chart instead of an average and range chart. If you took four or five measurements at one time from one batch of the liquid in the plating tank, you would obtain a range based mostly on the errors you made in measuring. For the same reason, it is not good practice to measure and record the thickness of a coating in more than one place on the same piece. A single measurement is enough in these situations, and an individual and range chart is appropriate.

You can also use the individual and range chart when you find that it's costly or time-consuming to test or measure the dimension.

DEVELOPING AN INDIVIDUAL AND RANGE CHART

The standard average and range chart form can be adapted easily for use as an individual and range chart. Just as with the median and range chart, cross out the words that don't apply to this chart and write in the words you need. (See Figure 3-25.)

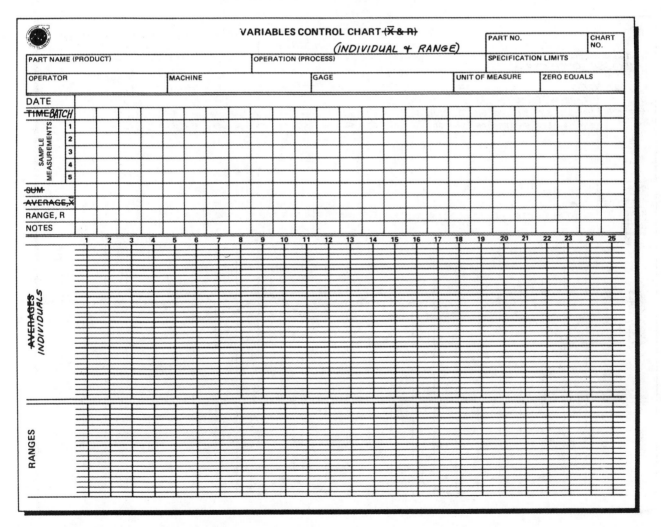

Figure 3-25. Individual and range (X-R) chart.

To demonstrate how to make an individual and range chart, we will use measurements taken from a rubber compounding process. In this process, the many ingredients that make up a batch of uncured rubber are mixed together. Small quantities of oils, various powders, and synthetic or natural rubber are mixed into a mass of uncured rubber called a "batch." These batches generally weigh about 350 pounds, and finishing a batch takes from several minutes to well over an hour. If you wanted to monitor and control the characteristics of this product, you would find that a fairly long time would elapse before you obtained four or five measurements to use on a typical average and range chart because you can obtain only one measurement per batch.

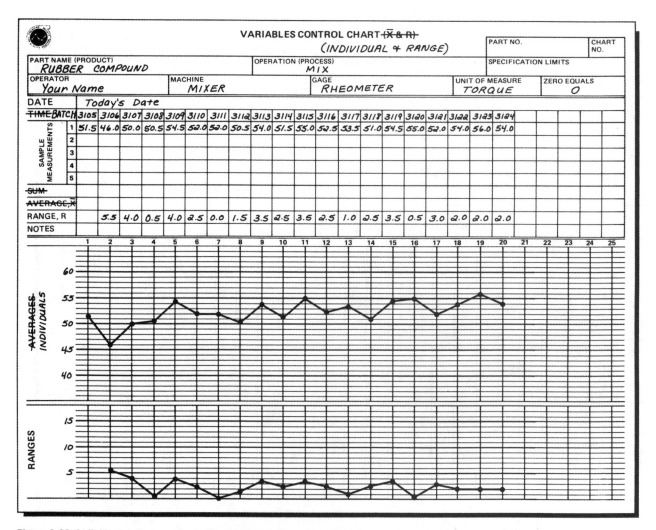

Figure 3-26. Individual and range chart with measurements and ranges.

To overcome this problem you can develop an individual and range chart with measurements that you obtain when you test samples from the batches. We will not describe the testing procedures; for this example you need to know only that the measurement numbers are called "torque units."

To set up an individual and range chart you will need twenty measurements. Record the torque values on the control chart as shown in Figure 3-26. Enter these values in the "SAMPLE MEASUREMENTS" row. Because this is an individual chart you will have only one measurement per batch. On this chart, the batch number is recorded in the row ordinarily used to record the time the sample was taken. Because the batches are numbered in order, the batch numbers are just as useful as times would be to show the order of the samples.

To figure the range (R) values, calculate the differences between the individual measurements. The first range is the difference between the first and second measurements (51.5 minus 46.0 equals 5.5). Record it in the "RANGE" row on the chart under the second batch measurement. There is no range value for the first batch, so there will always be one less range value than there are individual measurements. (See Figure 3-26.)

Set the scale for the "individuals" chart so that the difference between the largest and the smallest measurements will take up about half the space on the chart.

The "ranges" chart will start at zero. Each division on the scale should have the same value as a division on the "individuals" chart. (In this chart each division equals one torque unit.)

CONTROL LIMITS

Figure control limits in the same way you figured control limits for average and range charts. The upper control limit for ranges is calculated in this way:

$$UCL_R \text{ equals } D_4 \text{ times } \overline{R}.$$

The D_4 factor is the same as you use on an average and range chart when the sample consists of two pieces. This value is 3.268. (See Figure 3-14; n = 2.)

The value of $\overline{R}$ (the average range), as you already know, is calculated by adding all the ranges and dividing by the number of range values. In this case the total of the ranges is 46.5 and the number of range values is 19. (Remember that on the individual and range chart there is always one less range than the number of individual readings.)

On this chart (Figure 3-27) the upper control limit for ranges is calculated as follows:

$$\overline{R} = 46.5/19$$
$$\overline{R} = 2.45$$
$$UCL_R = D_4\overline{R}$$

D_4 times $\overline{R}$ equals 3.268 times 2.45 equals 8.01.

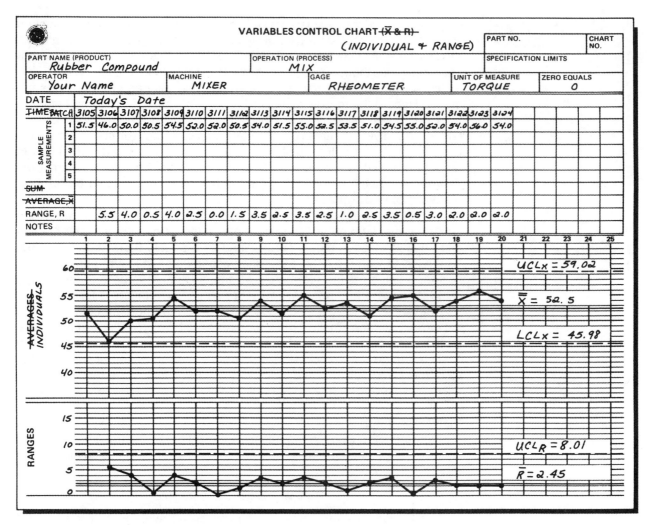

Figure 3-27. Individual and range chart with control limits.

The lower control limit for ranges is always zero on this type of chart.

To calculate the average of the individuals ($\overline{\overline{X}}$), add together all the individual measurements and divide by the number of individual measurements. On this chart (Figure 3-27) the sum of the individual measurements is 1050 and there are twenty measurements. The control limits for individuals are calculated as follows:

$$\overline{\overline{X}} = 1050/20 = 52.5$$

Upper control limit for individuals UCL_X:

UCL_X equals $\overline{\overline{X}}$ plus (2.66 times $\overline{R}$).

Be sure to multiply 2.66 times $\overline{R}$ and then add $\overline{\overline{X}}$.

$$UCL_X = 52.5 + (2.66 \times 2.45) = 59.02$$

Lower control limits for individuals LCL_X:

LCL_X equals $\overline{\overline{X}}$ minus (2.66 times $\overline{R}$).

Be sure to multiply 2.66 times $\overline{R}$ and then subtract the result from $\overline{\overline{X}}$.

$$LCL_X = 52.5 - (2.66 \times 2.45) = 45.98$$

The number 2.66, which is used to calculate the control limits, has been determined by mathematicians.

When you have calculated the upper control limit for the range, look at all the range values to see whether any of them are greater than the upper control limit. If three or more range values are greater than the control limit, throw out all the readings and start over. If one or two values are greater than the upper control limit, eliminate them from the group of range values and calculate a new average range ($\overline{R}$) and a new upper control limit for ranges. Be sure to throw out the corresponding individual measurements (X's). If any of the remaining range values are still greater than the new upper control limit, throw out all the readings and start over. If none of the remaining range values are greater than the new upper control limit, go ahead and calculate the upper and lower control limits for the individual readings.

Apply the same tests to the individual measurements. If three or more measurements lie outside the control limits, throw out the readings and start over. If one or two lie outside, refigure the control limits for individuals and check to see whether any more measurements are still outside the control limits. If so, start over with new measurements. When no measurements lie outside the control limits, go ahead and use the chart.

As shown in Figure 3-27, the range values and the individual measurements in the example all fall within the control limits, so you can use the control chart.

Once you have established the individual and range chart with proper control limits, you can use it as a tool to monitor and control the operation or process. Use it in the same way as other variable control charts, but remember—this is a control chart of *individual* measurements. The measurements you plot on the individual chart can be compared to the specification limits as well as to control limits.

When the points on the control chart fall outside the control limits, you have a floor solvable problem. Look for assignable causes and take corrective action. When the points on the control chart fall outside the specification limit but *not* outside the control limits, you have a management/team solvable problem. In this case you are doing things as planned and instructed, but the measurements are out of specification. To correct this situation requires a change in plans, instructions, or process.

If either of the control limits for the individual measurements falls outside the specification, you can predict that the operation or process will produce some pieces outside the specification. For this reason, be sure your prediction is accurate. To gain confidence in the accuracy of the control limits, it is good practice to recalculate the control limits as soon as you obtain more measurements.

When you have added twenty more measurements to the control chart, add them to the original group and refigure the control limits. Do this until you have calculated the control limits using at least 100 measurements.

SUMMARY

Control charts can tell you either to leave your process alone and make no adjustments, or to adjust or correct the process. In the first case, only inherent variation appears to be at work. In the second case, an assignable cause has probably disturbed the process.

Use an average and range control chart when you have variable data (data based on measurements).

To set up average and range charts you must collect samples; calculate $\overline{X}$'s and R's; calculate $\overline{\overline{X}}$ and $\overline{R}$; determine the control limits for ranges and know how to use them; and determine the control limits for averages and know how to use them. You must check to see whether the ranges are in statistical control before you calculate the limits for averages. A decision chart will help you to work with ranges and averages.

Points inside the control limits mean that only inherent variation is at work and no adjustments are required in the process. Points outside the control limits, as well as certain patterns within the limits, indicate assignable causes. In that case you must track down the cause—machine, material, method, environment, or production associate—and correct it.

When the process is in statistical control, determine whether the inherent variation is small enough so that your product can meet specifications. Remember that control limits have *nothing* to do with specifications.

A range chart tells you whether or not the process variation is stable. If it is stable, then you can check to see how well your product is meeting specifications. You will learn more about this in Module 5.

The median and range chart is easier to use than the average and range chart. The median is the middle value in a group of numbers, and can be found with little or no arithmetic. The range is easy to calculate because the points on the chart show clearly which is the largest and which is the smallest measurement. Sample sizes of three or five are easiest to work with.

You can use the median and range chart when you know that the frequency distribution of measurements from an operation matches the normal or bell-shaped curve. This is not as important when using the average and range chart.

The individual and range chart can be used in special circumstances, such as when a long time elapses between products or measurements or when you are monitoring processing conditions instead of a direct dimension on a product, such as solutions in plating tanks.

On the individual and range chart you record the measurements of individual parts or products, and you can compare the points on the individual chart to the specifications. This chart is easy to use, but it does not detect changes in the process as quickly as the average and range chart. The most important condition for the use of this chart is that the frequency distribution of the measurements from the operation to be charted should match the normal bell-shaped distribution.

PRACTICE PROBLEMS: VARIABLE CHARTS

Work through the following problems using the statistical techniques you learned in Modules 2 and 3. The solutions can be found in the "Solutions" section beginning on page 209.

Problem 3-1.

The following measurements are dial indicator readings of a pin diameter. The specification is .250 inch plus or minus .008.

Five pieces in a row were measured every fifteen minutes.

Does a frequency histogram of the measurements look normal?

Is the operation stable?

Pin diameter measurements (Problem 3-1)

Time

7:15	.249	.251	.251	.248	.250
7:30	.251	.246	.252	.248	.250
7:45	.250	.250	.246	.250	.251
8:00	.249	.253	.245	.254	.249
8:15	.250	.246	.251	.249	.250
8:30	.250	.250	.251	.251	.251
8:45	.247	.251	.253	.250	.249
9:00	.250	.251	.253	.249	.248
9:15	.246	.250	.248	.250	.251
9:30	.251	.248	.249	.249	.250
9:45	.251	.249	.249	.251	.252
10:00	.251	.255	.248	.247	.249
10:15	.250	.252	.252	.249	.251
10:30	.250	.251	.254	.251	.251
10:45	.252	.251	.248	.252	.251
11:00	.249	.250	.249	.251	.252
11:15	.250	.249	.250	.250	.250
11:30	.248	.250	.249	.251	.251
11:45	.251	.248	.250	.250	.252
12:00	.254	.251	.254	.247	.251

Problem 3-2.

Four pieces were taken from a lathe operation at fifteen-minute intervals. The dimension measured is an undercut diameter on a ball joint stud. The specification is .750 plus or minus .005 inches.

The following measurements were obtained. For convenience in recording, .750 inch was subtracted from each measurement before it was recorded, so a 5 is really .755 minus .750, a −1 is .749 minus .750, a 0 is exactly .750, and so on.

Time

7:00	5	5	5	4		10:15	6	6	6	8
7:15	5	6	4	7		10:30	3	4	4	7
7:30	6	4	3	4		10:45	2	2	2	6
7:45	6	5	6	4		11:00	5	4	6	6
8:00	3	4	5	3		11:15	5	4	4	1
8:15	4	7	7	6		11:30	0	4	2	−4

Time

8:30	5	5	4	7		11:45	−1	−1	0	0
8.45	4	4	4	7		12:00	8	8	4	5
9:00	6	5	6	4		12:15	4	6	4	7
9:15	1	5	7	6		12:30	4	5	6	6
9:30	5	5	1	3		12:45	3	3	4	9
9:45	7	8	7	6		1:00	7	4	6	5
10:00	3	4	7	7						

Does a histogram of the measurements look normal?

Does an average and range chart indicate that an assignable cause was present at any time? If so, what could it be?

Problem 3-3.

Look again at the shaft movement data in Problem 2-3. Construct average and range charts using the following groupings of the data. Use a subgroup sample size of five.

1. A, B, C, and D.
2. E, F, G, and H.
3. I, J, K, and L.
4. M, N, O, and P.
5. A, E, I, and M.

Do you see any differences among the averages ($\overline{\overline{X}}$'s)?

How do the averages compare to the averages from the frequency histograms?

How does the fifth control chart (A, E, I, and M) compare to the other four?

Problem 3-4.

Turn back to Problem 2-4 and construct a median and range chart from the measurements listed. Divide the measurements into five-piece subgroups for a total of 24 median points on the chart.

How does the estimated process average or the median of the medians ($\widetilde{\overline{X}}$) compare with the estimate of the process average you made using the histogram analysis?

4

Attribute Control Charts

When you are doing quality improvement work, you will be using or making charts based on two kinds of information. In Module 3, you learned to use and construct average and range and other kinds of control charts. The type of information you need for those charts is called *variable data.* Remember that when you measured the motor endplay, you found that the measurements varied from one piece to the next. Variable data come from things you can measure, such as motor shaft endplay, inside diameters of brake hoses, or resistance in a resistor.

Sometimes, though, you have a different situation in the manufacturing process. The unit of production has a characteristic you want to control, but you cannot measure it or it is difficult to measure. Yet the characteristic is important because of cost or acceptability to the customer.

When you're controlling for these characteristics, inspection or sampling shows whether the product meets standards, conforms to specifications, or has one or more defects. It's either O.K. or not O.K. You can see this when you examine a unit of production for visible defects: cracks or tears are present in trim molding, or they are not; flashing or burrs are present in a plastic part, or they are not; a painted surface has one or more dings, scratches, or dirty places, or it does not. Such nonmeasurable characteristics are called *attributes.* They provide *attribute* or *counting data.*

WHY USE AN ATTRIBUTE CONTROL CHART?

Whenever you need to monitor a nonmeasurable characteristic in your product, you can use a *p-chart,* an *np-chart,* or a *c-chart.* The p-chart helps you monitor and control the *percentage* of *defective pieces* in the production run. The np-chart helps you monitor the *number* of *defective pieces.* The c-chart helps you monitor the *number* of *defects* in the manufactured items. If you want to monitor the *percentage* of defective *parts,* in a production run, use a p-chart. If you want to monitor the *number* of defective *parts,* use an np-chart. If you want to monitor the number or *count* of defects in a part, use a c-chart. You can remember which is which if you keep in mind that "p" stands for "*p*ercentage," "np" stands for "*n*umber of defective *p*arts," and "c" stands for "*c*ount."

We are using the word "defective" to describe a piece or unit. The piece is either good (acceptable), or bad (not acceptable); that is, defective. Also, we are using the word "defect" in a special way. There may be one or more defects in a single piece, but the entire piece is defective whether it has one defect or more than one.

In this module, you will learn to use and construct all three kinds of attribute charts, beginning with the p-chart. (See Figure 4-1).

PERCENT DEFECTIVE p-CHARTS

Most p-charts use percentages. A percentage is the number of units out of 100 units that are defective or otherwise do not conform to specifications. We call this kind of p-chart a *percent defective p-chart.*

To find the percentage, p, use this formula:

p equals the number of defective pieces divided by the sample size. Multiply the result by 100 percent.

In a sample of 100 units where seven pieces are defective,

$$p = 7/100 \times 100\% = 7\%$$

On a percent defective p-chart, you plot points as percentages of defective pieces in the samples.

HOW TO USE p-CHARTS

As you did in Module 3, look first at a percent defective p-chart that a staff technician has set up. The technician developed the chart based on the previous day's production. He continued taking samples on July 12 and plotted the sample results as shown in Figure 4-2.

Your job is to take the sample, calculate p, enter the data on the p-chart, and plot the points. You will also have to understand what the chart is telling you, so that you can determine whether to continue running the process or whether to take corrective action.

In this case let's suppose you're checking samples of trim molding for auto deck lids. Your sample is 50 molding strips. You must check each strip

Figure 4-1. p-chart (Form developed by Robert and Davida Amsden and Howard Butler.)

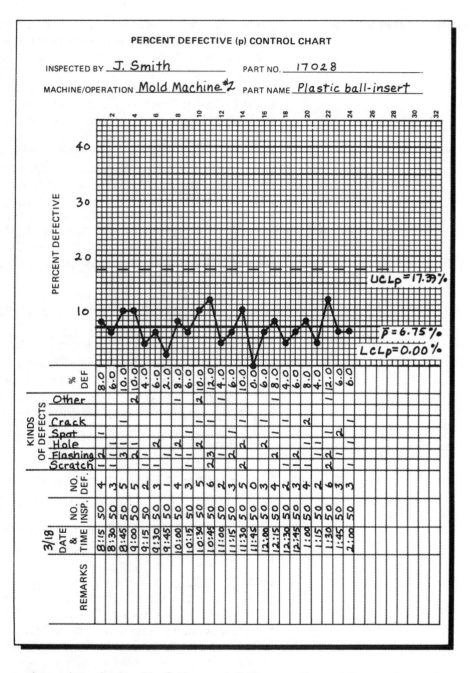

to determine whether it's O.K. or not O.K., regardless of the number or type of defects you find.

Since you will be inspecting the parts and filling in the chart for the rest of the shift, write your name above Baxter's and show the time you took over the chart. (See Figure 4-3.) Write in 9:00 under the "DATE & TIME"

Figure 4-2. p-chart already set up.

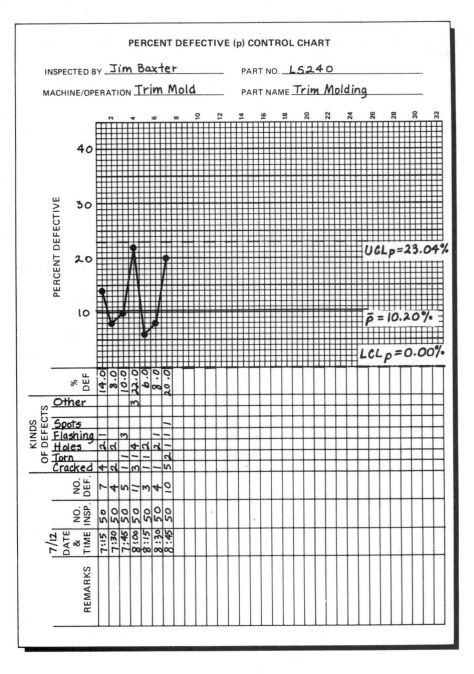

heading for the eighth sample (your first). At 9:00, make a visual check of the next 50 molding strips produced. You find six defective strips. Under the heading "NO. INSP." (number inspected) write 50; under "NO. DEF." (number defective) write 6.

Figure 4-3. p-chart with new data entered, 9:00.

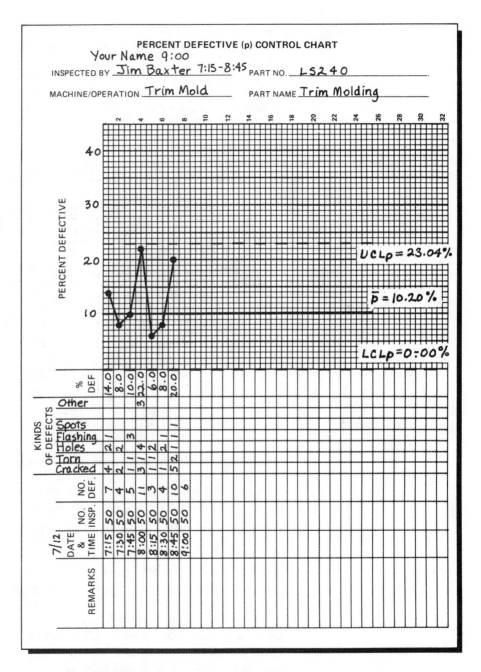

You probably have noticed divisions under the heading "KINDS OF DE-FECTS." You may also be asked to fill in the number of the particular kinds of defects such as "cracked," "torn," "holes," "flashing," "spots," and "other." To fill these in, count how many of each type of defect you find and write that number under the appropriate heading. Remember that one strip may have more than one kind of defect. It might be cracked *and* torn, for example. But even though this strip has *two defects,* it counts as only *one defective piece,* called a "defective."

In this sample of 50, two pieces have flashing, three pieces are torn, and two are cracked. (One of these defective pieces had two types of defects. It was cracked and torn.) Fill in the appropriate boxes under "KINDS OF DEFECTS." (See Figure 4-4.)

Figure 4-4. Portion of p-chart showing kinds of defects, 9:00.

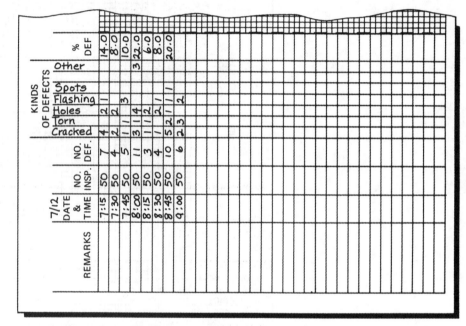

Once you have filled in the data, you are ready to calculate the percent defective in this sample of 50. Remember the formula:

p = number of defectives divided by sample size times percent.
$$p = 6/50 \times 100\% = 12\%$$

Write 12 under "% DEF" (percent defective) next to 9:00. (See Figure 4-5.)

Now plot the point as a large dot on the graph and draw a line connecting this dot with the last one. (See Figure 4-6).

As you remember from Modules 1 and 3, averages and ranges have upper and lower control limits, UCL and LCL. The same is true for p-charts. Keep this in mind when you look at what you plotted. You will learn how to set control limits later in this module.

Is the p where it's supposed to be? It's 12%, and that falls between the lower control limit of zero and the upper control limit of 23.04%, so it's all right.

What is this point telling you? When the percent defective is within the control limits, your process is in statistical control. The rule is: if the p, per-

Figure 4-5. Portion of p-chart showing percent defective, 9:00.

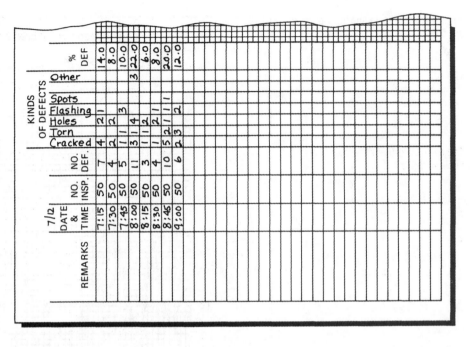

cent defective, for the sample is within the control limits, keep running the process without adjustments.

INTERPRETING PERCENT DEFECTIVE p-CHARTS
Now that you know how to figure the percent defective for the samples and how to plot the points, you can go on to interpret the charts.

PERCENT DEFECTIVE, p, INSIDE CONTROL LIMITS
Now that you have been taking the samples for a while, look at your p-chart in Figure 4-7. Since every point is inside the control limits, what should you do? Keep running the process. When all points are inside the limits, no corrections are needed. (The point plotted at 10:30 lies directly *on* the lower control limit. Consider any points *on* the control limit as inside.)

What do you do when a point is very close to the upper or lower control limit? If the point is inside or on the limit, make no adjustments and keep producing. But if the point is outside, an assignable cause is at work. Find that cause and correct it.

We have said before that a process is in statistical control when all points are inside the control limits, even if the points move up and down as they do in Figure 4-7. This movement most likely shows the natural variation in the process. As you learned in Module 3, this kind of variation is called inherent variation and is due to chance causes. Such causes are usually beyond the operator's immediate control, but they do cause the points to move up and down *inside* the control limits.

Figure 4-6. p-chart showing p plotted for 9:00.

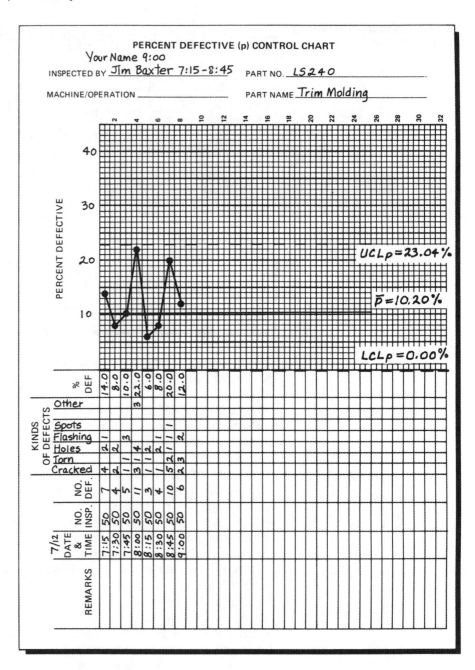

Figure 4-7. p inside control limits.

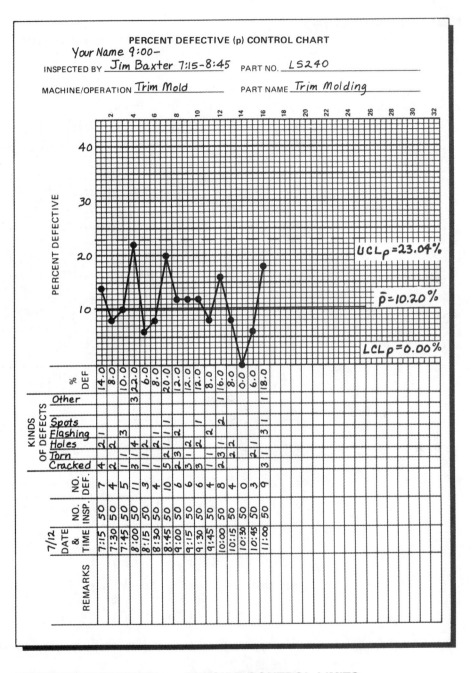

PERCENT DEFECTIVE, p, OUTSIDE CONTROL LIMITS

Figure 4-8 shows a p outside the control limits. Because it is outside, this process is now out of statistical control. An assignable cause is present, and something more than simple inherent variation is at work.

Figure 4-8. p outside control limits.

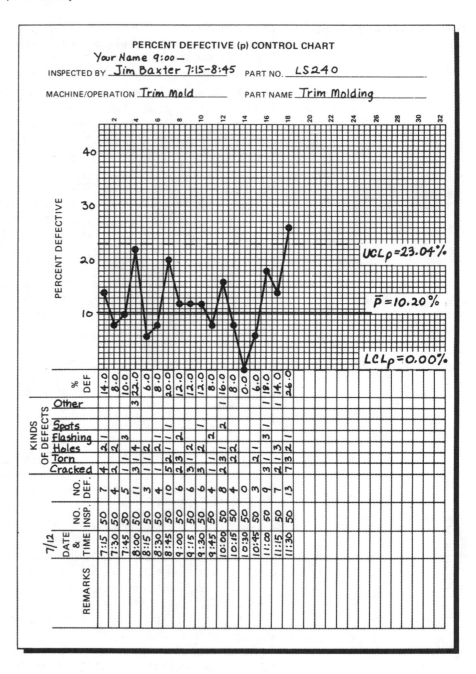

As you recall from Module 3, an assignable cause isn't always present. It's not natural to the process. But when it shows up on the control chart, you may be able to track it down.

Often a point outside the limits indicates a problem you can handle on the floor, such as changing a worn tool. At other times, however, such as when a chemical formulation changes, an engineer may be required. The important thing is not *who* is responsible, but *what* has changed and what needs to be done. The point outside the control limits simply shows you that a change has taken place and *when* it took place.

What do you do? The chart is telling you to correct your process. For some reason the process has shifted upwards, and it needs to be adjusted down.

In the case of the trim mold, the percent defective may have gone outside the limit because the air was extremely humid and not enough drying agent was added to the rubber mix, or the molding may have been in the press for less than the standard amount of time, and the time needs to be corrected.

OTHER INDICATIONS OF OUT-OF-CONTROL PROCESSES

As you recall from Module 3, the points you plot may show a pattern. One pattern we mentioned is seven consecutive points above or below the line marked $\bar{p}$. (We'll explain the $\bar{p}$ later.) Even though all the points are still inside the control limits, this pattern is giving you an indication—a weaker one—that the process is out of control.

Other patterns include longer runs of points, as well as too many or too few points close to the $\bar{p}$ line. To interpret these patterns we suggest that you look them up in the books we recommended in Module 3 on page 47.

TYPES OF ASSIGNABLE CAUSES

The point or points outside the control limits are your clearest indication that an assignable cause is at work in your process. Let's review the sources of assignable causes. (See Module 1, Figure 1-4, for the fishbone diagram.)

(1) Check the *machine.* Has something about the machine itself changed so that points are outside the limits? Look for worn tools, the jig setting, the level of coolant in a grinder, and so on.

(2) *Materials* are another item to check. When an assignable cause is due to materials, something is different about the stuff that is coming to the process. Chemicals may have been contaminated, for example, or a different strength thread is being used to stitch slippers.

(3) Another area to check is *method.* By "method" we mean the procedure followed in making the piece, such as the way you handle the trim molding when you take it out of the press.

(4) Also look at the *environment,* which includes such things as lighting, height of the work table, humidity or dryness, and dust.

(5) Finally, consider the *production associate.* Check training, hearing, eyesight, or arithmetic errors.

SETTING UP PERCENT DEFECTIVE p-CHARTS

Now you can try setting up your own percent defective p-charts for one of several purposes. *(1)* You may be using the charts for control. That is, they can help you determine whether to continue the process "as is" or whether you have to make corrections. *(2)* You could be using the charts for analysis to look for differences between materials, days, or shifts. *(3)* The charts may help in communication or documentation. Remember, charts can help focus attention on consistent quality.

We will use the example of the trim mold for auto deck lids to show you how to set up p-charts. It has been decided by a problem-solving team to control the percent defective in the molding strips. You're the production associate. The p-chart will help you control your process, and will also show you, your management team, and the engineers how well your process is doing.

Step 1. Take the sample.

Here are some guidelines for determining sizes of samples for p-charts:

— Use a sample size of at least 50 units.
— Use a sample size big enough to give an average of four or more defectives per sample.
— Avoid very large samples taken over a long period of time. If possible, break the sampling time period into smaller segments. Instead of plotting the percent defective for a day's production, break the day into two-hour or four-hour time periods and plot the percent defective for these shorter periods.
— If the sample sizes vary and one sample is more than 20% greater or 20% less than the average sample size, calculate separate control limits for that sample.

You want your sample to show only inherent variation. Remember, inherent variation means that defects in the trim molding are showing up at random. They're due to chance causes. If your sample shows only ordinary (inherent) variation, you can draw accurate control limits.

In order to have only inherent variation, you need to take your samples over a short period of time from a single source of production. This means you will sample pieces from *one* machine, *one* machine head, *one* production associate, and *one* batch of materials.

Now you're ready to begin taking your sample. A staff technician has established that the best sample size for p-charts on the trim molding process is 50 pieces. The process has been running at about 10 percent defective, so a sample of 50 should include about five defectives (10% of 50 is 5). Therefore a sample of this size should easily meet the guideline which calls for an average of at least four defectives per sample.

Take 50 pieces of the trim molding from your machine one after the other as they are produced. You are the only production associate, and you're taking a sample of 50 every fifteen minutes. As far as you can determine at this point, every sample of 50 pieces is as much like every other sample as possible. Any variation from sample to sample should be no more than inherent variation.

Sometimes, you may be asked to develop a p-chart using data from a 100% test or inspection operation. When you do this, your sample may be the result of inspection from an hour, half-a-day, or even a full day. Sample sizes taken in this way should be kept to the above guidelines as nearly as practical. Extremely large samples are impractical for this type of chart.

Figure 4-9. p-chart form.

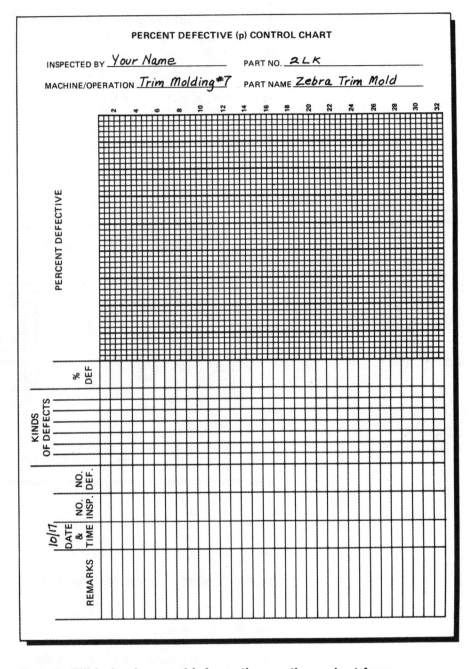

Step 2. Fill in background information on the p-chart form.

Figure 4-9 is the form for p-charts. This form makes it easy to write down all the necessary background information, such as part number and operation. It also has a graph for plotting points.

Fill in the background information.

Step 3. Collect samples and record data.

Your sample is 50 strips taken every fifteen minutes. We suggest you take at least 20 samples.

You have learned how to tell whether a strip of trim molding is defective or not, good or bad. You have been given small samples of molding that show various defects such as cracks, tears, and holes. Now, inspect each piece and write down the following information under the correct headings. (1) Record the date and the time. (2) Under "NO. INSP." (number inspected) write 50. This is your sample size. (3) Under "NO. DEF." (number of defectives) write 4, the number of defective pieces you found. (See Figure 4-10.)

Figure 4-10. Portion of p-chart showing first sample.

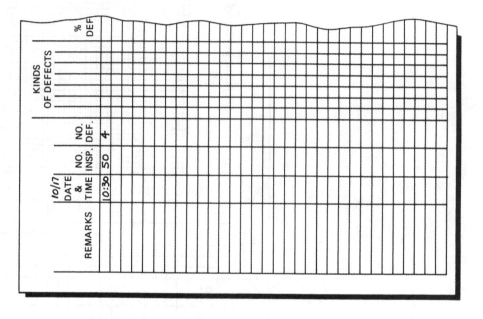

Don't worry about the divisions under "KINDS OF DEFECTS" for now. You will probably be too busy taking your samples. Once you have set up your p-chart, you can begin to collect information on kinds of defects.

Step 4. Calculate p, percent defective.

You have inspected the 50 molding strips and recorded all the data on the p-chart. The next thing to do is to calculate the p, the percent defective. Remember, the formula for p is:

p equals the number of defectives divided by the sample size times 100%.

For the first sample: p = 4/50 × 100% = 8%
For the second sample: p = 5/50 × 100% = 10%
(See Figure 4-11.)

Figure 4-11. p-chart with p calculated for each sample.

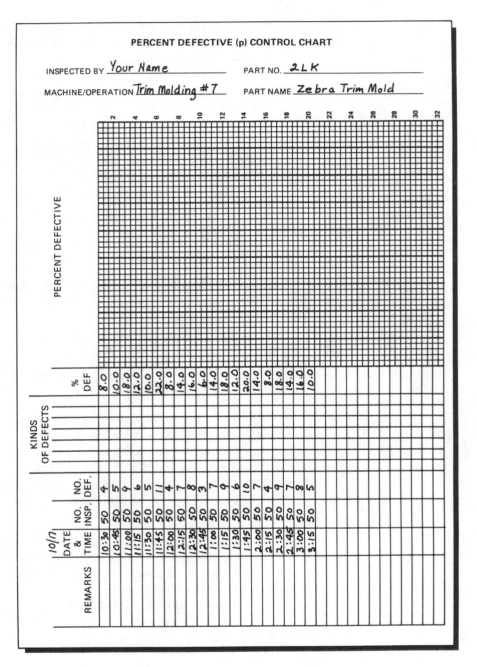

PERCENT DEFECTIVE (p) CONTROL CHART

INSPECTED BY *Your Name*   PART NO. *2LK*

MACHINE/OPERATION *Trim Molding #7*   PART NAME *Zebra Trim Mold*

	2	4	6	8	10	12	14	16	18	20	22	24	26	28	30	32

PERCENT DEFECTIVE

% DEF	8.0	10.0	18.0	12.0	10.0	22.0	8.0	14.0	16.0	6.0	14.0	18.0	12.0	20.0	14.0	8.0	18.0	14.0	16.0	10.0

KINDS OF DEFECTS

NO. DEF.	4	5	9	6	5	11	4	7	8	3	7	9	6	10	7	4	9	7	8	5
NO. INSP.	50	50	50	50	50	50	50	50	50	50	50	50	50	50	50	50	50	50	50	50

10/17

DATE & TIME	10:30	10:45	11:00	11:15	11:30	11:45	12:00	12:15	12:30	12:45	1:00	1:15	1:30	1:45	2:00	2:15	2:30	2:45	3:00	3:15

REMARKS

Step 5. Calculate the average percent defective for the process.

Add up all the numbers under "NO. DEF."
Number of defectives:

4, 5, 9, 6, 5, 11, 4, 7, 8, 3,
7, 9, 6, 10, 7, 4, 9, 7, 8, 5

Total number of defectives: 134.

Divide the total number of defectives by the total number of parts inspected. Then multiply by 100%. You have looked at 50 pieces twenty times, so you have inspected a total of 1000 parts.

Average percent defective for the process, $\bar{p}$:

134/1000 times 100% equals 13.4%

Don't enter the $\bar{p}$ on your chart yet. Make a note of it for the next step.
Check your arithmetic.

Step 6. Determine the scales for the graph and plot the data.

Set the scale for the graph so that the largest and smallest values for p can fit easily inside the ends of the scales. (Often the lower control limit for p is zero.) Be sure to leave enough room above the largest p for the upper control limit. Pick scales that make it easy to plot the data.

Largest percent defective (p): 22
Smallest percent defective (p): 6

You can run your scales from zero to 35. All the p's will fit easily and still leave plenty of room for the upper control limit. On your graph, there will be five lines between 5.0 and 10.0, so each line represents 1.0 unit. It will be easy for you to plot the p's. (See Figure 4-12.)

Now plot the p's and connect the plot points with straight lines.

Finally, draw a solid line across the graph at 13.4% for your average percent defective, $\bar{p}$, and label it "$\bar{p}$ = 13.4%."

Step 7. Calculate the control limits for percent defective charts.

Calculating control limits for p-charts is not quite as easy as calculating the limits for average and range charts. There is less work to do, but it is a little more difficult.

Here is the formula for calculating UCL_p, the upper control limit for p:

$$UCL_p = \bar{p} \text{ plus } 3 \sqrt{\frac{\bar{p} \times (100\% - \bar{p})}{n}}$$

$\sqrt{}$ is the symbol for the *square root,* a special calculation that mathematicians have worked out.
$\times$ is the symbol for "times."
n is the sample size.
$\bar{p}$ is the average percent defective.

Figure 4-12. p-chart with data plotted and p̄ drawn in.

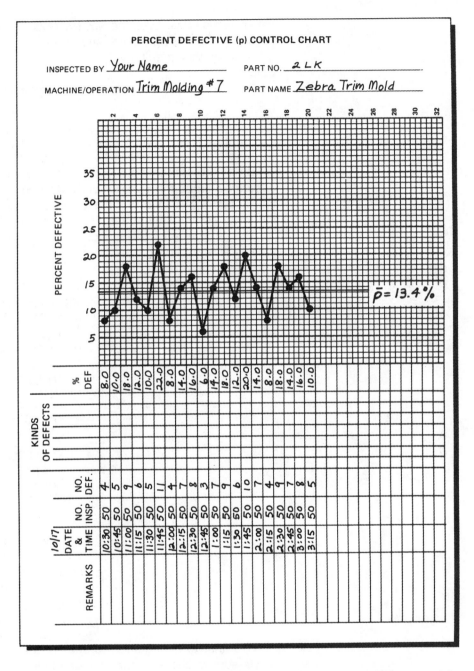

This looks like a lot of "chicken tracks," but it is not really too tricky. Read it this way: the upper control limit for p equals p̄ (the average percent defective) plus 3 times the calculation from the square root symbol.

Inside the square root symbol, first calculate 100% minus p̄. Then multiply the result by p̄. Divide that result by n, the sample size. Once you have calculated all this, take the square root by entering the number on a calculator and pressing the key marked $\sqrt{}$

Multiply this result by 3 and then add it to $\bar{p}$, the average percent defective.

The formula for LCL_p, the lower control limit for p, is:

$$LCL_p = \bar{p} \text{ minus } 3 \sqrt{\frac{\bar{p} \times (100\% - \bar{p})}{n}}$$

Do all the same calculations as for the upper control limit, but this time *subtract* 3 times the number you obtained from the square root symbol. If you obtain a negative number when you figure the lower control limit, set the lower control limit at zero.

This is how your calculations will look when $\bar{p}$ equals 13.4% and the sample size (n) is 50.

Upper control limit (UCL_p):

$$
\begin{aligned}
UCL_p &= \bar{p} + 3 \sqrt{\frac{\bar{p} \times (100\% - \bar{p})}{n}} \\
&= 13.4 + 3 \sqrt{\frac{13.4 \times (100 - 13.4)}{50}} \\
&= 13.4 + 3 \sqrt{\frac{13.4 \times 86.6}{50}} \\
&= 13.4 + 3 \sqrt{\frac{1160.44}{50}} \\
&= 13.4 + 3 \sqrt{23.2088} \\
&= 13.4 + 3 \times 4.818 \\
&= 13.4 + 14.45 \\
&= 27.85\%
\end{aligned}
$$

Lower control limit (LCL_p):

$$
\begin{aligned}
LCL_p &= \bar{p} - 3 \sqrt{\frac{\bar{p} \times (100\% - \bar{p})}{n}} \\
&= 13.4 - 14.45 \\
&= -1.05\%
\end{aligned}
$$

This answer is negative, so set the lower control limit at zero.

Be sure to check all the steps and all your arithmetic.

Now draw the control limits on your p-chart and label them UCL_p and LCL_p. Make a note of this step under "REMARKS." We suggest that you draw the limits as dashed lines or in color so that they are clearly visible. (See Figure 4-13).

Figure 4-13. p-chart with upper and lower control limits set.

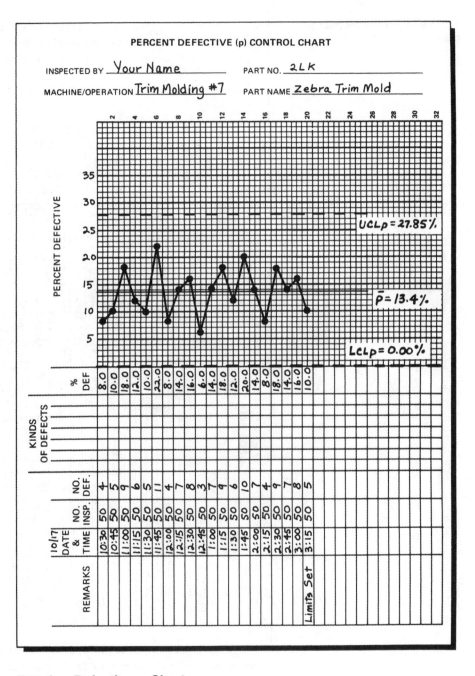

Fraction Defective p-Charts

Sometimes people set up another kind of p-chart that uses fractions instead of percentages, called *fraction defective p-charts* or *proportion defective p-charts.* This kind of p-chart shows how many parts are defective

Figure 4-14. Fraction defective p-chart.

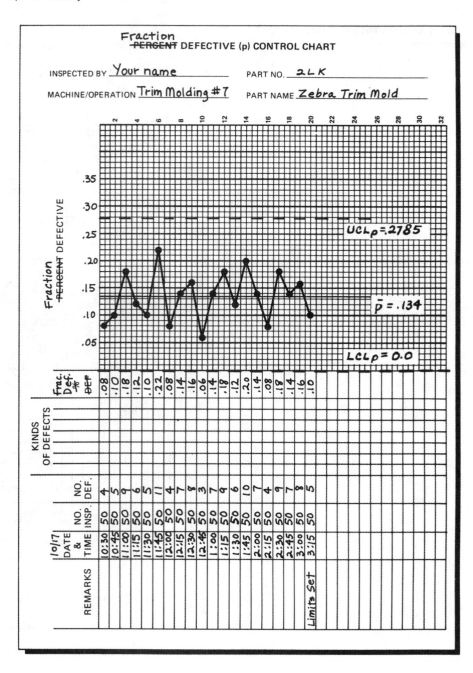

compared to the total in the sample. Figure 4-14 shows the chart for the trim molding data using fractions.

The fraction defective charts look just about the same as the percent defective charts, but there are three differences. (See Figures 4-13 and 4-14.)

The first difference is in the calculation of p, the fraction defective. The formula for p using fractions, not percentages, is:

p equals number of defective pieces divided by sample size.

For the trim molding, the first p would be:

$$p = 4/50$$
$$= .08$$

The next p would be:

$$p = 5/50$$
$$= .10$$

Do the remaining calculations for p in the same way. When you calculate p you are *not* multiplying by 100%, as you did in the percent defective chart. You get the same answer but the decimal point is two places to the left. Calculate $\bar{p}$ in the usual way: add up all the defectives and then divide by the total number of pieces inspected. In the trim molding example, the number is the same, but the decimal point is two places to the left:

$$\bar{p} = 134/1000$$
$$= .134$$

(Note that this is not a percentage, but a decimal fraction.)

The second difference is in how you calculate the upper and lower control limits. The formula for the upper limit for p, fraction defective, is:

$$UCL_p = \bar{p} + 3 \sqrt{\frac{\bar{p} \times (1 - \bar{p})}{n}}$$

The numbers inside the square root symbol are different. You are using 1 instead of 100%, and $\bar{p}$ is a decimal fraction, not a percentage. Otherwise you make the same calculations as in the percent defective chart.

This is how all the "chicken tracks" look when you work out the UCL_p for the trim molding case using fraction defective:

$$UCL_p = .134 + 3 \sqrt{\frac{.134 \times (1 - .134)}{50}}$$
$$= .134 + 3 \sqrt{\frac{.134 \times .866}{50}}$$
$$= .134 + 3 \sqrt{\frac{.116044}{50}}$$
$$= .134 + 3 \sqrt{.00232088}$$
$$= .134 + 3 \times .04818$$
$$= .134 + .1445$$
$$= .2785$$

You see that you have the same answer except for the decimal point, which is two places to the left.

Figure the lower control limit with this formula:

$$LCL_p = \bar{p} \text{ minus } 3 \sqrt{\frac{\bar{p} \times (1 - \bar{p})}{n}}$$
$$= .134 - .1445$$
$$= -0.0105$$

Set your lower control limit at zero because the final calculation is negative.

The third and last difference is that the scale for the fraction defective p-chart is shown in decimals, not percentages. Your scale for the p-chart in our example will read .05, .10, .15, and so on. Be sure to cross out "PERCENT" on the form and write in "FRACTION."

We are telling you about the fraction defective p-chart only because you may run into it once in a while. Most people prefer to do their calculations for p-charts in percentages, not in fractions. It's easier to think in terms of percentages—8% defective or 12% defective—than in terms of decimals—.08 defective or .12 defective.

Step 8. Interpret the p-chart.

When you are interpreting the p-chart, there are three possible situations you need to consider. Either all the percents defective, p's, are inside the control limits; or there are one or two p's outside the limits; or three or more p's are outside the limits. (You have already seen this kind of decision making in Module 3.)

If *all* the p's are within the control limits, the process is in statistical control. Only inherent variation is at work, as far as you can tell.

If one or two p's are outside the limits, the usual practice is to throw out those one or two p's and the samples from which they come. Completely refigure the average percent defective, $\bar{p}$. Then, using the new $\bar{p}$, calculate new control limits.

Once you have recalculated the control limits, there are two situations to check. If one or more of the remaining p's are still outside the new control limits, your process is not in statistical control. Assignable causes are disrupting the process. Find and remove them. Then take new samples and data and set up the p-chart again, using limits based on this new information.

On the other hand, if all the p's are now inside the new control limits, go ahead and run your process. But be careful! Some assignable causes may still be around to cause trouble later on.

If three or more p's are outside the limits, your process is clearly out of statistical control. First, you must clean out the assignable cause or causes that are upsetting your process. Then you can start again. Collect new data and set up new p-charts.

Figure 4-15 is a decision chart to help you understand this process. This is similar to the decision charts you saw in Module 3.

Figure 4-15. Decision chart for working with p's.

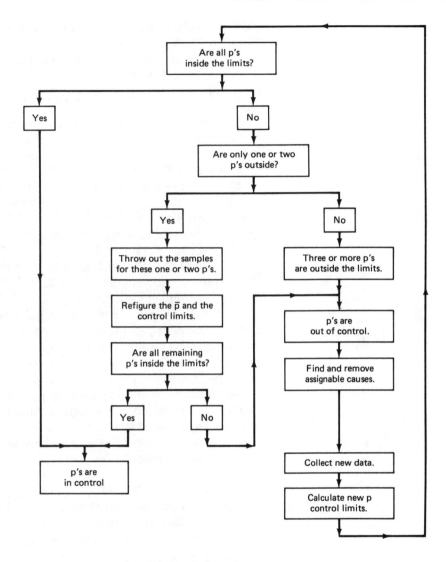

Figure 4-13 shows the p's for the trim molding. Every p lies between the upper control limit of 27.85% and the lower control limit 0.0%. Therefore the p's are in statistical control.

Step 9. Fill in the kinds of defects.

Now that the p's are in control you can begin to collect information about the different kinds of defects. Under "KINDS OF DEFECTS," write headings such as "cracked," "torn," "holes," and any other defects you find. Now you can begin to count the specific defects. Remember, this total count of defects may be larger than the number of defective pieces because a defective piece may have more than one defect.

HOW TO USE A NEWLY DEVELOPED p-CHART IN CONTINUED PRODUCTION

Once the percentages of defectives are in control, you can say that your process is in statistical control. That is, it appears that only inherent variation is at work and is present because of chance causes. Apparently, *no* assignable causes are present.

A word of warning: even though the process is in control, it may not be doing what you want. The level of the $\bar{p}$ may not be acceptable because of cost or customer dissatisfaction. You and your management team will have to work that out.

Now that the p-chart is set up and the percents defective are in control, you can use the chart in an ongoing manner. Once you have determined your control limits, you can use them to tell whether defects are due to chance causes or to assignable causes.

Review your p-chart periodically to make sure you're still operating where you think you are. You will need to review the p-chart if you have tried to make some improvements, or if you think something is different about the process. Looking at the chart again is a way to check. Take ten new samples of 50 pieces as close together as possible. Find the new p values and calculate the new average ($\bar{p}$). Now you can compare the old $\bar{p}$ with the new one to see how the process is going.

THE np-CHART

Sometimes you will find it convenient to use a control chart that plots the *number* instead of the percentage of defective parts in the sample. This kind of "counting" chart is called an np-chart.

One rule must be followed strictly when you use an np-chart. The size of every sample must be the same.

SETTING UP THE CHART

Setting up the np-chart is very similar to setting up a p-chart. The only difference is that the number of defective parts is recorded instead of the percent defective or fraction defective.

Step 1. Take the sample.

The sample size for the np-chart should be large enough to make sure that you will see defective parts in each sample. A good rule to follow is to set your sample size so that the average number of defective parts per sample will be four or more. Take your sample in the same way and with the same frequency as you would for a p-chart.

Step 2. Fill in the form for data and graph.

You can use the same chart form for the np-chart as you use for the p-chart. Simply cross out the words "PERCENT DEFECTIVE" and write in "NUMBER DEFECTIVE" to identify the chart as an np-chart. Nothing will be written under "% DEF."

Figure 4-16. Percent defective p-chart. Kinds of defects have been filled in and control limits have been set.

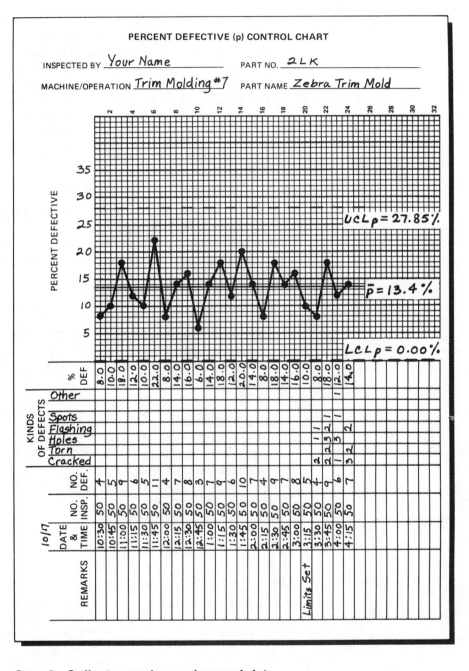

PERCENT DEFECTIVE (p) CONTROL CHART

INSPECTED BY *Your Name*   PART NO. *2LK*

MACHINE/OPERATION *Trim Molding #7*   PART NAME *Zebra Trim Mold*

$UCLp = 27.85\%$

$\bar{p} = 13.4\%$

$LCLp = 0.00\%$

Step 3. Collect samples and record data.

This step is identical to the p-chart procedure except that "NO. INSP." will have the same number for each sample. Plot the number of defective parts in each sample on the chart.

Step 4. Calculate the $n\overline{p}$.

To calculate the *$n\overline{p}$,* or the *average number defective for the process,* add up the total number of defective parts found in the samples and divide that total by the number of samples. Remember, that in the np-chart, if you look at (say) 50 pieces at a time, those 50 pieces make up a single sample. The total number of samples is the total number of times you looked at pieces. It is *not* the total number of pieces inspected.

The formula for finding the $n\overline{p}$ looks like this:

$n\overline{p}$ equals the number of defective parts in all samples divided by the number of samples taken.

$n\overline{p}$ is the average number of defectives for the process.

Let's use the inspection data shown in Figure 4-13 to make an np-chart. The number of defectives has been transferred to Figure 4-17, along with the other information from Figure 4-13.

To calculate the process average number defective for our example, add all the numbers under "NO. DEF.", which total 134. Then divide 134 by the number of samples, which is 20. The result is 6.7, the $n\overline{p}$. Draw a solid line on the chart at the 6.7 level and write in "$n\overline{p} = 6.7$."

Step 5. Determine the scale for the graph and plot the np's.

Set the scale so that the largest and smallest np's will fit on the graph, and pick a scale that makes it easy to plot the data. Be sure to leave extra space for the upper control limit. (The lower control limit will often be zero.)

Step 6. Calculate the control limits for number defective.

The formula for calculating the control limits for np, number defective, is about the same as the formula for finding the control limits for p, percent defective, on the p-chart. This is how your calculations will look when $n\overline{p}$ equals 6.7: ($n\overline{p}$ is the average number defective and n is the sample size.)

Upper control limit for np:

$$UCL_{np} = n\overline{p} + 3\sqrt{n\overline{p} \times (1 - n\overline{p}/n)}$$
$$UCL_{np} = 6.7 + 3\sqrt{6.7 \times (1 - 6.7/50)}$$
$$= 6.7 + 3\sqrt{6.7 \times (1 - .134)}$$
$$= 6.7 + 3\sqrt{6.7 \times .866}$$
$$= 6.7 + 3\sqrt{5.8022}$$
$$= 6.7 + 3 \times 2.4088$$
$$= 6.7 + 7.2264$$
$$UCL_{np} = 13.9264$$

Draw the upper control limit on the chart as a dashed line. (See Figure 4-17.)

Figure 4-17. np-chart.

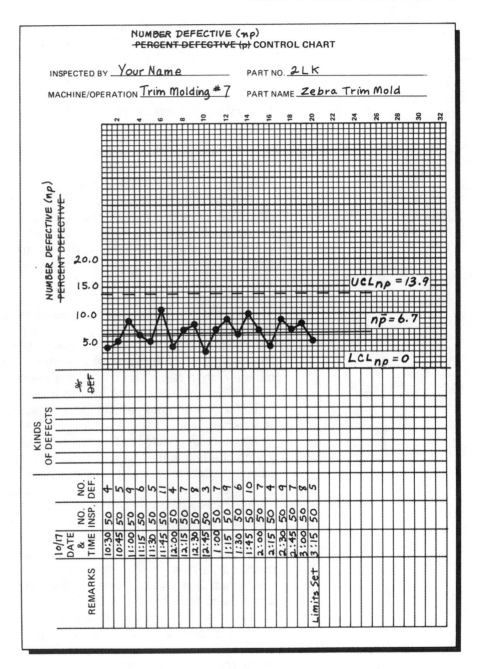

To find the lower control limit for number defective, use this formula:

$$LCL_{np} = n\,\bar{p} - 3\sqrt{n\bar{p} \times (1 - n\bar{p}/n)}$$
$$= 6.7 - 7.2264$$
$$LCL_{np} = -0.5264$$

Because the answer is a negative number, set the lower control limit at zero.

Step 7. Interpret the np-chart.

Interpret the newly developed chart in the same way you did the p-chart. (See Step 8, "Interpret the p-chart.")

This control chart looks very much like the p-chart in Figure 4-13. The difference is that the p-chart shows the *percent* defective in the sample and the np-chart shows the *number* defective in the sample. You may choose which chart you use as long as each sample for the np-chart is the same size.

c-CHARTS

Earlier in this module, we told you that you can control a nonmeasurable characteristic in your product by using a p-chart, an np-chart, or a c-chart. The p-chart helps you control the percentage of defective pieces in production and the np-chart helps you to control the number of defective pieces, but the c-chart helps you control the number of defects in a *single part or assembled unit.* It's a good idea to use a c-chart when there are opportunities for one or more defects to be present in a part or a unit. Figure 4-18 is a c-chart.

The c-chart should not be confused with the np-chart. As you remember, the np-chart plots the *number of defective parts* in the sample. The c-chart plots the *number of defects* in the *inspection unit.*

As you know, the p-, np-, and c-charts all use attribute or counting data. For the p-chart and np-chart you counted how many pieces in your sample were defective; that is, were not good. For the c-chart, you will be counting how many specific defects there are in each inspection unit. An inspection unit may consist of one part, such as a painted surface on a car door; or it may consist of a group of parts, such as a printed circuit board with its transistors. One part or group of parts may have any number of defects, or it may have none at all.

It is very easy to calculate c: just count up all the *defects* in each piece or group of pieces. There is no formula.

HOW TO USE c-CHARTS

Earlier in this module, we looked at a p-chart that somebody else had already set up. Now we will do the same thing with c-charts.

As with the other attribute charts, your job is to take the sample, count the number of defects, write that data on the c-chart, and plot the points.

Figure 4-18. c-chart (Form developed by Robert and Davida Amsden and Howard Butler.)

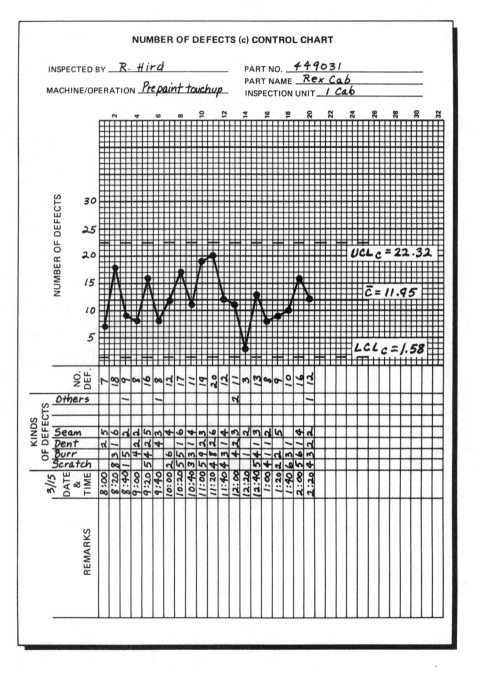

You have to understand what the chart is saying so that you'll know whether to keep producing or to make corrections.

The c-chart in Figure 4-19 deals with polyurethane foam seat cushions for passenger cars. Your job is to check a seat cushion and to count the

Figure 4-19. c-chart already set up.

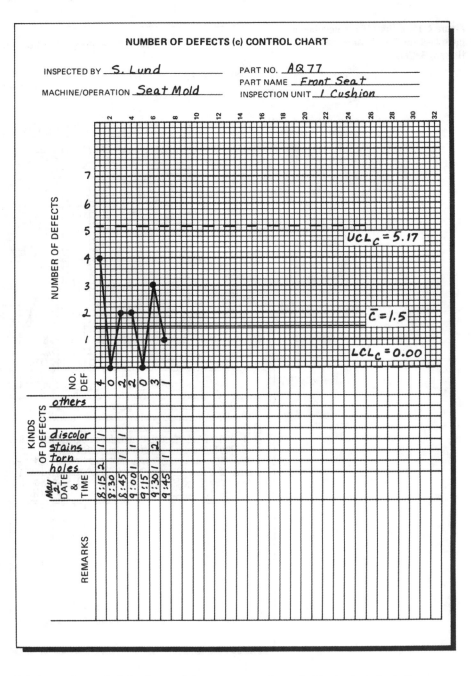

total number of defects and how many of each kind of defect there are. Somebody else set up the chart originally and marked the first few samples for you.

You will be marking the chart for this shift. At 10:00, take a seat cushion from production and inspect it for defects. Write your name above Lund's

Figure 4-20. c-chart with new data added.

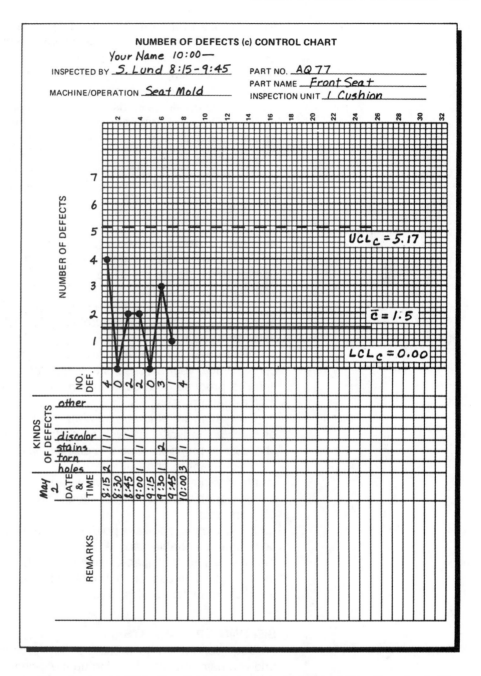

on the chart and fill in the time when you started marking the chart. (See Figure 4-20.)

On the chart are several readings under "KINDS OF DEFECTS." The kinds of defects are more important in the c-chart than in the p-chart because a defective piece may have more than one defect. Each heading has room for one of the particular kinds of defects that you are looking for and counting: "holes," "torn," "stains," "discolor," and "other." You know that a seat may have more than one kind of defect: it may have stains, holes, and discoloration. Simply count up how many of each defect you find and write that number in the proper place.

Now add up all the kinds of defects you have found and write this number under "NO. DEF." (number of defects). There are three holes, one stain, and nothing else. The sum of these defects is 4. Write this number, 4, under "NO. DEF."

When you have filled in the data, you can plot the point as a large dot on the graph. Connect this dot with the previous dot by drawing a straight line. (Figure 4-21).

INTERPRETING c-CHARTS

Just as averages, ranges, and percents defective have upper and lower control limits, so do c's (defect counts). Remember this when you check your plot.

Ask yourself, "Is the c where it's supposed to be?" In this case the c is 4. It's between the upper control limit of 5.17 and the lower control limit of zero, so it's O.K.

What does the chart tell you? When your c (defect count) is within the control limits, your process is in statistical control. This means you can continue to produce seat cushions without making any corrections or adjustments to the process.

Everything we said about points inside the control limits, near the limits, or outside the limits, as well as patterns of points, applies as much to c-charts as to p-charts. (See this discussion in the p-chart section of this module.) You want to find out whether your process is in control, whether only inherent variation due to chance causes is present, or whether there are any assignable causes of variation. The c-chart provides you with this kind of information.

If the c-chart shows a point or points outside the limits, you must hunt down the assignable causes and remove them. You have already learned the sources of assignable causes: machine, method, materials, environment, production associate. We talked about these sources in Module 3 and the p-chart section of this module.

SETTING UP c-CHARTS

Your department is running a new process for making seat cushions, and you have the job of setting up the c-chart. A c-chart for this process will do several things. It will help you monitor the process and keep track of the number and kinds of defects. It will also document what is happening and communicate all this to you, your team leader, the quality assurance department, and anyone else who wants to know.

Figure 4-21. c-chart with new point plotted.

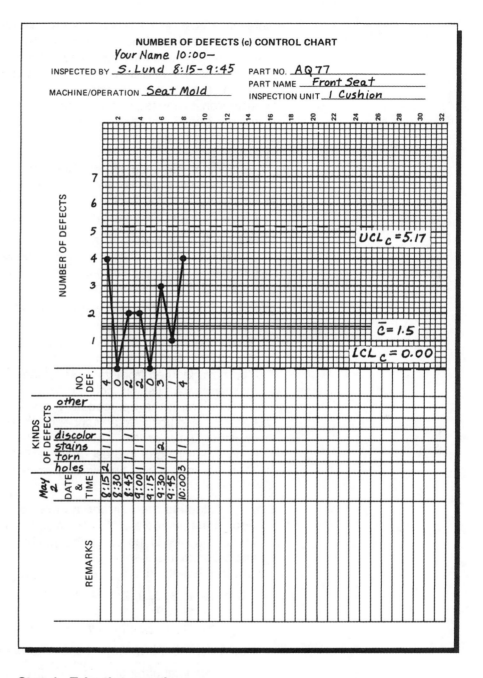

Step 1. Take the sample.

You want your sample to show only inherent variation. To do this, the sample must represent only one source of data. Therefore you will take the sample from one machine, one production associate, one batch of raw materials. Because this process is new, you will probably want to inspect a piece about every 15 minutes. When the process shows that it's settled down, you won't need to sample so often.

The inspection unit is the sample you take. In Figure 4-18 the inspection unit is one truck cab. In Figures 4-19 through 4-21 the inspection unit is one seat cushion, because you are inspecting one cushion every fifteen minutes. If your company manufactures integrated circuits, your inspection unit might be one ceramic wafer, and the wafer itself might contain several hundred individual circuits.

Remember that once you establish the inspection unit, you must stick to it. If the inspection unit is one seat cushion, always take *one* seat cushion as your sample. If you decide to use five seat cushions as the sample unit, then always inspect five cushions in each sample.

Step 2. Fill in background information on the c-chart form.

The layout of the c-chart is similar to the p-chart. (See Figure 4-22.) The c-chart has a place for information such as machine, part number, and inspection unit. Fill in this background information.

Step 3. Collect and record data.

Follow the plan you established and inspect one piece every 15 minutes.
Follow the standards for determining defects.
Record the data on the chart.

You have learned from your customers what defects to look for. When you inspect each cushion, count how many of each defect you find. Write these numbers in the appropriate places under the heading "KINDS OF DEFECTS." Add up the total number of defects for the first sample and write that number, 3, under "NO. DEF." This total, 3, is what we call "c," or count. Note down anything of interest under "REMARKS."

Continue in this way until you have recorded data for twenty samples. (See Figure 4-23.)

Step 4. Calculate the average number of defects for the process.

Add all the numbers of defects, c's, under "NO. DEF."
Divide the total of the c's by the number of inspection units. In this case an inspection unit is a seat cushion.
Check the arithmetic.

Defects, c: 3, 0, 2, 2, 1, 3, 6, 4, 4, 2, 2, 0, 2, 1, 1, 0, 2, 3, 1, 0
Total of c's: 39
Number of c's: 20 (the number of cushions examined)

Now calculate the *average number of defects for the process, $\bar{c}$:*

$\bar{c}$ equals total of all defects (c's) divided by number of inspection units
$\bar{c} = 39/20$
$= 1.95$

Make a note of the $\bar{c}$. You will add it to the chart later.

Figure 4-22. c-chart with background information.

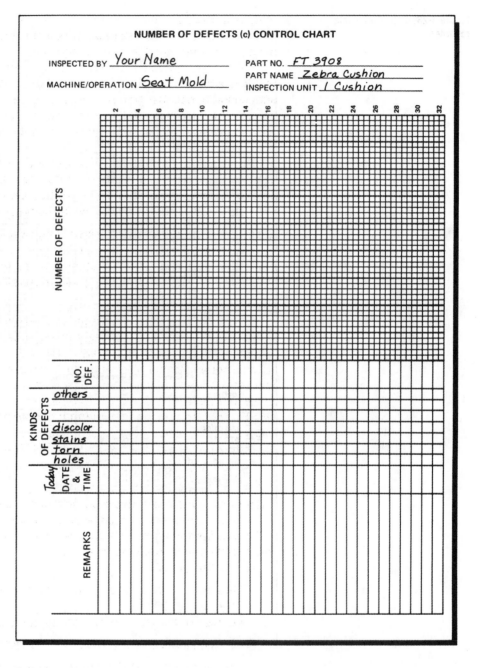

Step 5. Determine the scales for the graph and plot the data.

Find the largest and smallest c. The largest c is 6 and the smallest c is 0.

Set scales on the graph so the largest and smallest c's can fit easily. Allow enough room for the control limits. (See Figure 4-24.)

Figure 4-23. c-chart with data recorded.

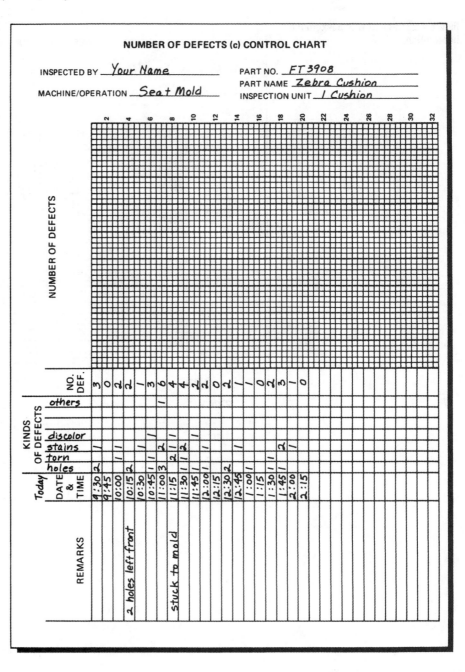

NUMBER OF DEFECTS (c) CONTROL CHART

INSPECTED BY _Your Name_   PART NO. _FT 3908_

MACHINE/OPERATION _Seat Mold_   PART NAME _Zebra Cushion_

INSPECTION UNIT _1 Cushion_

You can run the scales from zero to 8. All the c's will fit, and you'll have room for your upper and lower control limits. On the graph the first dark line will be 1, the next dark line 2, and so on.

Plot the c's and connect the points with straight lines. Now draw in the overall mean, $\bar{c}$, and label it 1.95.

Figure 4-24. c-chart with points plotted.

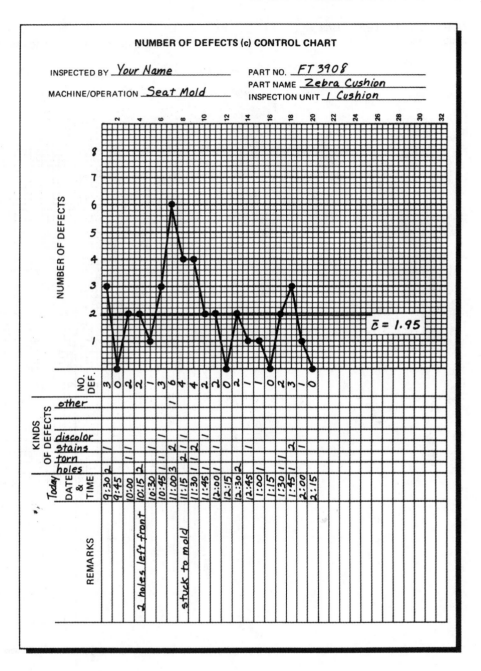

Step 6. Calculate the upper and lower control limits.

The arithmetic for calculating the control limits for c-charts is easier than for p-charts. This is the formula for the upper control limit for c:

$$UCL_c = \bar{c} + 3\sqrt{\bar{c}}$$

Figure 4-25. c-chart with control limits added.

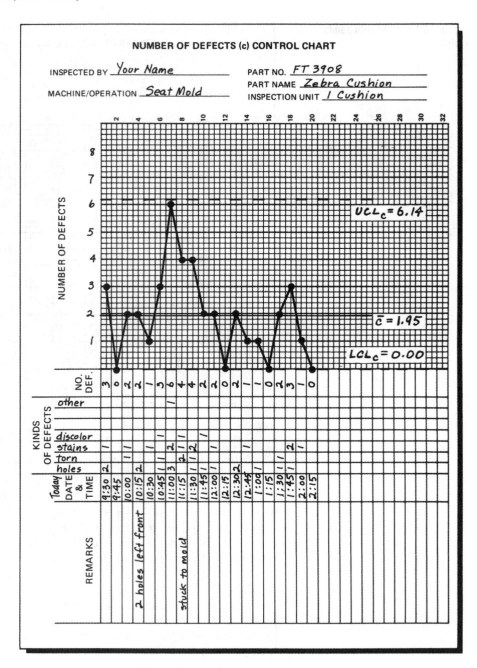

The upper control limit for c equals $\bar{c}$ plus 3 times the square root of $\bar{c}$. (To do square roots easily, use a calculator.)

To figure the lower control limit, use this formula:

$$LCL_c = \bar{c} - 3\sqrt{\bar{c}}$$

The lower control limit for c equals $\bar{c}$ minus 3 times the square root of $\bar{c}$.

Remember, you are *subtracting* the term 3 times $\sqrt{\bar{c}}$ from $\bar{c}$ when you figure the lower control limit. If your answer is a negative number, set it at zero.

This is how your calculations will look when $\bar{c}$ equals 1.95:

Upper control limit for c:

$$UCL_c = \bar{c} + 3 \sqrt{\bar{c}}$$
$$= 1.95 + 3 \sqrt{1.95}$$
$$= 1.95 + 3 \times 1.396$$
$$= 1.95 + 4.188$$
$$= 6.138$$

Round off 6.138 to 6.14.

Lower control limit for c:

$$LCL_c = \bar{c} - 3 \sqrt{\bar{c}}$$
$$= 1.95 - 3 \sqrt{1.95}$$
$$= 1.95 - 4.188$$
$$= -2.239$$

The answer is negative, so set the lower limit at zero.

Check your arithmetic at every step. You don't want to be an assignable cause!

Draw in the control limits on your c-chart and label them UCL_c, 6.14 and LCL_c, 0.00. Show these as dashed lines or use color so that they are highly visible. (See Figure 4-25.)

Step 7. Interpret the c-chart.

Once you have completed the c-chart, there are three possible situations, just as with the p-charts. Either all the c's are inside the control limits; or one or two c's are outside the control limits; or three or more c's are outside the control limits. As you did for p-charts, take the appropriate action depending on the number of c's outside the control limits.

As you can see in Figure 4-25, all the c's for the foam seat cushion are in control. Because all the c's are in control, you can use your c-chart to continue monitoring and controlling your process.

SUMMARY

When you need to adjust or monitor quality characteristics in your process, you may use an attribute control chart. These charts are based on attribute or counting data. An attribute is not measured; it's either there or it's not.

The three most important kinds of attribute charts are the p-chart, the np-chart, and the c-chart.

Use the p-chart when you want to control the percent or fraction defective of the units produced. If you want to monitor the number of defective units, use the np-chart. To control the number or count of defects in the inspection unit, use the c-chart.

A piece or a unit is defective if it is not good (not acceptable). A defective unit may have one or more defects, such as a scratch or a hole, which makes the unit unacceptable or defective.

You must know what your control charts are telling you. Points inside the control limits mean that as far as anybody can tell, only inherent variation is affecting your process. Therefore no corrections or adjustments are necessary. If one or more points lie outside the limits, however, or if certain patterns of points appear, then assignable causes are disrupting your process. At this point some adjustment or correction will be required.

A point outside the control limits tells you that something about the operation has changed. It does not tell you *what* happened, only *when* it happened.

PRACTICE PROBLEMS: ATTRIBUTE CHARTS

Work through the following practice problems using the statistical techniques you learned in Module 4. The solutions to these problems can be found in the "Solutions" section beginning on page 230.

Problem 4-1.

For a long time you have noticed that your panels have many dirt and grease spots when they are packed and shipped out of your department. The customer says that something must be done to improve the situation. Can this problem be solved by the people on the production floor, or must a management team take the necessary action to bring about improvement?

Someone took the time to inspect 48 parts at the final packing operation each day for twenty days. Using this data, try to determine whether the problem is due to assignable causes or due to the way the process is set up.

Day	No. Defectives	Day	No. Defectives
1	30	11	25
2	27	12	20
3	34	13	24
4	23	14	23
5	20	15	16
6	33	16	19
7	22	17	32
8	24	18	26
9	18	19	25
10	34	20	25

Problem 4-2.

A wiring harness manufacturer uses high-speed machinery to cut wires to a predetermined length and install terminals on the ends of the wires.

These products are basically all the same: the wire is brass with an insulation coating and the terminals installed on the wire are made of brass. The length and diameter of the wire and the shape of the terminals may vary, but the types of defects are the same for all sizes and shapes.

The production associate makes a tour of the machines and visually inspects the output of the machines that are running at that time. (Several machines perform this assembly operation, but all of them do not run all the time.)

One hundred pieces are inspected visually at each machine that is running, and the number of defects found in the sample is recorded. If the machine is not running, the record is left blank.

Make a control chart for each machine. Which machines need attention?

The following is a listing of data from six of the machines.

Inspection Round	Mach. No. 1	Mach. No. 2	Mach. No. 3	Mach. No. 4	Mach. No. 5	Mach. No. 6
1	0	—	6	0	—	1
2	0	—	6	1	—	0
3	0	1	—	0	—	0
4	0	0	—	0	—	1
5	—	—	—	5	0	—
6	6	0	4	—	3	0
7	0	—	—	—	—	—

8	0	0	—	0	0	0
9	2	0	—	0	0	0
10	1	0	—	0	0	0
11	1	0	—	0	0	0
12	—	2	—	1	0	0
13	0	0	0	0	0	0
14	—	0	3	—	4	0
15	—	0	1	2	1	1
16	—	0	2	0	5	1
17	—	0	—	0	5	0
18	—	0	—	0	0	0
19	—	0	6	0	0	0
20	—	0	1	0	0	1
21	—	2	7	1	0	—
22	4	0	8	0	0	—
23	12	0	2	0	0	2
24	8	0	1	0	0	1
25	—	0	3	2	1	2
26	—	0	1	0	0	2
27	—	0	1	0	0	1
28	—	1	3	0	0	1
29	—	0	—	—	0	0
30	—	—	—	—	0	—

Problem 4-3.

Your company has started a drive to improve the quality of the products you manufacture. You and your co-workers want to help this effort, so you get together and discuss what you can do as a group.

You decide to analyze some inspection results to find out where to start. The products are processed and packed in groups of 100. The inspection results are recorded in such a way that if a part is found to have one or more scratches, it is recorded as one defective unit. Likewise, if a part is found to have one wrinkle or more or one crack or more, it is recorded as one defective unit. In the inspection data listed below, the first line shows 14 units with scratches and 10 units with wrinkles. These might or might not have occurred on the same pieces. Each classification of defect is separate from the others. Only the sample size—100—is the same for all. What recommendations would you make for improving quality?

Sampling data for Problem 4-3.

Sample	Scratches	Wrinkles	Bent	Cracks	Wrong Part
1	14	10	5	1	0
2	16	7	5	0	1
3	13	10	2	2	0
4	12	6	5	1	0
5	12	10	9	5	0
6	11	6	4	0	2
7	17	6	3	0	0
8	20	12	1	1	0
9	11	6	5	1	1
10	9	10	7	0	0
11	6	7	7	2	0
12	8	6	8	3	0
13	21	6	3	3	0
14	17	7	3	3	0
15	15	11	2	3	0
16	10	10	4	2	0
17	9	9	3	3	0
18	17	5	2	3	1
19	12	11	2	1	0
20	14	7	5	4	0

Make a control chart for each category of defect. What will be your recommendation to the management team.

Machine and Process Capability

Once the assignable causes have been eliminated from a process or operation, we can say it is stable. The "floor solvable" portion of the quality problem has been eliminated. Most statistical process control techniques, the "tools of quality", measure the stability of machine or process or operation.

After we make a process or operation stable, we must answer the question, "Has this process or machine been designed and installed in such a manner that no quality problems will arise once the assignable causes are eliminated?" In other words, is the machine or process capable of producing parts within the specification? If it is not, we have identified a problem that must be solved by a management team.

In this module we will learn two ways to measure the capability of a machine or process and to compare it to the product tolerance. These two methods are the average and range chart and the *probability plot*. They should be used together to give the best estimate of *machine capability* or *process capability*.

The analysis techniques for machine capability and process capability are almost the same. The difference lies in how the measurements are obtained.

You will be concerned mainly with the capability of a machine or an operation. You will probably be concerned with the capability of the process as a whole after the job is in production, but more often you will need to make machine capability studies to determine the effects of a change in materials or methods or tools. We will discuss machine capability first.

MACHINE CAPABILITY

A machine is generally considered a part of the total process. The total process is subject to variation from such sources as the production associates, the methods they use, the materials fed into the process from suppliers, the surrounding environment, and the machines used to make the product. (See the fishbone diagram in Module 1, Figure 1-4.)

A machine capability study is performed on a single machine or operation. The measurements used to measure that capability should show only the variation caused by the machine and not the variation caused by other parts of the process: the production associate, the methods, the incoming materials, or the environment. You cannot eliminate completely the effects of these other factors, but you can minimize them by collecting the measurements over as short a period of time as practical. When you do this, you can make the best possible estimate of machine capability.

AVERAGE AND RANGE CHART METHOD

A machine capability study is concerned with one dimension of a product at a time. One purpose of the study is to make an estimate of the average dimension produced by the machine or operation. Then you can compare this average with the part print to see how close you came to the print specification.

A second purpose of the study is to make an estimate of how the dimension is clustered around the average. As we saw in Module 1, this pattern is called the process spread. The process spread is measured in terms of the standard deviation of the operation. Standard deviation is simply a number that we can use to describe the process spread.

To develop an average and range chart we use measurements of parts from the operation being studied. We need these measurements because we must know how stable the operation is when we make our estimate of capability. Our estimate of capability will be based on the statistics obtained from the operation when all conditions are normal or stable. The best way to determine stability is to make an average and range chart and look for the presence of assignable or floor solvable causes. If the chart shows points out of control, we have a signal that some assignable cause is distorting the normal distribution of the dimension. We must eliminate the assignable causes whenever possible. If we cannot do this, we will be less able to make an accurate estimate of machine capability.

As you saw in Module 2, a frequency histogram can be used to estimate the average of a dimension and its spread around the average. You can place the design specification on the histogram, and in this way you can obtain an estimate of the capability of the machine. The histogram is often satisfactory if you need a quick check and if you're sure that no assignable causes are present, but the average and range chart is more precise and more reliable for predicting machine capability.

When all assignable causes are identified and eliminated, you can say that the operation is stable and predictable. Once the operation is stable, you can proceed to make a capability study to see if it will produce all parts within print tolerance. A typical machine capability study is illustrated in Figure 5-1 and Figure 5-2. In this operation a bushing is pressed into a door hinge. Figure 5-1 shows the control chart developed during the capability study.

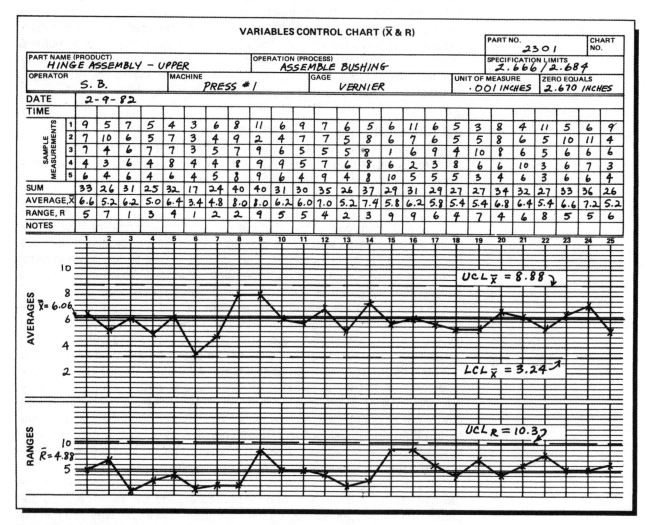

Figure 5-1. Average and range chart, machine capability study.

Figure 5-2. Back of average and range chart, showing "limits for individuals," upper right.

CALCULATION WORK SHEET

CONTROL LIMITS	LIMITS FOR INDIVIDUALS
	COMPARE WITH SPECIFICATION OR TOLERANCE LIMITS

SUBGROUPS INCLUDED __25__ _____

$\bar{R} = \frac{\Sigma R}{k} = \frac{122}{25} = 4.88$ _____ =

$\bar{\bar{X}} = \frac{\Sigma \bar{X}}{k} = \frac{151.6}{25} = 6.06$ _____ =

OR

$\bar{X}'$ (MIDSPEC. OR STD.) = _____ =

$A_2\bar{R} = .577 \times 4.88 = 2.82$ × = _____

$UCL_{\bar{x}} = \bar{\bar{X}} + A_2\bar{R} = 8.88$ =

$LCL_{\bar{x}} = \bar{\bar{X}} - A_2\bar{R} = 3.24$ =

$UCL_R = D_4\bar{R} = 2.114 \times 4.88 = 10.3$ × =

LIMITS FOR INDIVIDUALS (right column):

$\bar{\bar{X}}$ = 2.6761

$\frac{3}{d_2}\bar{R} = 1.29 \times .00488 = .0063$

$UL_x = \bar{\bar{X}} + \frac{3}{d_2}\bar{R} = 2.6824$

$LL_x = \bar{\bar{X}} - \frac{3}{d_2}\bar{R} = 2.6698$

$US = 2.684$

$LS = 2.666$

$US - LS = .018$

$6\sigma = \frac{6}{d_2}\bar{R} = .0126$

MODIFIED CONTROL LIMITS FOR AVERAGES

BASED ON SPECIFICATION LIMITS AND PROCESS CAPABILITY. APPLICABLE ONLY IF: US − LS > 6σ.

US = LS =

$A_M\bar{R} =$ × = _____ $A_M\bar{R} =$ = _____

$URL_{\bar{x}} = US - A_M\bar{R} =$ $LRL_{\bar{x}} = LS + A_M\bar{R} =$

FACTORS FOR CONTROL LIMITS

n	A_2	D_4	d_2	$\frac{3}{d_2}$	A_M
2	1.880	3.268	1.128	2.659	0.779
3	1.023	2.574	1.693	1.772	0.749
4	0.729	2.282	2.059	1.457	0.728
5	0.577	2.114	2.326	1.290	0.713
6	0.483	2.004	2.534	1.184	0.701

NOTES

$\bar{R} = \frac{122}{25} = 4.88$ (IN THOUSANDTHS OF AN INCH = .00488)

$\bar{\bar{X}} = \frac{151.6}{25} = 6.06$ (IN THOUSANDTHS OF AN INCH = .00606)

ZERO = 2.670; THEREFORE $\bar{\bar{X}}$ IN INCHES EQUALS 2.670 + .00606 = 2.6761

$\frac{3}{d_2}$ IS SELECTED FROM THE TABLE OF FACTORS FOR CONTROL LIMITS. FOR A SAMPLE SIZE (n) OF 5 THIS IS 1.290

$\frac{3}{d_2}\bar{R} = 1.290 \times .00488 = .0063$

$\frac{6}{d_2}\bar{R} = .0063 \times 2 = .0126$

As you learned in Module 2, you can use what you know about the operation to help simplify the job. In this example we "coded" the measurements, using 2.670 inches as zero. (See "zero equals" space on chart, Figure 5-1.) That is, when we measured a part and found that it measured 2.673 inches, we recorded a 3 on the chart. When we found that a part measured 2.680 inches, we recorded a 10, and so on. In this way we could use smaller numbers when recording the measurements and when making the calculations.

In this study we measured 125 consecutively made parts and recorded these measurements on the control chart in the order in which they were made. We did this in as short a time period as possible; in this way we kept down variation due to causes other than the assembly press.

After we recorded all the measurements, we made calculations to determine the average range ($\overline{R}$); the upper control limit for the range (UCL_R); the average of the sample averages ($\overline{\overline{X}}$); and the upper and lower control limits for the average (UCL_x and $LCL_{\overline{x}}$). Just as in any average and range chart, we developed the range chart first and determined that there were no out-of-control points on that chart before proceeding with the average chart.

Fortunately there were no points outside the control limits (see Figure 5-1), but this is not always the case. Often it is very difficult to find and eliminate the assignable causes. But even if all assignable causes cannot be eliminated, it is often worthwhile to proceed with the capability study. When you do this, you should be very cautious in making your capability estimate. Keep in mind that assignable causes tend to distort the normal frequency distribution curve. When this happens you are less able to predict accurately the capability of the process or machine.

VARIATIONS DUE TO ASSIGNABLE CAUSES TEND TO DISTORT THE NORMAL FREQUENCY DISTRIBUTION CURVE!

LIMITS FOR INDIVIDUALS

Once you have established the average and range chart with control limits, you must estimate the upper and lower limits for individual parts. This is a simple calculation that you can perform using a form on the back of the average and range chart. The formulas are supplied; you just put in the numbers. Use the form headed "Limits for Individuals." (See Figure 5-2.)

To help you understand and use this form, we have defined or identified a number of terms. Some of these terms are new, and some you have met earlier in this book.

$\overline{\overline{X}}$ — overall average or mean of the process or operation.

$\overline{R}$ — average range of the operation.

σ — "sigma," the standard deviation of the process or operation. One of the divisions of the distribution around the average of the normal curve. (See Module 1.)

d_2 — a factor used in combination with the average range ($\overline{R}$) to determine the standard deviation (σ). (See d_2 under "Factors for Control Limits," Figure 5-2.) 1σ equals $\overline{R}$ divided by d_2; 3σ equals $3\overline{R}$ divided by d_2.

UL_x — upper limit for individuals; the estimated largest individual part to be produced by the operation under study. This is not to be confused with the upper control limit ($UCL_{\overline{x}}$), which is the limit for averages. UL_x equals $\overline{\overline{X}}$ plus ($3\overline{R}$ divided by d_2).

LL_x — lower limit for individuals; the estimated smallest individual part to be produced by the operation under study. LL_x equals $\overline{\overline{X}}$ minus ($3\,\overline{R}$ divided by d_2).

US — upper specification limit.

LS — lower specification limit. US minus LS equals specification limit or tolerance. $6\overline{R}$ divided by d_2 equals 6σ—formula for process spread (machine capability).

Figure 5-3. Process spread is normal; coincides with specification limits.

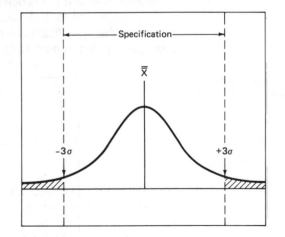

If the upper limit for individuals (UL_x) is equal to or less than the upper specification limit (US); and if the lower limit for individuals (LL_x) is equal to or greater than the lower specification limit (LS), you can say that the operation or machine is capable of meeting the specification. Remember, this is true only if the measurements show the operation to be stable and normal. Figure 5-3 illustrates a capable condition: (1) the process spread and the specification limits are the same and (2) they coincide. Most of the parts (99.73%) produced in an operation like this will be within specification. You can see that if anything changes in such an operation, parts will be produced outside the specification.

In a case where the process spread is greater than the specification limits, the machine or operation must be declared not capable of meeting the specification. (See Figure 5-4.)

Figure 5-4. Process spread is greater than specification limits.

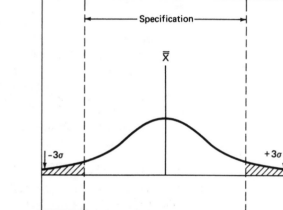

In a case where the process spread is less than the specification spread but the upper limit for individuals (UL_x) or the lower limit for individuals (LL_x) is outside the specification limits, an adjustment is required in the process average or process mean ($\overline{\overline{X}}$). In Figure 5-5 the curve has the same spread

Figure 5-5. Process mean is high; upper limit is above upper specification limit.

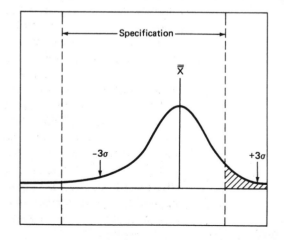

as in Figure 5-3, but the process mean ($\overline{\overline{X}}$) is on the "high" side of center. As a result, the lower 3σ limit is well within specification, but the upper 3σ limit is well above the specification limit. This process could be brought within the specification limits if an adjustment could be made to shift the process mean to a lower value.

Figure 5-6. An ideal condition; the process is centered on the specification and the process spread is less than the specification.

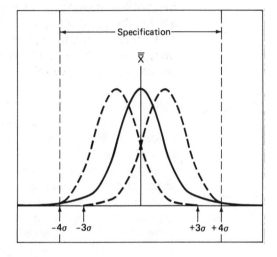

A much better situation is shown in Figure 5-6. The process is centered on the specification and the process spread is such that 8σ is equal to the specification. In this case, the operation can change somewhat and the parts being made will still be within specification.

This is your goal. The dimension created by the machine or operation being studied must be centered on the specification and the process spread must be as small as possible. Keep in mind that the capability of a machine or operation is only one part of a total process. Over a period of time other sources of variation will affect the output of this machine. These other sources will cause the process spread to be greater than the estimated process spread caused by the machine alone.

The variability built into one machine must be small enough to allow for other sources of variation to enter the total process and still keep the process output within 3σ above and 3σ below the mean. This situation is expected and required when you perform a machine capability study.

When you use the average and range chart to predict process or machine capability, you have the advantage of seeing how stable the operation is because the chart shows whether or not assignable causes were at work during the time the measurements were taken. However, you can't always be sure about the shape of the distribution of the original measurements. Whether or not the individual measurements form a normal distribution, the distribution of the *sample averages* plotted on the average and range chart is nearly normal. We assumed the frequency distribution was normal, as shown in Figure 5-3, when we compared the operation spread to the specification. When we made calculations (Figure 5-2) to estimate the upper and lower limits for individual parts and to determine the operation spread, we assumed here, too, that the distribution was normal.

The charts shown in Figures 5-1 and 5-2 are typical of a machine capability study. The measurements were taken on a continuous basis to minimize the variation due to outside sources. As a result, the variation shown on the chart is due mostly to the machine that created the dimension under study, namely the width across the bushings of a door hinge. No points were outside the control limits, so the operation was considered stable enough to continue with the study.

THE PROBABILITY PLOT

Is this a good estimate of capability? A simple way to test the estimates made from the control chart measurements is to use a probability plot to estimate the shape of the distribution formed by those measurements.

In the probability plot we take the measurements used to make the average and range chart and plot them in such a way that we can estimate how well they fit a normal curve. We use this technique together with the average and range chart method, discussed above, to make the best estimate of machine capability.

This method makes use of a special graph paper called *normal probability paper*. (See Figure 5-7.) The form of the graph paper used in this technique has been developed over the years through the efforts of many people in the field of statistical process control. Each step in the development of this paper has helped to simplify its use. If you can't find the form for the normal probability chart used in this book, you can use some other form or make copies of the form used here.

Using normal probability paper we will be able to show the following:

— The center of the frequency distribution curve (where most of the measurements are).
— The spread of the frequency distribution curve (how the measurements cluster around the middle).
— The general shape of the frequency distribution curve.
— The percentage of measurements beyond the specification limits.

In the following pages you will learn how to construct a probability plot on normal probability paper.

Step 1. Gather the information and fill in the heading.

As in normal in-plant practice, use the first twenty subgroups of measurements from the chart shown in Figure 5-1, for a total of 100 measurements. You could estimate the normality of the process with fewer measurements. Fifty would be enough, and in fact, many estimates of normality and capability have been made with as few as 25 measurements. But if you

Figure 5-7. Normal probability chart. (Form developed by Howard Butler.)

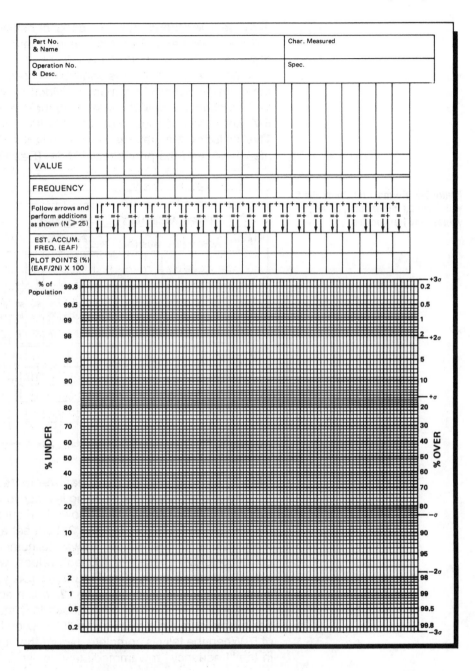

ever use fewer than 50 you run a higher risk that your estimate will be wrong. On the other hand, it's hardly worth the trouble to make more than 100 measurements.

Since the information is available, you might as well take advantage of the greater degree of accuracy provided by the larger sample.

The chart you will use in making the capability study is shown in Figure 5-7. Enter the information pertinent to this study in the heading of the chart. This includes the part name and number, the operation, the dimension measured, and the print specification. (See Figure 5-8.)

Figure 5-8. Normal probability chart with heading information, tallies, values, and frequencies.

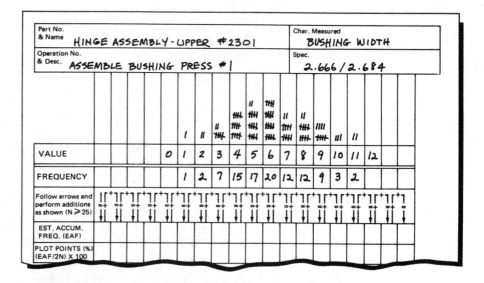

Step 2. Make a tally of the measurements.

Immediately under the heading is a section in which to make a frequency tally of the data. (This is also shown in Figure 5-8.) To make this tally, use the method described in Module 2. First set a scale that will give you about ten divisions. In the "value" row write numbers beginning with 0,1,2, and going up to 12. These are "coded" values, which you recorded on the average and range chart. (See Figure 5-1.) As you remember, 0 equals 2.670, 1 equals 2.671, and so on up to 12, which equals 2.682.

As you make the tally, enter each tally mark in the appropriate section. For example, make a mark in the "5" section for each sample measurement of 5. When the tally is complete, record the number of tallies in each division in the "frequency" row immediately below the "value" row.

Step 3. Find the estimated accumulated frequencies.

To place the plot points on the graph, you must transform the frequency of each measurement value (1,2,7,15, and so on), which you obtained from the frequency histogram tally, to the *estimated accumulated frequencies*

(EAF). Then you must convert the estimated accumulated frequencies to percentages of the total sample. This may sound confusing at first, but with use, you will find that it is a simple way to convert measurements into a form you can use to estimate how normally the measurements are distributed around the average.

This is how to calculate the estimated accumulated frequencies (EAF), as shown in Figure 5-9.

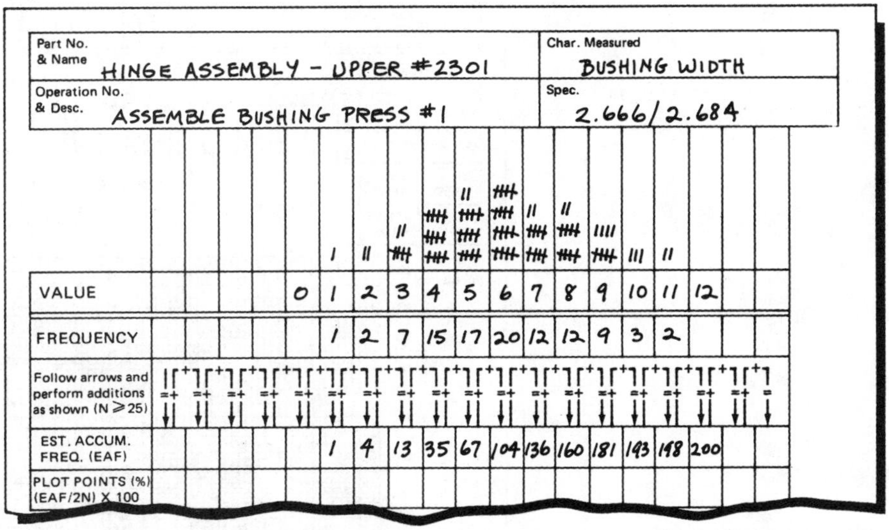

Figure 5-9. Normal probability chart showing estimated accumulated frequencies (EAF).

Transfer the first frequency on the left to the EAF space or *cell* two rows below it. In this case, the number is 1.

For the second entry, start with the EAF you just entered (1), follow the arrow up past the plus sign to the "frequency" row, and add the first frequency (1). Follow the arrow to the right past the next plus sign to the second frequency (2) and add that number; follow the arrow down past the equal sign and enter the total (4) in the EAF cell. In our example, 1 + 1 + 2 = 4.

For the third entry, follow the next arrow upward, starting with the second EAF value (4), and add the two frequency counts (2 and 7) to obtain 13, the third EAF. In our example, 4 + 2 + 7 = 13.

Follow the arrows and add the numbers until you have added all the frequency counts. The last arrow in our example starts with the EAF of 198. Follow the arrow up to the last frequency count, 2, and add it to the 198. Then move to the next frequency cell, which is blank, and continue down to the EAF cell and record the total of 200. At this point, we can check our addition simply by comparing the highest EAF to the sample size. This value is always twice the sample size. In our example, the highest EAF value is 200 and the sample size is 100.

Figure 5-10. Normal probability chart showing plot points.

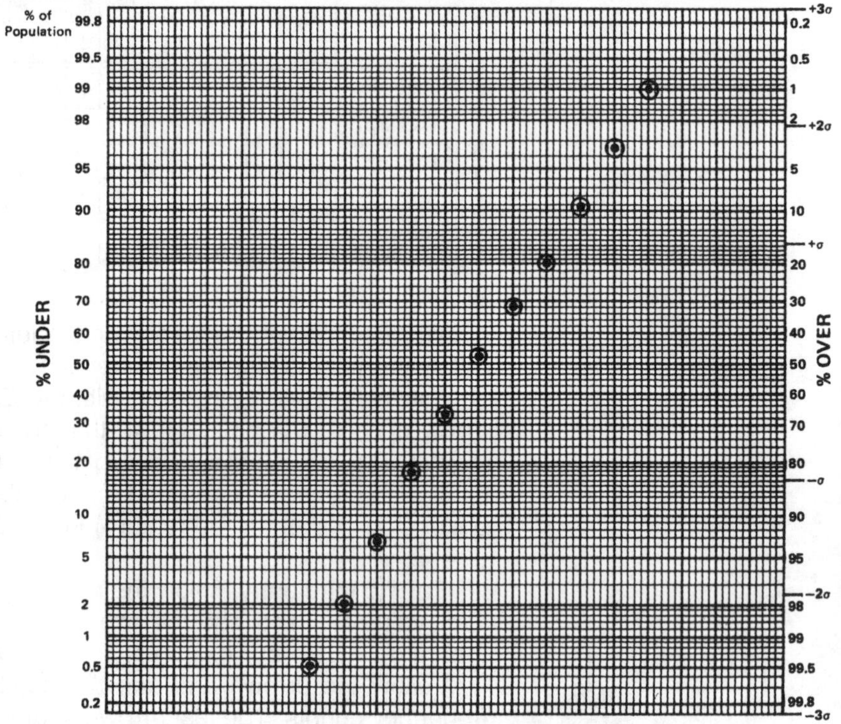

Step 4. Place the plot points.

Now you can use the estimated accumulated frequencies to place the *plot points* on the probability graph. To obtain the points to be plotted on the graph paper, convert the estimated accumulated frequencies to percentages of the total sample that formed the frequency distribution. (See "plot points" row in Figure 5-10.)

To determine the plot points, use the formula in the "plot points" row. Divide each EAF by twice the sample size (2N) and multiply the result by 100.

Plot points (%) equals EAF divided by 2N, all times 100.

In our example, N equals 100 and so 2N equals 200. The first EAF is 1. Therefore the first plot point is $1/200 \times 100 = 0.5$. The second plot point is $4/200 \times 100 = 2$; the third is $13/200 \times 100 = 6.5$; and so on, as shown in Figure 5-10.

Now record the plot points on the graph portion of the chart, as follows. On the left-hand edge of the graph, which is marked "% under," find the number that matches the number in the "plot points" box. On this chart, the number in the first box in the "plot points row" is .5, so locate the number .5, or 0.5, on the "% under" scale. Follow the horizontal line that corresponds to 0.5 until you reach the heavy vertical line that runs up to the first "plot points" box. Place a point where these two lines meet and draw a small circle around the point so that you can see it more clearly. (See Figure 5-10.) The number in the next "plot point" box is 2, so find 2 on the "% under" scale. Follow the horizontal line across until you reach the line that runs up to the "plot point" box containing the number 2, and plot the point. Continue doing this until you have plotted the point for the "plot point" box containing the number 99. (See Figure 5-10.)

Step 5. Draw the line of best fit.

Now draw a line that best fits the plot points. This is called the *line of best fit*. If the measurements used in this study are distributed normally around the average, the points will fall in a straight line on this graph paper. Any trend away from a straight line is a sign that the normal distribution is distorted. A line has been fitted to the plot points in Figure 5-11.

At this point you can judge the accuracy of the estimate of the process spread, which you made using the average and range chart. If the line of best fit is straight or nearly straight, you can be highly confident about the estimate of the mean and standard deviation based on the average and range chart. If the line of best fit is more irregular, you should have less confidence in the estimate.

Step 6. Estimate the process spread.

Now extend the line of best fit beyond the points you plotted on the graph until it crosses the horizontal lines at the top edge and at the bottom edge of the graph. You can use the dimensions represented by these two

Figure 5-11. Normal probability chart showing line of best fit.

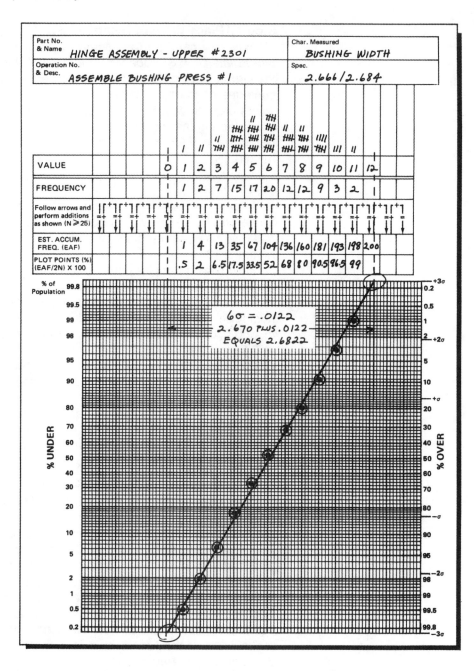

intersection points to estimate the process spread. (See Figure 5-11.)

In Figure 5-11, the line of best fit crosses the bottom edge of the graph at a vertical line which, when followed up to the top of the graph, ends at the middle of the division with a value of zero. When you look back at the average and range chart with the measurements on it (Figure 5-1), you see in the "zero equals" section that zero equals 2.670. This is the lowest value you can expect from this operation.

Where the line of best fit crosses the top edge of the graph, it also crosses a vertical line which is one gradation beyond the middle of the "value row" box with a value of 12. (On the scale we are using for this graph, each heavy vertical line ends at the middle of a box in the "value" row.) The unit of measure as recorded on the average and range chart in Figure 5-1 is .001 inch. (See "unit of measure" box, Figure 5-1). Each heavy vertical line is .001 inch on the graph, and each of the other vertical lines represents .0002 inch, or .001 divided by 5 (there are five divisions between each two heavy lines). With this information, you can now determine that the line of best fit crosses the top edge of the graph at one division beyond the heavy vertical line that ends at the value box marked 12. The 12 is equal to .012 (see "unit of measure" box, Figure 5-1) and one division beyond the heavy vertical line is equal to 0002, so this value added to .012 equals .0122. As you will remember, "zero" is equal to 2.670. If you add .0122 to 2.670, the result is 2.6822, the largest measurement you can expect from this operation.

This spread from 2.670 to 2.6822 is "six sigma" (6σ)—the spread of the measurements from this operation. Machine capability is the expected spread of measurements from the operation when no assignable causes are present. In this example you found that the 6σ or the capability of this operation is .0122 inches.

ESTIMATING THE PROPORTION OF PARTS OUT OF SPECIFICATION

The graph obtained by the probability plot method can be used to estimate the proportion of parts that will be out of specification. The specification limits can be drawn on the graph, as shown in Figure 5-12. If the line of best fit crosses a specification limit line before it crosses the top or bottom edge of the graph, you can estimate the percentage of parts out of specification by reading the percentage above the upper specification limit on the vertical scale on the right-hand side of the graph ("% over"), opposite the place where the line of best fit crosses the upper specification line. You can estimate the percentage below the specification by reading the percentage on the left vertical scale ("% under"), opposite the place where the line of best fit crosses the lower specification line. These estimates can be used even if the line of best fit is not a straight line, but the estimates won't be quite as good.

Figure 5-12 shows that the operation of assembling the bushing into the hinge is capable of meeting the specification because of the following:

— The operation is well centered on the specification at 2.676 inches versus a specified 2.675 inches.
— The process spread of .0122 inch (6σ) is less than the tolerance of .018 inch.
— The upper limit for individuals (UL_x) is less than the upper specification limit (USL_x), 2.682 versus 2.684.

— The lower limit for individuals (LL_x) is greater than the lower specification limit (LSL_x), 2.670 versus 2.666.

Figure 5-13 shows a probability plot of another machine capability study. The dimension measured for this study is a diameter, which is specified

Figure 5-12. Normal probability chart showing specification limits. Operation is within limits.

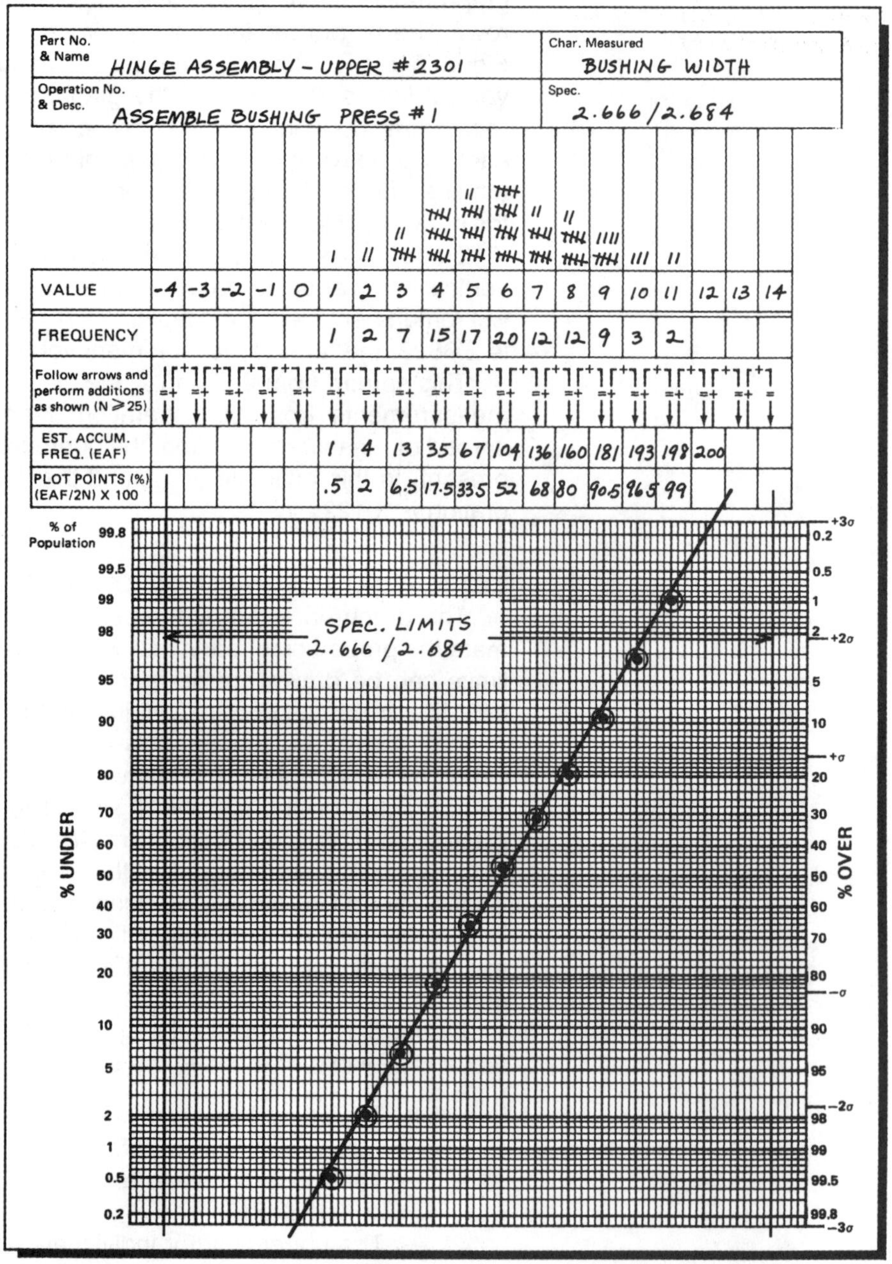

Part No. & Name	HINGE ASSEMBLY – UPPER #2301															Char. Measured BUSHING WIDTH		
Operation No. & Desc.	ASSEMBLE BUSHING PRESS #1															Spec. 2.666/2.684		
VALUE	-4	-3	-2	-1	0	1	2	3	4	5	6	7	8	9	10	11	12	13	14
FREQUENCY						1	2	7	15	17	20	12	12	9	3	2			
EST. ACCUM. FREQ. (EAF)						1	4	13	35	67	104	136	160	181	193	198	200		
PLOT POINTS (%) (EAF/2N) X 100						.5	2	6.5	17.5	33.5	52	68	80	90.5	96.5	99			

Follow arrows and perform additions as shown (N ≥ 25)

SPEC. LIMITS 2.666 / 2.684

as 1.00 to 1.035. In this study zero equals 1.00, so the specification is marked on the graph with vertical lines at zero and 35 on the "value" row scale.

Figure 5-13. Operation is 32% over upper specification limit.

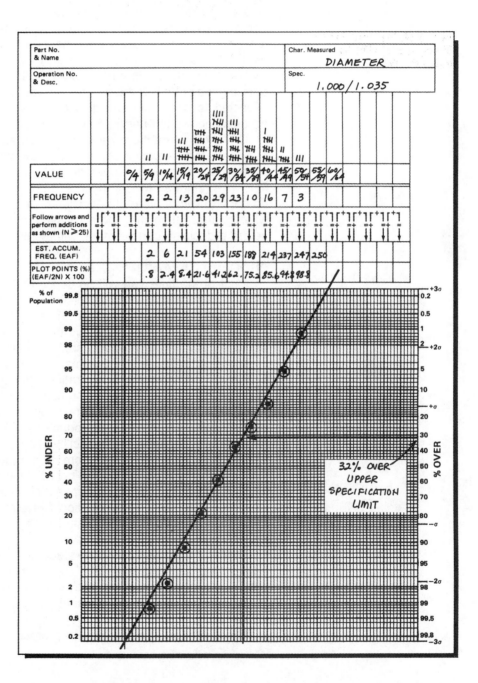

The line of best fit has been drawn on this graph, and it is plain to see that it crosses the upper specification limit line before it crosses the top edge of the graph. The point at which the line of best fit crosses the upper specification limit line is even with 32% on the "% over" scale on the right-hand side of the graph. That is, you would expect 32% of the parts from this operation to be over the specification limit. Any operation that produces such a high percentage of parts over the specification limit would *not* be considered capable.

If the line of best fit had crossed the lower specification limit line before crossing the bottom of the graph, you would estimate the percentage of parts expected to be below specification by seeing where the crossover point occurred on the left-hand ("% under") scale.

One word of caution: we chose these examples of probability charts to demonstrate the technique, and so they show almost ideal conditions for capable and noncapable operations. You will rarely find that the line of best fit is as straight as it is in these examples. In fact, many capability studies do not end with a clear-cut decision of "capable" or "not capable," but only with the realization that more measurements and information are needed before a decision can be made with confidence.

PROCESS CAPABILITY

Most of the time you will be concerned with machine capability, but on some occasions you will need to know the capability of the whole production process as it relates to your operation.

The basic difference between machine or operation capability and process capability is that machine capability is concerned with the variation in measurements caused by one machine or operation, and *only* the variation caused by that machine or operation. Process capability is concerned with the variation caused by *all* the sources of variation: the machine, the material used, the methods employed, the production associates involved, and the environment as it affects the product. (See fishbone diagram, Figure 1-4.)

If you want to know the capability of a process, your measurements must include the chance variation from *all* sources. This includes the variation that is built into the process but occurs only over a relatively long period of time. Changes in incoming shipments of material, shifts in temperature, tool wear, work by different production associates, small changes in methods are all part of the process and should be included when you estimate process capability.

To make a process capability study, you must collect measurements over a fairly long period of time from the machines you studied for machine capability. Once you have recorded the measurements, the analysis of these measurements is similar to the analysis you made for the machine capability study.

These are the steps in making a process capability study:

Develop an average and range chart by sampling the process over a long period of time. Thirty days is usually long enough to obtain measurements that include variation from all sources.

Identify and make notation of assignable causes, especially those that cause the range to go out of control.

Make a probability plot of the measurements used to develop the average and range chart.

Estimate the process spread from the probability plot and evaluate the process capability by comparing the process spread with the specification limits.

The average and range chart will give a sense of the stability of the process. The range is a measure of the process spread at the time the sample was taken. The range is considered most often to reflect machine capability, while the average is affected most often by variation from sources other than the machine.

Over a long period of time we would expect the range to be constant unless something happens to the machine. Over the same period we would not be surprised to see the average move up or down as new shipments of material are used, as the weather changes, as the tools wear, or as other things happen on the production floor.

It is often necessary to revise the control chart to adjust for the long-term changes in the average. You can do this as long as the process is still capable of producing parts to the specification.

Because the range tends to show only the machine variation and because the average is affected by variation from all sources, you must estimate *process* capability using the individual measurements that make up the averages.

As you saw in the machine capability study, the probability plot can help you estimate the shape of the distribution of measurements around the average. This is also the recommended method for estimating process capability. If the probability plot is a straight line, or nearly straight, you can use it to estimate the process average and process spread. (There are also many more complicated ways of estimating process capability, but we leave those to the mathematicians and engineers.)

Figure 5-14 is an average and range chart developed during a process capability study. The dimension measured in this job is the relative alignment or concentricity of two diameters on a crankshaft. The specification is .060 inch total indicator reading (TIR). This tolerance was considered large enough to allow for variations in incoming shipments of raw forgings, the changing condition of the tooling, the different production associates on the job, and the degree of maintenance on the lathe. The measurements were obtained over a two-month period.

The control chart shows that the process is statistically stable. At one period (6/12 to 6/21) the sample averages seem to be at one level, and at

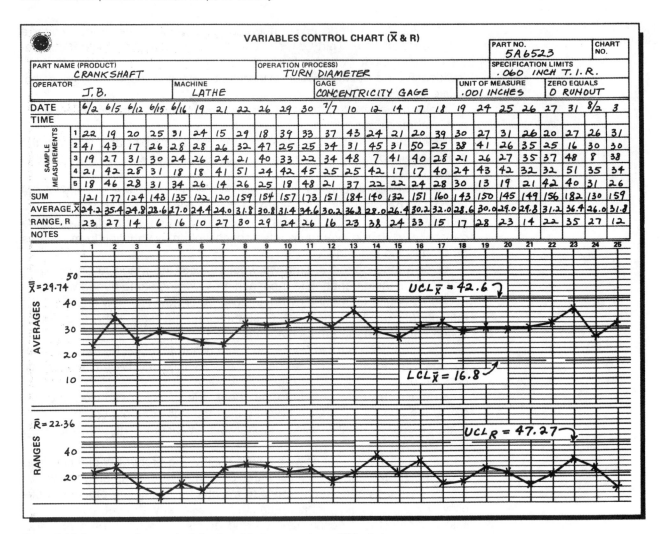

Figure 5-14. Average and range chart developed during process capability study.

another period (6/22 to 7/10) they move to another level. This variation may have been due to a new lot of material, new tooling or fixtures, or many other long-term variables, but it did not cause any instability or any out-of-control points.

The "limits for individuals" calculations shown in Figure 5-15 shows that the process uses most of the tolerance but appears to be capable; this estimate, however, is based on the average range ($\overline{R}$), which reflects mainly machine variation. The capability of the total process must be estimated using the individual measurements.

Figure 5-15. "Limits for individuals" calculations, upper right.

CALCULATION WORK SHEET

CONTROL LIMITS

SUBGROUPS INCLUDED ___25___ ═══════ ═══════

$\bar{R} = \frac{\Sigma R}{k} = \dfrac{559}{25} = 22.36$ _____ =

$\bar{\bar{X}} = \frac{\Sigma \bar{X}}{k} = \dfrac{743.4}{25} = 29.74$ _____ =

OR

$\bar{X}'$ (MIDSPEC. OR STD.) =   =

$A_2\bar{R} = .577 \times 22.36 = 12.90$ x   = _____

$UCL_{\bar{x}} = \bar{\bar{X}} + A_2\bar{R}$ $= 42.64$ =

$LCL_{\bar{x}} = \bar{\bar{X}} - A_2\bar{R}$ $= 16.84$ =

$UCL_R = D_4\bar{R} = 2.114 \times 22.36 = 47.27$ x   =

LIMITS FOR INDIVIDUALS
COMPARE WITH SPECIFICATION OR TOLERANCE LIMITS

$\bar{\bar{X}}$ $= .0297$

$\frac{3}{d_2}\bar{R} = 1.290 \times .0224 = \underline{.0289}$

$UL_x = \bar{\bar{X}} + \frac{3}{d_2}\bar{R}$ $= .0586$

$LL_x = \bar{\bar{X}} - \frac{3}{d_2}\bar{R}$ $= .0008$

US $= .0600$

LS $= \underline{.000}$

US − LS $= .060$

$6\sigma = \frac{6}{d_2}\bar{R}$ $= .0578$

MODIFIED CONTROL LIMITS FOR AVERAGES	**FACTORS FOR CONTROL LIMITS**

MODIFIED CONTROL LIMITS FOR AVERAGES

BASED ON SPECIFICATION LIMITS AND PROCESS CAPABILITY. APPLICABLE ONLY IF: US − LS > 6σ.

US   =   LS   =

$A_M\bar{R} =$ x   = _____ $A_M\bar{R}$ = _____

$URL_{\bar{x}} = US - A_M\bar{R}$ = $LRL_{\bar{x}} = LS + A_M\bar{R}$ =

FACTORS FOR CONTROL LIMITS

n	A_2	D_4	d_2	$\frac{3}{d_2}$	A_M
2	1.880	3.268	1.128	2.659	0.779
3	1.023	2.574	1.693	1.772	0.749
4	0.729	2.282	2.059	1.457	0.728
5	0.577	2.114	2.326	1.290	0.713
6	0.483	2.004	2.534	1.184	0.701

NOTES

Figure 5-16 is a probability plot of the measurements, and it shows that the measurements are normal. The line of best fit crosses the bottom edge of the graph at the value of 1 (.001 inch TIR), and it crosses the top edge of the graph at the value of 59 (.059 inch TIR). The process spread can now be estimated to be between .001 inch TIR and .059 inch TIR, or .058 inches.

Figure 5-16. Probability plot showing a capable process.

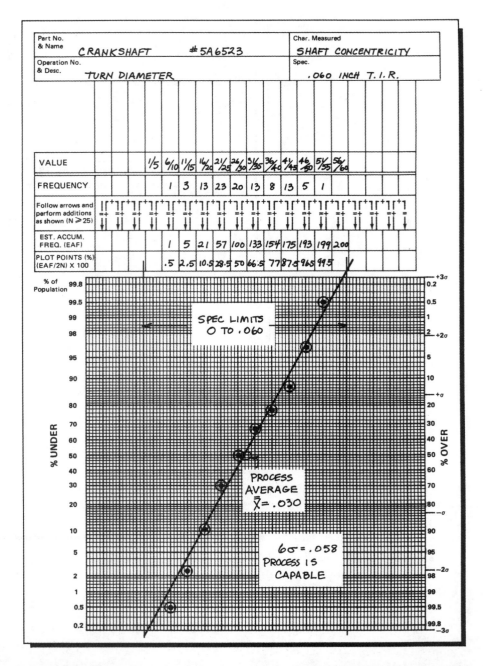

Like all process spreads, this spread is equivalent to six standard deviations (6σ) of the process.

The *estimated process average* is the value shown at the point where the line of best fit crosses the horizontal 50% line on the chart. This value is 30 (or .030 inch TIR), halfway between .001 inch TIR and .059 inch TIR.

As in a machine capability study, the specification limits are drawn on the graph and the line of best fit is compared to these limits. In this chart the total process spread (6σ) is less than the specification spread, as shown by the fact that the line of best fit crosses the upper and lower edges of the graph *before* it crosses either specification limit line.

This process can be judged capable because the analysis shows the following:

— The process is well centered on the specification.
— The process spread is less than the tolerance.
— The upper limit for individuals is less than the upper specification limit.
— The lower limit for individuals is greater than the lower specification limit.

Note that this job is estimated to use a substantially larger portion of the tolerance than the door hinge operation in the machine capability study. It could well be that if the door hinge operation were studied over a two-month period, it, too, would use a larger portion of the tolerance.

CAPABILITY INDEX

Once a process or operation has been determined to be stable (in statistical control) and distributed normally, the capability must be evaluated. As you have seen, you must first calculate the process spread using an average and range chart and then analyze the shape of the distribution with a probability plot.

The capability of a process or a machine can be expressed as a number, which is referred to as the *capability index.* This is a handy way to talk about the capability of any process or machine, whatever the products or processes may be. As you will see below, you find this index number by comparing the process spread to the specification spread, and express it in terms of the standard deviation.

One form of capability index (C_p) is simply the ratio of the specification spread or tolerance to the machine or process spread, or six standard deviations (6σ) of the process. A C_p of 1.0 or greater means that the machine or process is capable of producing parts with a spread less than the tolerance.

This is the formula for the capability index:

C_p equals the tolerance divided by 6σ of the machine or process.
$$C_p = \text{tolerance}/6\sigma \text{ of the machine or process}$$

A machine or process with 6σ equal to the tolerance would have a C_p of 1.0.

A machine or process with a total tolerance of .018 inch and a machine or process spread of .012 inch would have C_p of 1.5 (C_p = .018/.012 = 1.5).

The C_p index does not tell the whole story, though. With this method, you could show a C_p larger than 1.0 which indicates that the spread is less than the specification tolerance and therefore capable. Still, such a machine or process could be producing all parts outside the tolerance. The C_p index does not take into account where the process is centered with respect to the tolerance of the part.

A second type of capability index, the C_{pk}, is now used by many companies. This capability index will result in a negative number if the machine or process average is outside the specification tolerance. Any number less than one is an indication of a noncapable machine or process.

This C_{pk} is calculated as the smaller of these two values:

> The upper specification limit minus the machine or process average, all divided by three standard deviations of the process, or

> the machine or process average minus the lower specification limit, all divided by three standard deviations of the process.

> C_{pk} equals smaller of:(USL minus $\overline{\overline{X}}$) divided by 3σ, or
> ($\overline{\overline{X}}$ minus LSL) divided by 3σ.

Remember that the process spread is 6σ, so half the spread, or 3σ, will fall on each side of the process average. (See Figure 5-17.)

Figure 5-17. Two possible sources of C_{pk}. True C_{pk} is the smaller of these

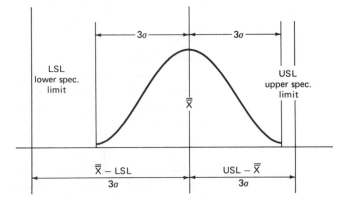

CAPABILITY RATIO

Some companies use the *capability ratio (CR)* to express machine or process capability. This ratio is the ratio of the machine or process spread (6σ) to the specification tolerance, which is then multiplied by 100 to convert it to a percentage. CR equals 6σ divided by specification tolerance, all times 100%.

A capability ratio of more than 100% indicates a noncapable machine or process. This expression of capability does not consider the machine or process average in relation to the tolerance. Quoting the spread (6σ) as a percentage of the specification tolerance does not say whether or not the machine or process is presently producing parts in tolerance. It only tells how capable the machine or process is when the average is centered on the specification mean. (See Figure 5-18.)

Figure 5-18. Two processes showing the same capability ratios (CR). The upper curve is not centered on the specification; the lower curve is centered on the specification.

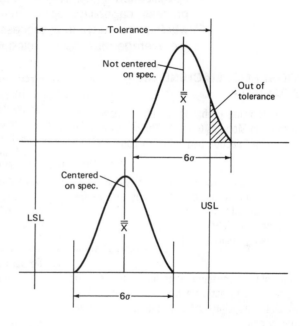

SUMMARY

Capability analysis is divided into two types: machine or operation capability studies and total process capability studies.

The statistical methods used in these two techniques are the same and are based on the six basic principles of statistical methods of process control.

A machine capability study analyzes the variation in a dimension caused by one machine or operation. This machine is generally only one part of the total process. A study of machine capability covers a relatively short period of time.

A process capability study analyzes the variation in a dimension caused by all parts of the total process. A process capability study analyzes the output of a process over a fairly long period of time, usually thirty days or more.

The estimate of capability of a machine or operation is based upon the average range of measurements in small samples taken from the operation. The estimate of capability of a total process is based upon the distribution of the individual measurements around the overall mean.

The capability of machines and processes can be described by the capability index and the capability ratio. Both these methods use numbers to describe the machine or process spread in relation to the specification tolerance.

The capability index also indicates the relationship of the mean to the specification limits. When a capability ratio is used to describe machine or process capability, some additional explanation is needed to indicate whether the machine or process is capable as currently operating or whether the average must be adjusted to a new level to achieve capability.

PRACTICE PROBLEMS: MACHINE AND PROCESS CAPABILITY

Work through the following problems, which are based on the material you learned in Modules 3 and 5. The solutions can be found in the "Solutions" section beginning on page 245.

Problem 5-1.

Turn back to the pin diameters listed in Problem 3-1 and estimate the machine capability using the average and range chart method and the probability plot method.

What is the machine capability index (C_{pk})?

What is the machine capability ratio (CR)?

Problem 5-2.

Turn back to the table of measurements listed in Problem 3-2. Can this data be used to estimate machine capability? If so, estimate the machine capability, using an average and range chart and a probability plot.

Does the capability index (C_{pk}) indicate that the machine is capable?

Does the capability ratio (CR) indicate that the machine is capable?

Problem 5-3.

Turn back to the shaft movement data in Problem 2-3. Estimate the capability of each of the five groups of data.

The specified dimension for the shaft movement is .080 inch maximum. Use a minimum dimension of .040 inch as the lower specification limit.

Are the machine setups all capable as they were running when the study was made? Should adjustments be made?

How do the averages estimated from the probability plots compare to the averages obtained from the average and range charts (Problem 3-3) and the frequency histograms (Problem 2-3)?

Problem 5-4.

Using the measurements from Problem 2-4, make a process capability analysis.

How does the estimated process average compare to the median of medians obtained in Problem 3-4?

How does the estimated process average compare to the estimate obtained using the frequency histogram in Problem 2-4?

Is the process capable? What is the C_{pk}?

6 Quality Problem-Solving Tools

Problems crop up in almost every situation. If you don't have a problem, you probably don't understand the situation! Maybe your job goes smoothly most of the time, but haven't you ever asked yourself, "Why is there so much scrap from this process?" "Why are the radiator hoses cracking along this one bend?" If you ask questions like this, you have opportunities to solve problems and make changes.

In this module you will learn methods and procedures that will help you get a handle on your production problems. Even though this book is concerned mainly with statistical tools, we are including five methods for problem solving.

These methods are useful for solving *chronic* production *problems,* where the same thing happens over and over again. For example, you may constantly find misalignment of holes between the brake pads and brake shoes, or the consistency of the cement slurry may be different from one day to the next. (Another type of problem, the *sporadic problem,* happens only once in a while, as when a machine breaks down or a key ingredient is left out of the mix for glass. In this module, however, we are concentrating on ways to solve chronic problems.)

Finding solutions to chronic problems, the ones that keep happening, will result in breakthroughs to new and better operating levels and so will bring about improvements in quality, productivity, and customer satisfaction. Success in solving problems will give you, the solver, real satisfaction.

BRAINSTORMING—A DOWNPOUR OF IDEAS

In the problem-solving process, you need to identify problems as well as determine their causes. *Brainstorming* will help you to do both. It's an excellent way of identifying problems, such as those you see on your job, and it's also a good way to gather many possible explanations for a specific problem.

Brainstorming is a group problem-solving method. It taps people's creative ability to identify and solve problems, and brings out a lot of ideas in a very short time. Because it is a group process, it helps build people as human beings. For example, brainstorming encourages individual members to contribute to the group and to develop trust for the other members.

WHAT IS NEEDED FOR BRAINSTORMING?
A group willing to work together.

In order to begin a brainstorm, you must have a group of people who are willing to work together. You may feel that this is impossible, that the group you work with will never be a team. However, brainstorming can be a key to building a team! Furthermore, it is a great tool for the group which is already working together.

Who should be included in the group? Everyone who is concerned with the problem, for two reasons. First, the ideas of everyone concerned with the problem will be available for the brainstorm. Second, those people can take an active part in solving the problem. In that way you can get them to support the solution.

A leader.

Anyone can lead the brainstorm: the manager, one of the regular members, or even an outsider. The important thing is that there *must* be someone who can and will lead.

The leader is needed to provide some guidance so that the brainstorm will produce ideas. The leader has to exercise enough control over the group to keep it on the track, and at the same time must encourage people's ideas and participation. He or she puts aside personal goals for the benefit of the group. In this sense the leader both leads and serves, and must walk the fine line between control and participation.

A meeting place.

The group should have a meeting place where they will not be interrupted or distracted. In some manufacturing plants there are rooms set aside for group meetings. In other plants, groups use a foreman's office, an area on the production floor, or even the executive conference room.

Equipment.

The group will need flipcharts, markers, and masking tape to put the charts up on the wall.

HOW DOES A BRAINSTORM WORK?

Here are some general rules for a good brainstorming session.

1. Choose the subject for the brainstorm.
2. Make sure that everyone understands what the problem or topic is.
3. Each person is to take a turn and express one idea. If somebody can't think of anything, he or she says "Pass." If someone thinks of an idea when it is not his turn, he may write it down on a slip of paper to use at his next turn.
4. Have a recorder who will write down each idea as it is expressed. Be sure the recorder has a chance to give his or her idea.
5. Write down *all* the ideas.
6. Encourage wild ideas. They may trigger someone else's thinking.
7. Hold criticism until after the session—criticism may block the free flow of ideas. The aim of the brainstorm is quantity and creativity.
8. A little laughter is fun and healthy, but don't overdo it. It is O.K. to laugh with someone, but not at them.
9. Allow a few hours or a few days for further thought. The first brainstorm on a subject will stimulate people to start thinking, but an incubation period allows the mind to release more creative ideas and insights.

Once everybody has reviewed the rules, the leader may simply say, "Let's begin the brainstorm." Sometimes you can place a time limit on the brainstorm, maybe from twelve to fifteen minutes. Although this may seem too short, we suggest that you start with short periods and lengthen them only after your group is used to working together. Then you can use longer sessions when they're needed.

Let's illustrate the brainstorm with a skit. This group includes five people: Sharon, the leader; Fred; Jan; George, the recorder; and Aaron. Since they have been meeting for only a short time and the members have not had much experience with brainstorming, the leader has to do most of the work of keeping them on the track. As the group gains experience, other members should begin to share the work of leadership.

Sharon: I think it's time to brainstorm for causes of defective capacitors. That's the problem our group chose to work on last time. George, since you're good at the flip chart, could you help us there?

George: As long as you help with my spelling.
(laughter)

Sharon: Yours is as good as mine! The others will help. Our subject, which George is writing down, is defective capacitors. Let's put a fifteen-minute time limit on the session. And don't forget the rules:

We'll go around from person to person, one idea at a time.

Don't worry if your ideas sound strange. After all, even if your idea is a wild one, it may stimulate somebody else.

No evaluations. No "That's good" and no "That's dumb." We'll have plenty of time afterward to look at the ideas.

O.K. Are we ready? (Everybody agrees.)

Fred, your turn.

Fred: Vendor. (George writes VENDOR.)

Jan: I've seen dents in some of them. And I think that a dent on the outside means something breaks or gets squeezed or somehow messed up inside. . . .

Sharon: Jan, you're saying "dents." Is that right?

Jan: No, I mean dents show us there's a problem inside.

Sharon: Can we abbreviate it to read: "Dents show inside problem"?

(Jan nods "O.K.")

Sharon: George, it's your turn.

George: I think I'll pass this time.

Aaron: The leads to the capacitors sometimes don't get soldered well. So that makes it look like a defective capacitor.

George: How do I write that? "Soldering of leads"?

Aaron: Yup, that's O.K.

Sharon: My turn. I'll build on Fred's idea of "vendor." Maybe it's only one of them that is really the problem and not all of them. George, write "one vendor."

Fred: Seems to me the shape of the AX12's is the problem. They remind me of toilet seat covers. (Much laughter)

Sharon: Let's get back to the subject. Fred may have something there. So George, write "shape of AX12's."

And so it goes. The brainstorm is fun. It's creative. Everybody is involved. Put-downs are carefully discouraged while healthy laughter is accepted. The group develops a fairly exhaustive list of possible reasons for the problem. Probably, no one knows at this point what the real cause is, but the brainstorm will give valuable guidance in finding one or several major causes. The group has begun to participate actively in solving the problem.

PRODDING TECHNIQUES

Sooner or later the downpour of ideas in the brainstorm dries up. What do you do to get it going again? Or what do you do with the silent member who doesn't participate? In the following sections we will suggest some ways to deal with these problems. But be careful! Know your group. And remember that you are developing a group process, which is exciting and powerful, but fragile.

Encouraging ideas: Priming the pump again.

If the brainstorm seems to slow down, the leader may suggest *piggybacking.* Piggybacking is building on others' ideas. In the skit, Sharon suggested "one vendor" as a piggyback to Fred's idea of "vendor." To give another example of piggybacking, the "shape of the AX12's" might be such that sometimes they "go in backwards." Fred's wild idea has led to a useful one.

Another technique is to suggest opposites. The leader says, "We've got a lot of ideas on the flipchart. Now can you give some opposites?" If somebody says "too little solder" on the leads, the opposite would be "too much solder."

You can also try quick associations. The leader gives a word and the members respond as quickly as possible with an associated word which might apply to the problem in some way. For example:

Sharon: Charged.

Fred: Short-circuited.

Jan: Lightning.

George: Cheap.

Aaron: Electrons.

Sharon: Now try a new word. Metals.

Fred: Weak.

Jan: Rotten.

George: Fried.

Aaron: Pass.

Sharon: Now let's get back to our regular brainstorming. Fred?

Fred: Sure. Some metal particles short-circuited the capacitors.

Jan: I think lightning struck the line and blew them up.

The leader may also prod the brainstorm by tossing out ideas in certain directions. He or she may ask the group to work on a new area of possible causes or pursue one area in greater depth. We might see something like this:

Sharon: O.K., we've looked at some pretty general things so far. Now let's think about possible causes that happen during manufacture.

George: You mean in the fabrication of the capacitors?

Sharon: Right, George. Why don't you begin?

George: Well, the crimp at the end of the capacitor may sometimes be done wrong.

The silent member.

When a member of the group doesn't speak up, the best advice we can give is "Be patient!" Sometimes a member will be very quiet for meeting after meeting, and then he or she will begin to open up. When this happens it's very exciting, so give that person time. Maybe he or she will always be quiet, but will serve the group in other valuable ways. Once we invited a brainstorming group to give a presentation. The quiet member had the job of operating the overhead projector. Later, he was the one who privately gave us a compliment. We suspect he does the same kind of building-up with his group.

There's a simple but effective method to help bring out the silent member. Remind the whole group that when each person's turn comes in the brainstorm, he or she just says "Pass" if not ready with an idea. That gets people off the hook, but it also breaks the sound barrier: they hear their own voices and participate by saying "Pass."

The direct question is another method, but you must use it with care. Something like the following may be appropriate: "Sandy, you know this process well. Do you have a suggestion?" But as the leader you have to know your group, and know whether putting someone gently on the spot will help or hinder development.

The second pass.

After the initial brainstorm and some time for further thinking, it's a good idea to have another session in order to capture additional ideas. These ideas come to mind as the group members think over the problem and consider what was said.

You can handle the second pass in two ways. One way is to gather the group together and go through a second brainstorm with a time limit of ten or twelve minutes. The same rules apply as in the first pass. The main purpose of this session is to record all the ideas that have come to mind since the first brainstorm.

Another technique for the second pass is to post the brainstorm sheets in the workplace so that people can jot down their ideas as they have them. Posting the sheets has another advantage: it allows people who work in the same area to contribute, even though they are not a regular part of the problem-solving group. In this way they feel that they are not being left out.

COMPLETING THE BRAINSTORM—A THOROUGH SOAKING

How do you make sure that your brainstorm has covered all possible causes for a problem? Well, you can't. Sometimes you're up against really tough problems. Sometimes the solution lies in a research lab, where only a highly trained expert has a chance of digging it out. Often, though, the solutions are right on your doorstep.

Even if you don't solve the problem right away, you can make sure that you have covered all the general areas of possible causes. Make up a list of the general areas and then make sure your group has examined every one of them.

Such a list would include a number of subjects. In Module 3, we told about some major factors that go into an operation: machine, method, material, environment, and people. (See also the fishbone diagram, Figure 1-4, Module 1.) *Machine* includes the type of machine, the maintenance, and the setting. *Materials* are the elements that come to the process, whether they are raw materials, subassemblies, components, or partially processed materials. *Method* concerns the process itself. Are machine screws turned automatically in the proper direction before being fed to a hand-gun screwdriver? Does the production associate manually lift an automobile fender off the feeder line and place it on the chassis? How does he or she do this? *Environment* may be important, too. Humidity or dust can affect a process. Finally, *the person* doing the job. Factors connected with the person could include training, eyesight, and level of skill.

Other general areas may also apply to the problem. Your group might want to consider factors that aren't shown on the fishbone diagram in Module 1, such as money, management, competition, sampling, and arithmetic errors.

DIFFICULTIES WITH BRAINSTORMING AND WHAT TO DO ABOUT THEM

You're stepping on my turf!

In a brainstorm, some people may be very close to the problem and some may not. For example, a production floor group may be led by their team leader and a design engineer may be sitting in. When an idea comes from the "outsider," the "insiders" may resent it. What do you do?

Training the group is one answer, and it is a must. While training your group in the goals for brainstorming—self-development of each person, solving problems, and development of team spirit—you need to explain that we all have blinders on. Each of us sees only part of the problem and its causes. Also, remind the group that an outsider may see things that insiders can't. That's one reason we need outsiders' views. It's a matter of perspective.

Criticism.

Above all, build a constructive, positive environment in the group. Do this by criticizing *problems,* not *people.* Make sure that ideas, not persons, are evaluated. Be especially careful that mistakes are not publicized and never appear in anyone's personnel file.

The difficult member.

Some people are difficult to deal with in a group. They talk too much; they get off track; they criticize people instead of ideas or they shoot down the ideas. How do you handle this kind of person?

You need to be firm but friendly. First try talking to the person privately. Explain how his or her actions—for example, talking too much or shooting down ideas—disrupt the group's work or put down individual members. Give the difficult person special jobs to do for the group. Sound out his or her feelings about what the group is doing. Don't fight them; draw them in.

At other times, direct confrontation may be necessary. When a person gets the discussion off track, gently direct the conversation back to the topic. In dealing with criticism of people or ideas, remind the group as a whole of the ground rules.

In our experience, difficult people usually do one of two things: they either become your strongest supporters or they leave.

CAUSE AND EFFECT DIAGRAMS—ORGANIZING THE BRAINSTORM

Once you have finished the brainstorm session and your team's ideas are written on a flipchart, you may ask "What next?" Very likely your brainstorm list is a mixed-up jumble of ideas. It needs some organizing so that you can use it effectively.

At this point you can use a second problem-solving method, the *cause and effect (C and E) diagram.* This diagram shows in graph or picture form how one idea from the brainstorm relates to another.

Figure 6-1 is a cause and effect or fishbone diagram. You'll notice that it's the same kind of diagram as in Module 1, Figure 1-4. In the box at the far right is the "effect" or problem: variation in coating thickness. Everything to the left of the boxed-in effect is a *possible* cause of the effect. We emphasize "possible" because at this point we don't know for certain the real cause or causes.

Those possible causes all came from a brainstorm session. In that session let's suppose that you, as the leader, asked your group members to brainstorm possible causes of the variation in coating thickness. Your group came up with seventeen possible causes.

In the C and E diagram, you have organized the brainstorm list of causes under several main headings. Under "material," for example, you listed "formulation," "variation," and "wrong, defective." These three terms came from the brainstorm list, and all three describe incoming materials. That's why you drew them as branches off the main arrow, "material."

You will see four other main arrows: method, machine, environment, and production associate. All the other ideas from the brainstorm fit under one of these main arrows. For example, "speed" may fit under "machine" and "formulation" may fit under "material."

WHY USE THE C AND E DIAGRAM?

There are several reasons for using the cause and effect diagram. First, it organizes the ideas of your brainstorm session and helps to sort them out into basic categories. Second, it shows relationships between ideas. The

Figure 6-1. Cause and effect diagram.

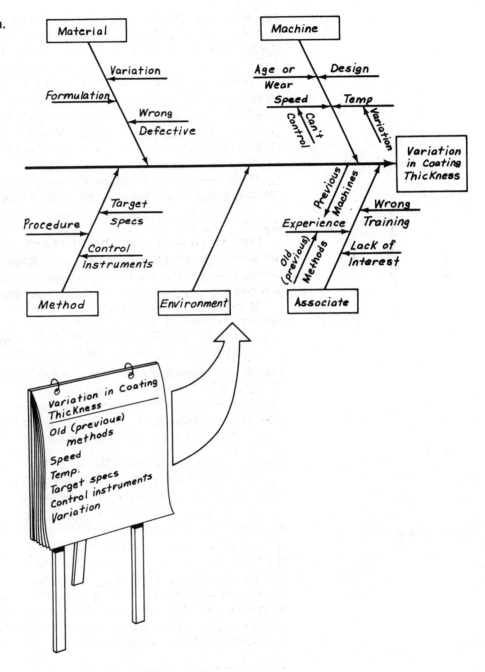

speed of the machine may be causing the variation in coating thickness, but the cause of the speed may be lack of control. So the relationships are as follows:

"can't control ♦ speed ♦ machine ♦ variation in coating thickness."

Grouping the ideas under main headings also helps to complete the brainstorm. When you and your team look over the C and E diagram, you may see some gaps that need filling. For example, you might find that there are no ideas under "environment," which would suggest that "environment" was forgotten during the brainstorm session.

Finally, the C and E diagram helps your team to keep track of where they are in the problem-solving process. It serves as a record of the brainstorm. C and E diagrams can be used wherever a group of people are solving problems.

HOW TO CONSTRUCT A CAUSE AND EFFECT DIAGRAM

The C and E diagram is fairly simple to construct. As you and your team work on it, you will see more relationships between various ideas.

Step 1. Gather the material.

You will need a big flipchart or large sheets of paper, masking tape, flipchart markers with fairly broad points, and the brainstorm idea list.

Step 2. Call together everyone involved with the problem.

Generally this group will include the leader and the members of the brainstorm group, but it may also include outside experts such as engineers, sales representatives, or people from quality assurance. One person may volunteer to act as a recorder and draw the diagram.

Step 3. Begin to construct the diagram.

On the right-hand side of the paper, write down the problem or effect. State it clearly so that everyone understands what they will be discussing.

Figure 6-2. The problem.

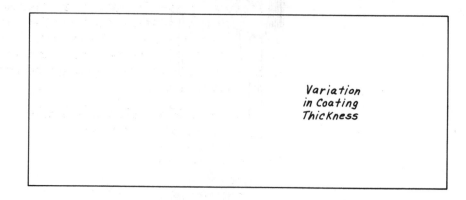

Next, draw a box around the problem.

Figure 6-3. The problem boxed in.

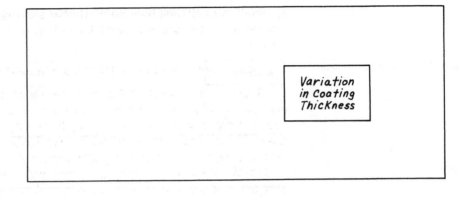

Step 4. Draw in the spine of the "fishbone."
Begin at the left-hand side of the paper and draw an arrow to the box.

Figure 6-4. The spine of the "fishbone."

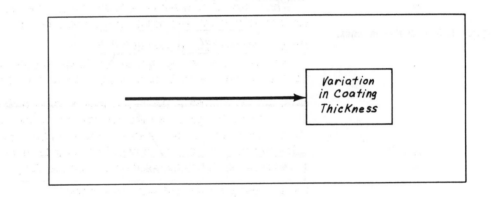

Step 5. Add the main causes.
"Machine," "method," "material," and "production associate" are the four main headings most often used, but you and your team might decide that others are also appropriate. For instance, as we suggested earlier, you might want to add "environment" because many ideas from the brainstorm seem to concern factors like temperature, humidity, and dust. Other possible causes might include:

    bias or error in measuring or inspection
    causes outside the process
    sampling errors
    arithmetic errors
    money
    management
    gauges or gauging

Your diagram will now begin to look like Figure 6-5:

Figure 6-5. Main causes or "bones" of the fishbone.

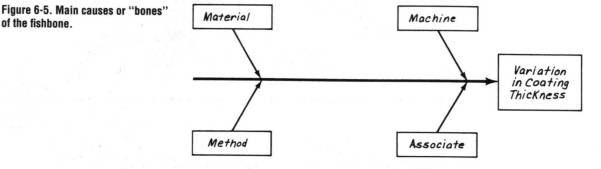

If the team has decided to use additional causes, your C and E diagram will look like Figure 6-6:

Figure 6-6. Additional main bones.

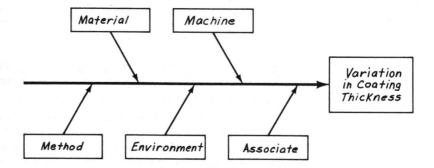

Step 6. Add the brainstorm ideas.

At this point you begin to sort through your brainstorm ideas and to group them logically under the appropriate headings. These ideas may be subdivided further. (See Figure 6-7.)

THE PROCESS OF CONSTRUCTING THE CAUSE AND EFFECT DIAGRAM

The ideas for the cause and effect diagram can come from a previous brainstorm session, or you can suggest the ideas as you build the diagram. If you suggest the ideas as you go along, the process of constructing the C and E diagram is like brainstorming. You need a leader to guide the session and someone to serve as a recorder. The basic rules of brainstorming apply here, too. Make contributions in turn, pass when you don't have an idea, refrain from criticism.

As in brainstorming, working out the diagram requires effort and guidance from the leader. There are many decisions to make about which ideas

Figure 6-7. Completed cause and effect diagram.

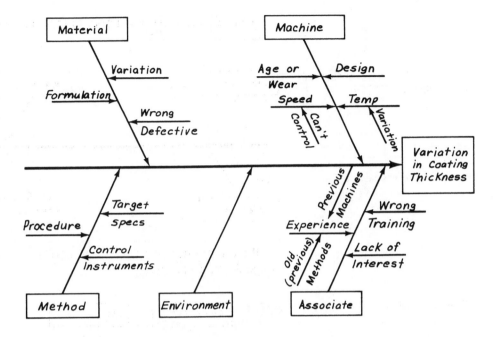

go where. The leader may need to ask "When does this happen? Why does this take place?" At the same time, the emphasis must always be on *how to solve the problem,* not on who's to blame.

There are two ways to fill in the ideas under the causes. The team can brainstorm in a freewheeling manner and cover all the headings at once, or work through each cause in turn. If one area does not receive much attention, the team can concentrate on it for a few minutes.

What do you do when an idea seems to fit under more than one heading? Include it under every heading where it seems to fit.

TYPES OF CAUSE AND EFFECT DIAGRAMS

The most commonly used C and E diagram is the fishbone diagram, as in Figures 1-4 and 6-1. This diagram organizes and relates the causes of the problem.

Another type of C and E diagram is the *process C and E diagram,* which follows the product through each step of the manufacturing or assembly process. The team looks at each stage of production and determines which factors are involved in each stage. (See Figure 6-8.) To construct a process C and E diagram, the group brainstorms the first stage, "weigh raw materials," for whichever factors apply—in this case materials, machine, method, and production associate. Then they go on to do the same for the next stage, "mix raw materials." In this stage the factors are production associate, method, machine, and environment.

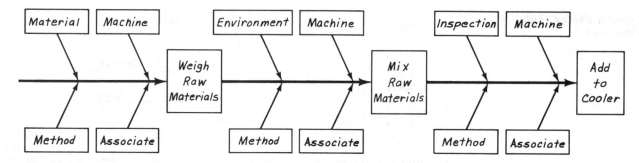

Figure 6-8. Process cause and effect diagram.

Brainstorming and cause and effect diagrams are two methods for finding the causes of production problems. Both methods can be used at several stages in the problem-solving process, such as finding possible causes and developing trial solutions.

PARETO ANALYSIS

A third method, *Pareto* (pa-RAY-toe) *analysis,* is particularly useful in dealing with chronic problems because it helps you decide which of several chronic problems to attack. You can also make a Pareto analysis at the end of your problem-solving process to see whether your solution worked.

You've probably heard the saying, "It's the squeaking wheel that gets the grease." In choosing problems to solve, it's often the same way. The problems that seem biggest or most urgent are the ones that attract our attention. To be an effective problem solver, however, you must be able to sort out the few really important problems from the more numerous but less important problems. Pareto analysis will help you do this.

You may already know the idea behind Pareto analysis, even though you haven't heard it called by that name. You see it when twenty percent of your customers account for eighty percent of your business. To give another example, it's when only a few kinds of parts in an automotive store—mufflers, fan belts, and spark plugs—make up most of the inventory.

Problems tend to sort themselves out this way, too. When you do some investigating, you usually find that of the twelve or so problems you have looked at, only one or two, maybe three cause the most dollar loss, happen the most often, or account for the most failures.

Figure 6-9 is a special type of bar graph called a *Pareto diagram.* In this example, a problem-solving team has collected data about defects in a small motor produced by their department. The team looked at the past month's inspection reports and recorded the data in a Pareto diagram (see Figure 6-9). Among the 145 defects recorded, they found 53 cases of endplay, 31 cases of binds, 28 cases of tilt, 16 missing wheels, 8 switch problems, 5 dead motors, and 4 "other" defects. Endplay accounted for 53 defects out of the total of 145, or 36.6 percent.

Figure 6-9. Pareto diagram.

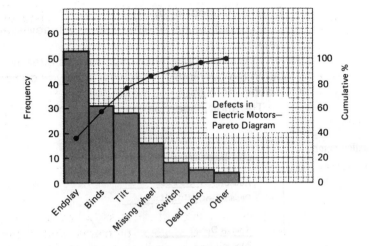

If this team wants to improve the quality of the motors, which problem do you think they should tackle first, dead motors or endplay? A dead motor is an obvious problem, but the team discovered that endplay was far more frequent. Therefore, to improve both quality and productivity, the best approach to reducing defects in this motor is to tackle endplay, the biggest problem. Pareto analysis helped the team make this decision.

What is the difference between Pareto analysis and a Pareto diagram? As we said before, a Pareto diagram is a special type of bar graph. In this graph, the problem that occurs most frequently is shown by the first vertical bar at the left, the tallest bar. The next most frequent problem is represented by the second tallest bar. The third bar shows the third most frequent problem, and so on. "Frequency" might mean cost in dollars, number of defects (as in polyurethane foam seat cushions), or how often a failure occurs. Each bar represents a specific kind of defect, part, day of the week, or even production associate.

Pareto analysis will help you see that there is a need for change and improvement, and the Pareto diagram is the picture part of the analysis. Pareto analysis helps set priorities on problems that need to be solved and helps bring agreement on what to do first. It helps you make decisions based on data, not on "squeaking wheels."

HOW TO CONSTRUCT A PARETO DIAGRAM
Step 1. Specify your goal clearly.

Let's suppose your company supplies seats to a major automotive firm. Your department makes the polyurethane foam seat cushions that go in the seats. Since your company wants to produce the highest-quality seats of any supplier, your department will do its share by producing the best cushions.

Your goal is to improve the quality of the seat cushions and, in particular, to reduce the rate of defective cushions.

Step 2. Collect data.

First determine whether data is already available. If not, then collect the data.

In our example, inspection reports already tell what kinds of defects occur in the cushions. In a few minutes you can get all the data you need (and maybe more than you want!).

The audit inspection report for the month of August is shown in Figure 6-10.

Figure 6-10. Audit inspection report.

AUDIT INSPECTION REPORT

Auditor: L. Miller
Department: Molding
Shift 2
Product: Seat Cushions
Date: Aug. 19, 1985

Kind of Defect	8/12	8/13	8/14	8/15	8/16
Poor mix	2		3	1	
Holes	8	4	7	3	5
Dent		1			
Not enough component	1		1		
Deformed					1
Torn through handling	1			1	
Oil/grease stains		1	1	1	

Step 3. Tally the data.

Count the defects in each category. When you have finished counting, you have the numbers shown in Table 6-1.

TABLE 6-1
Tally of data.

Poor mix	6
Holes	27
Dents	1
Not enough component	2
Deformed	1
Torn through handling	2
Oil/grease stains	3
Total defects	42

Step 4. Rank the categories of defects by frequency.

List the most frequent defect first, then the next most frequent, and so on. When you have rearranged the categories with the most frequent defect at the top, your list will look like Table 6-2.

You are now ready to organize the data into a Pareto diagram.

TABLE 6-2
Tally of data, rearranged in order of frequency.

Holes	27
Poor mix	6
Oil/grease stains	3
Not enough component	2
Torn through handling	2
Dents	1
Deformed	1
Total Defects	42

Step 5. Prepare the chart for the data.

First draw horizontal and vertical scales. Then mark the numbers on the left-hand vertical scale so that the largest category will fit comfortably. Your largest category is "holes," with 27 defects, so run your vertical scale up to 35. Label the scale "Frequency."

Next, subdivide the horizontal scale into equal width intervals so that you have enough intervals for your categories. You may decide to combine the smallest categories into a single group called "other." We recommend that the total of the categories under "other" not be greater than 10 percent of the overall total.

You have seven categories or kinds of defects. The two smallest, "dents" and "deformed," only have one case each, so they can be combined into one category, "other." As a result, you will need only six equal width intervals. (See Figure 6-11.)

Step 6. Draw in the bars.

For the first interval on the left, draw in a bar to represent your largest category. "Holes" is the largest category with 27 cases, so draw it with a height of 27 and label it "holes."

For the second interval from the left, draw in a bar for "poor mix," the next largest category, at a height of 6. Label it.

Continue in this manner with all the other categories.

Figure 6-11. Pareto diagram with scales set.

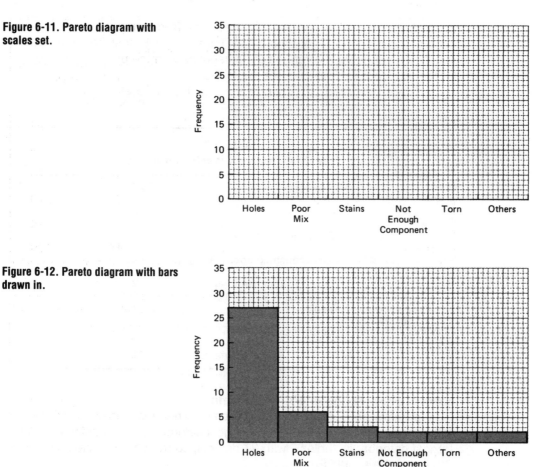

Figure 6-12. Pareto diagram with bars drawn in.

Step 7. Make calculations based on tallies.

First add the tallies, starting with 27 ("holes"), the largest. Add the next largest entry, 6 ("poor mix"), for a total of 33. When you add frequencies for "holes" and "poor mix," the *cumulative frequency* is 33. The third entry, 3 ("stains"), gives a cumulative frequency of 36 because you have added "holes"—27, "poor mix"—6, and "stains"—3. Make a note of each cumulative frequency and keep adding until you reach the last entry. The last cumulative frequency should be 42, the total number of defects. (See Table 6-3.)

Now that you have calculated the cumulative frequencies, the next step is to find the *cumulative percentage* for each entry. To do this you use a simple formula:

Cumulative percentage equals cumulative frequency divided by the total frequency times 100%.

| | | CUMULATIVE | |
	FREQUENCY	FREQUENCY	%
TABLE 6-3			
Cumulative frequencies and percentages.			
Holes	27	27	64
Poor mix	6	33	79
Stains	3	36	86
Not enough component	2	38	90
Torn	2	40	95
Others	2	42	100

As you have already seen, the first cumulative frequency is 27. Divide 27 by 42, the total frequency (total number of defects); the result is .64. Multiply this figure by 100% to find the cumulative percentage.

$$27/42 = .64$$

$$.64 \times 100\% = 64\%$$

To find the second cumulative percentage take 33, the second cumulative frequency, and divide by 42. The cumulative percentage is higher this time because now you are using the cumulative frequencies from *two* categories of defects.

$$33/42 \times 100\% = 79\%$$

Continue in this way to find the cumulative percentage on the basis of each cumulative frequency, and make a note of each cumulative percentage. Each percentage will be larger than the one before. The last one should equal 100%.

Step 8. Complete the Pareto diagram.

Finally, set a scale on the diagram to show the cumulative percentages. You can use ten major subdivisions of graph paper. We recommend that you (1) use an easy method and (2) use a scale that is easy to read, fits the graph well, and looks good. The following method is simple and clear.

Draw a vertical scale for cumulative percentages on the right-hand side of the graph. Label it "Cumulative %." Mark off ten divisions to represent ten percentage points each. Mark some cumulative percentages on it—at least 0%, 50%, and 100%—so that the reader will understand the scale.

Next, draw in the cumulative percentages. Over the bar for "holes" mark a small circle at a height of 64%, your first cumulative percentage. Over the "poor mix" bar draw a circle at 79%, and so on. Then connect the circles with straight lines to make the chart easier to read.

Finally, label the chart "Pareto Diagram of Defects, Injection Molding Dept., 8/12—8/16." This completes the Pareto diagram.

Figure 6-13. Completed Pareto diagram.

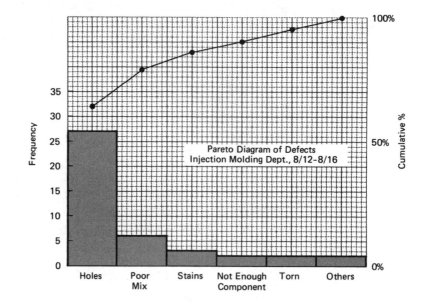

HOW TO INTERPRET THE PARETO DIAGRAM

Your Pareto diagram (Figure 6-13) is a document of the quality problems in the process: it can be duplicated, put on an overhead transparency for a presentation, or otherwise copied and stored.

The Pareto diagram is also a communication tool based on data, and it should help to bring agreement about which problems to solve first. The diagram allows the process to tell its own story without politics or personal feelings. In Figure 6-13, for example, anyone—managers, team leaders, production associates—can see that holes are by far the most frequent defect in the time period you studied and should be tackled before anything else.

Finally, the Pareto diagram serves as a way to compare problems that existed before you worked to improve the process with problems that exist after you have worked on the process. After you tackle the problem of holes in the seat cushions, a new Pareto diagram should show holes as a minor or nonexistent problem.

PROCESS FLOW CHARTS

Have you ever asked, "Why does it take so long to get a simple request for machine maintenance approved?" or "Why do we have so many steps to follow in assembling this wiring harness? Isn't there a simpler way?" The *process flow chart* helps you answer such questions.

The process flow chart is a special kind of diagram that depicts the steps of a particular job in sequence. This diagram helps track the flow of subassemblies, parts, raw materials, information, or people through the system of manufacturing a product. The flow chart may show that the system is more complex than anyone realizes. If you or your problem-solving team can analyze how a raw material or subassembly moves through the system, you may be able to come up with a simpler way. Once you are aware of all the actual steps in the process you are studying, you probably can find ways to combine or eliminate repeated or unnecessary ones. Simplifying the system that delivers the product is a good way to begin improving quality, efficiency, and productivity.

One important use of the flow chart is in identifying the points in the process that need to be controlled. One or more steps may be critical to ensuring the quality of a subassembly or ensuring that it gets to the next workstation on time and in an effective manner. Or you may discover where in your process trouble usually happens. Both critical and troublesome steps should be controlled. The flow chart helps you find the most effective point to control. (See Modules 3 and 4 for a discussion of the methods for controlling a process.)

PROCESS FLOW CHART SYMBOLS

A process flow chart is fairly easy to construct. But first, you need to know the flow chart symbols.

Operation: This is the work that is required to complete a task. An associate is doing something, such as torquing a bolt, weighing an ingredient, welding spokes to a steering wheel rim, or loading a banbury.

Move: Something—ingots, a motorcycle chassis, raw material—travels from one point to another. For example, various inks go from central receiving to the staging area beside the printing press. A technician takes a sample of a chemical to the lab where it will be checked for purity. Conveyors carry tires to the station where they are to be mounted on rims.

Inspection: Someone tests or verifies that the raw material, part, subassembly, or activity is correct and meets the requirements. This person decides whether the part, raw material, subassembly, or activity should continue to the next step or if a correction, addition, or some other change is needed.

Delay: A delay means waiting; for some reason the subassembly, part, or raw material cannot go immediately to the next step in the process. A delay can occur before an operation, inspection, or move, as well as after. For example, the technician has to wait for the gage before measuring a part. Or, subassemblies sit in shipping containers waiting to be shrinkwrapped.

Decision: This symbol is sometimes used to indicate a place where alternative actions may be taken. For example, a technician may have to decide to either pass a machine part on to the next step or return it to the previous step if the part does not meet specifications.

Storage: At this point in the process, some element is being stored in a holding area. Computer printouts sit in an in-basket until the shift leader comes for them. Steel rods are stacked on pallets after cutting. Design changes are stored on microfilm.

Connector: This symbol indicates a continuation of the process. If you run out of room on a page, place a connector symbol at the end of the line and at the beginning of the next. When you have more than one set of connectors, write the same number inside each pair of connectors.

CONSTRUCTING A PROCESS FLOW CHART

Step 1. Defining the process.

You may think that defining your process is a lot like trying to eat an elephant! Where do you start? But it really is not too difficult if you identify the beginning and end of the process you want to study. Ask yourself, "What is the first thing I do?" and make a note of this step. Then ask, "What is the last step?" and note that. For the moment, do not be concerned with the activities between the beginning and the end points. If you think of an earlier step, add it. Approaching the study of a process in this way is not overwhelming. You can begin to "eat the elephant."

Step 2. Identify the steps in the process.

The easiest way to identify the steps is to mentally walk through the process as it normally happens. In this way, you will add the steps between the beginning and the end of the process. A new step begins when a new kind of activity is required.

Write down the steps on a sheet of paper. You may actually need to go where the activity happens, observe, and take notes. You can also make a video of the process for use in identifying each step. A step begins when a new kind of activity is required. Be sure to include every operation, move, decision, point of inspection, storage area, and delay. It is important to list all elements of the process regardless of the amount of time needed to complete each one. However, try to avoid the magnifying glass approach when you first develop your flow chart—that is, don't try to describe all aspects of the step, such as an inspection, in minute detail. You can do this at a later time, if it's necessary.

Step 3. Draw the flow chart.

Once you have defined the process and have identified all the steps, you are ready to draw the flow chart. Choose the correct flow chart symbol for each step and draw that symbol on a sheet of paper, flipchart, or chalkboard. Briefly identify each step, telling who does it, what it is, and where it is done. Connect the steps with a line. As you are putting the diagram together, the line may become too long for the page. Use the connector symbol and start another line. Continue in this manner until you have covered all the steps in the process.

Sometimes the flow chart may branch. This can happen in a number of different ways. Sometimes, several operations need to occur at the same time. For example, in Figure 6-14 car bodies are painted and dried, together with the doors. The doors advance for the assembly of the windows and door panels while the car bodies continue through their assembly steps. At a later point in the process doors and bodies come together for the final steps of assembly. Another type of branch results from an "if," or conditional, situation. If the amount of additive A is below a certain percentage, more is added to the batch. If A is above this amount, no more is added. The decision symbol is used to indicate a conditional situation, as in Figure 6-15. The chart can also branch as a result of an inspection. If after inspecting the grinding of a machine part the production associate determines that the part is still too large, the part is returned to the grinding step, as seen in

Figure 6-14. Branch in flow chart showing parallel operations.

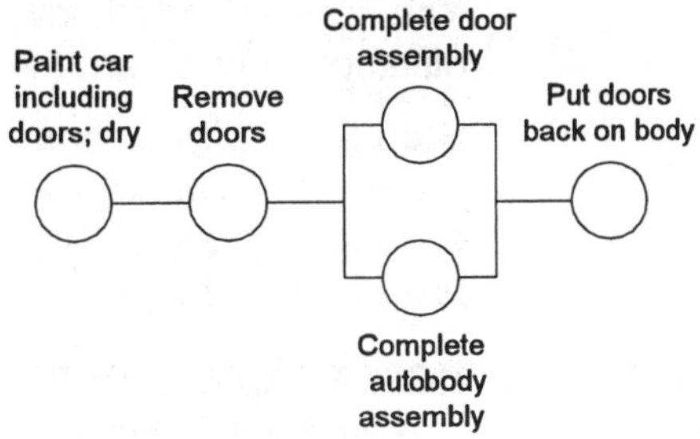

Figure 6-15. Branch in flow chart resulting from an "if."

Figure 6-16. Branch in flow chart resulting from an inspection.

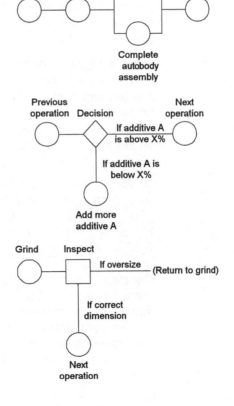

Figure 6-16. If the dimensions of the part are correct, it continues to the next operation.

Step 4. Determine the time or distance for each step.

In order to improve the process flow, it is important to know the amount of time it takes to complete each step. This helps you find where you can reduce or eliminate wasted time.

When determining how long a step takes, note its start and finish. Then time it. You may already have an idea of the time based on your own experience. Another thing to try is actually tracking a part through the process. If the time it takes to complete a step varies a great deal, you may need to record times for a week or a month to determine the step's average completion time. This could happen if a machine breaks down frequently and the part has to wait for repairs.

Write the appropriate times beneath each step. Remember to record the time for delays and storage. These are good places in the process flow to target for improvement.

In addition, you may want to record the distance required for each move. You may already know how far it is from one area to another. A move's distance may be another area where you can improve your process.

Step 5. Assign a cost for each step.

You may want to assign a cost to each step in the process, but this is optional and will depend on you particular situation. Cost information may provide incentive to eliminate unnecessary or repetitive steps.

HOW TO USE THE PROCESS FLOW CHART

Once you have drawn the flow chart and have determined times, distances, and costs for the different steps (where applicable), you can begin to use the chart in one of two ways—to control the process or to improve it. The flow chart helps you decide what steps need to be controlled and where the overall process requires improvement.

Controlling the process.

As you analyze the flow chart, you may find that many of the steps seem to be working well. For the time being, these steps should remain unchanged—however, they need to be monitored or controlled so that change does not occur. The flow chart can also help you find the points in the process that are giving you trouble—that is, unwanted change. Once you identify such points, consider using a process cause and effect diagram to examine the elements of your process steps. By looking at the method, the equipment, or people involved in the process steps, you may be able to find the causes of the problem.

Trouble points probably require some type of control chart to ensure that the process performs as you want. Control charts, described in Modules 3 and 4, are statistical tools that help control processes.

Improving the process.

Improving the process means that you will deliberately change it in some way. Can you eliminate any repeated operations? Are there ways to shorten or eliminate delays and moves? How can you shorten the time that things like parts, electrical components, or supplies are in storage? Consider using brainstorming or process cause and effect diagrams to improve your process.

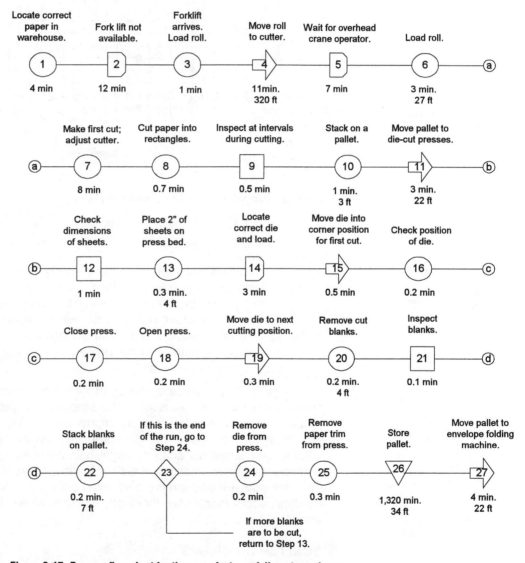

Figure 6-17. Process flow chart for the manufacture of die-cut envelopes.

Figure 6-18. Scatter diagram of cement strength vs. percentage of ingredient.

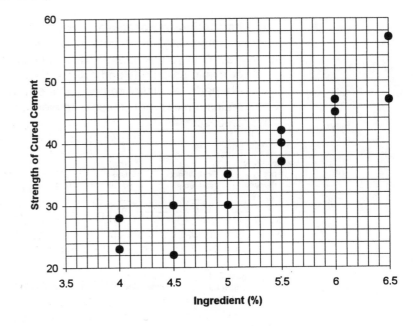

Here are some points to keep in mind:

1. Is there a point in the process that slows or restricts the flow of material, work, or information? What can you do to improve this situation?
2. How can you improve the sequence of the operations to make the process more effective? Would a change in the workplace layout or the flow of components increase effectiveness?
3. Can you improve how you do the operation or activity?
4. Can you reduce or eliminate the need to correct, change, add, or recycle something in the process?
5. Is there a better way?

Figure 6-17 is a process flow chart for manufacturing die-cut envelopes. Numbers in the symbols refer to the steps of the process. The flow chart reveals several areas for possible improvement. Two activities, "adjust cutter" (step 7) and "move die into corner for first cut" (step 15), are places where some statistical analysis might help. How often does this cutting operation really need to be adjusted? Is it currently in or out of statistical control? Ask yourself why are there so many delays in this process? What could be done about them? Are there other places where this process could be improved?

SCATTER DIAGRAMS

Another quality tool used for solving problems is the *scatter diagram.* Let's start with an example. A team and their facilitator suspected that the higher the percentage of a certain ingredient, the stronger the cement would be when it was fully cured. To settle the issue, they recorded data on the strength of cured cement. Along with the strength, they recorded different percentages of this particular ingredient. Then they plotted their data on the chart shown in Figure 6-18, which shows that the strength of cured cement usually does correspond to higher percentages of the ingredient.

A scatter diagram is a kind of graph that indicates how two variables may be related. By plotting data on a scatter diagram, you can see whether there is a relationship between the variables. If there is a relationship, then by controlling one variable, you may be able to control the other. In the cement example, if you control the percentage of the ingredient added to the batch of cement, you may have more control over the strength. Even if you cannot exactly control the strength, you may still have a good idea how strong the cement will be if you simply know how much of the ingredient has been added to the dry cement.

WHEN TO USE A SCATTER DIAGRAM

Scatter diagrams are useful for determining how one variable relates to another. For example, in a cutting operation, you might relate the speed of the cutter to variation in the length of reinforcing rods. Or you might want to see how the length of time between maintenance of injection molds compares to the frequency of breakdowns or stoppages. In a training situation, you could relate the number of hours of safety instruction to the number of shop floor accidents.

HOW TO CONSTRUCT A SCATTER DIAGRAM

Each point on a scatter diagram represents two variables. If you look at the strength and percentage example, any one point on the graph represents a particular percentage as well as a specific value for strength. For example, the point in the lower left corner represents 4% of the ingredient and a strength of 23. This means that when that batch of cement contained that percentage of the ingredient, it measured a strength of 23 after curing. Another batch of cement, made with the same percentage of the ingredient, would most likely be slightly more or less strong, because there is variation involved.

The data you use in scatter diagrams should be variable data. *Variable data* comes from things that you can measure, such as time, length, and temperature. You can measure time to the hour, to the minute, or if necessary, to the second. Time is a variable. Length is variable as well, and can be measured to the foot, inch, or fraction of an inch.

Step 1. Is the problem suitable for a scatter diagram?

Check whether you really have the right kind of problem for a scatter diagram. First, does each point you are going to plot come from variable data—that is, is it measurable? Second, are there two things you can measure—that is, two variables? Third, are you trying to see if the two variables directly affect each other?

Step 2. Collect your data.

Sometimes the data you need are already recorded. Other times you will have to collect them. When collecting data, record any interesting or peculiar things that happen. For instance, if you noticed that the ingredients came from different lot numbers when you were collecting data for the study, you should record the lot numbers of the ingredient for each data point. That extra information could be useful later on.

Step 3. Determine the scales for the graph and plot the data.

Start with the vertical axis and decide which variable it will represent. Usually, we plot the *dependent variable* on the vertical axis. When one variable results from or depends upon another variable, this kind of variable is called the dependent variable. In our cement example, the different values for the strength probably resulted from different amounts of the ingredient. That is, the strength differs depending on the amount or percentage of the ingredient. In our example, the vertical axis represents the dependent variable, the strength.

Now find the largest and the smallest values of the dependent variable, the one you will plot on the vertical axis. Set the scale for the axis so that the largest and smallest values fit inside, not on, the edges of the chart. In our example, the highest value for strength is 57, the lowest is 22. So the vertical axis runs from 20 to 60. It is helpful to use scales that are easy to work with. We marked the vertical scale with the numbers 20, 30, 40, 50, and 60. This makes the diagram easy to construct and to read.

Next, find the largest and smallest values for the other variable. Set the scales of the horizontal axis so that the largest and the smallest values of that variable fit inside, but not on, the edges of the chart. Now you can plot the data.

Step 4. Do the corner count test.

After you use a scatter diagram a few times, you will develop the ability to tell from a glance whether it shows a straight-line relationship between the variables, whether it is clear from the diagram that such a relationship does not exist, or whether you must conduct a corner count test to determine the relationship. Without doing the corner count test, you could work for a long time without knowing the true situation. The reason for learning this step is to help you avoid wasting time and become an effective problem solver.

The corner count test helps you determine whether there is a straight-line relationship between the variables or if there is only a jumble of plotted points with no real relationship. If a relationship does exist between the variables, it may be a cause and effect one. If there is a true cause and effect relationship, you can predict one variable by knowing the other. Furthermore, if there is a cause and effect relationship *and* you are able to control one variable, you will be able to control the other.

What is a *straight-line relationship?* The ideal straight-line relationship is one where an increase in one variable results in an increase or decrease in the other variable, and the amount of the change is always the same. A good example of this is shown in Figure 6-19, where we plotted temperature in degrees Centigrade versus temperature in degrees Fahrenheit.

Figure 6-19. Scatter diagram of degrees Centigrade versus degrees Farenheit.

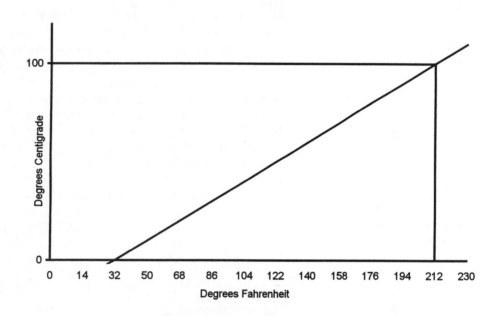

For every degree increase in Centigrade temperature, the Fahrenheit temperature always rises 1.8 degrees. This example is ideal in that all points fall exactly in a straight line, since degrees Fahrenheit and Centigrade were set up in this way. Usually, the data you plot will not fit as neatly as this and you will have a situation more like the scatter diagram for strength of cured cement versus percentage of ingredient. Use the following steps to do a corner count test.

A. Do you have enough data?

You need at least 10 points on the scatter diagram for the corner count test to work effectively. In our example in Figure 6-18, we have 13 points, enough to conduct the test.

B. Find the medians.

Find the *median* for the first variable. The median is the point at which half of the measurements are above and half are below. The median is represented on the diagram by a vertical or horizontal line where half the points are on one side of the line and half are on the other side.

To draw the horizontal median, set a ruler on the bottom of the chart so that all the points are above it. Move the ruler up slowly. As you move it up, count the points as they disappear beneath the ruler. Stop when you reach half the count. If the number of points is odd (13 in our example) divide the count in half. This gives you 6.5 plot points. Round it off to 7.0 by adding 0.5. Stop your ruler on the scatter diagram and draw a horizontal line through the seventh point. In our example the line goes through the point representing strength at a value of 37. Six points fall below the line, and six are above it. This horizontal line is the median for strength, the dependent variable. When the number of points is even, say 14, divide the count in half. Move your ruler until you have covered half, or 7, of the points. Now position the ruler between the 7th point and the next one. The horizontal line you draw across the diagram is the median line because half the points lie above it and the other half are below.

Once you have drawn the horizontal median, find the vertical one. Proceed in the same way as for the horizontal median, but start your ruler at the right-hand vertical edge of the scatter diagram. Move the ruler in from the right side of the chart. Stop the ruler when you reach half the count. Then draw a vertical line to represent the median. See Figure 6-20.

Figure 6-20. Strength of cement with corner counts.

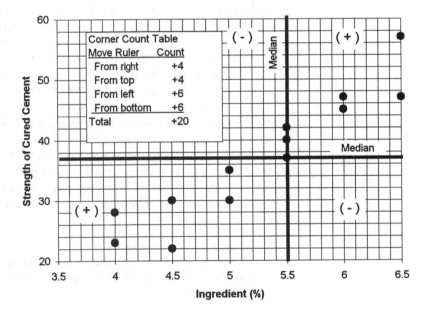

Once you have drawn these lines, you will find that half the points are below the horizontal line, and half are above it; half the points are to the left of the vertical line and half to the right. Sometimes the median line has more than one point on it. That is OK.

C. Label each corner of the chart.

The two median lines have divided the scatter diagram into four parts, or quarters. Mark the upper right quarter with a "+" sign or write in the word "plus." Mark the upper left with a "−" sign or write in the word "minus." Mark the lower left with "+" and the lower right with "−". See Figure 6-20 as an example.

D. Do the corner counts.

This is the tricky part, so be careful. Place your ruler vertically on the right side of the chart. Slowly move it toward the left side of the chart. Stop at the first point you come to and note the sign (either plus or minus) of the quarter where the first point lies. Then slowly move the ruler toward the left. If the next point is in the *same* quarter as the first point, count the point. Continue in this fashion, counting the points as they disappear under your ruler. Move your ruler until you come to a point that is in a *different* quarter or is on a *median* line. Stop and write down the total number of points you have counted so far. Don't count the stopping point (i.e., the one on the median or in a different quarter). In front of this number, write the sign of the quarter where you started counting.

In our example, as we move our ruler in from the right, we find one point in the upper right quarter. It is in a plus quarter. The second point is also in this first quarter. We continue counting until we come to the fifth point, which is on a median line, so we don't count it. We stop at a count of 4. Since our first point is in a plus quarter, we assign a plus to this count. The first count is +4.

Now place your ruler horizontally at the top of the scatter diagram and move it toward the bottom of the chart. Count as before. In our example, we count one point in the upper right quarter. As we move our ruler further down, we meet three more points. But the next one, the fifth, is on the vertical median. So, we stop counting at four. Since the points we've counted are in a "plus" quarter, we write down +4.

Next, count in the same way coming in from the left side of the diagram. This gives a count of +6. Then count up from the bottom of the scatter diagram toward the top. This also gives a count of +6. Sometimes you will count a point twice. Some of the points you will not count at all. Both of these situations are O.K.

E. Total the corner counts.

Add all your counts together. If some are pluses and some are minuses, subtract the minus values from the plus values. The results of our example are as follows:

Count from right	+4
from top	+4
from left	+6
from bottom	+6
Total	+20

F. Compare the total of the counts.

Once you have totaled the counts, remove the sign from the total. If it is plus, as in our example, write down 20. If the total is −20, simply write 20. The important thing is how big the total is, not whether it is plus or minus.

Now compare your result to the number "11." Eleven is a figure that statisticians have worked out as a comparison figure for scatter diagrams (as long as there are at least 10 data points). If your result is 11 or higher, you probably have a straight-line relationship between your two variables. But if your result is smaller than 11, there may not be a straight-line relationship. Your data simply do not tell.

In our example, the total is 20, so we can say there is a straight-line relationship between the two variables. The team has statistical evidence that there is a straight-line relationship between strength and the percentage of the ingredient. The data back up their opinion that the higher the percentage of the ingredient, the stronger the cement is when it sets up.

G. Some special problems.

Sometimes when doing a corner count, you may encounter a situation in which you have a "tie," i.e., two or more points fall on the same horizontal or vertical line, but in different quarters. Or you may find that one of the points falls directly on a median line. The rule is to stop counting in these cases. Following this rule will work in most situations—a scatter diagram is used mainly as a rough tool to determine whether two variables are related. However, in some instances you may need to use a scatter diagram as a more precise tool than is discussed in this book, such as when an important decision involves a great deal of money or a serious safety issue. In such cases we recommend that you consult Ellis Ott's book *Process Quality Control,* listed in the Recommended Readings section at the end of this book.

SUMMARY

Control charts can tell you whether or not your process is in statistical control, but they can't tell you how to improve your process. There are other powerful tools for improving a process: brainstorming, cause and effect analysis, Pareto analysis, flow charts, and scatter diagrams. These problem-solving tools are especially useful in attacking and solving chronic problems.

Brainstorming is a method by which a group can identify problems and gather many suggestions about the causes of the problems. The brainstorming process encourages creativity and participation by everyone in the group. Brainstorming allows room for wild ideas and piggybacking—building on someone else's idea. The proper place for criticism is after the session, and then it is concerned with ideas, not people.

The cause and effect (C and E) diagram organizes brainstorm ideas in categories such as machine, method, material, environment, and person. This organization shows how the different brainstorm ideas relate to each other. The C and E diagram completes the brainstorm because it reveals areas that may have been overlooked during the brainstorm. It also helps you keep track of where you are in solving a problem. Any group of people who are working to solve problems can use the C and E diagram.

The process C and E diagram is useful for tracking a product through the sequence of manufacturing or assembly operations. This type of diagram can be used to analyze each stage of the operation.

Pareto analysis helps separate the few, important problems from the many, unimportant ones. The Pareto diagram is the picture part of Pareto analysis. When completed, it serves as a document of quality problems and as a tool for communication. The Pareto diagram can be the basis for comparing the situation before and after the problem is solved.

The process flow chart is a special diagram that tracks the flow of work, materials, information, or paper through the system of manufacturing a product. The diagram depicts the sequence of steps in a job. Once you have characterized each step as an operation, move, decision inspection, delay, or storage, you can use the flow chart to analyze the process in order to make it more efficient and effective. Another important use is helping to pinpoint trouble areas in the process that may need to be monitored or controlled with a control chart. The flow chart can be used by an individual or a problem-solving team to identify process problems and to make improvements.

The scatter diagram is a type of graph that helps you determine how one variable may relate to another. Each point on the diagram represents the two variables you are studying. The corner count test is a simple test to see whether, in fact, there is a straight-line relationship between the variables. If the corner test results in a count equal to or greater than 11, there is probably a straight-line relationship, and a cause and effect relationship may exist between the two variables.

PRACTICE PROBLEMS: QUALITY PROBLEM-SOLVING TOOLS

Work through the following problems, using the problem-solving techniques you learned in Module 6. The solutions can be found in the "Solutions" section beginning on page 264.

Problem 6-1a.

Brainstorming requires a group in order to work well. You need other people to make the creative ideas flow. If you don't have a group, try a brainstorm session with your family or several friends at lunch. Even a ten-minute session can be fun and productive.

If your group is new to brainstorming or if the members are not used to working together, try a fun brainstorm first. This will accustom the members to the rules of brainstorming and it will show them that brainstorming can be both productive and creative. Try one of these topics:

Uses for old books.
Uses for a large (2-foot-by-2-foot) red bandanna.
Uses for old tires.

It is not unusual for brainstorm groups to think of thirty or more uses for each article. Pick one of these topics as a fun brainstorm and see if your group can beat the record.

Problem 6-1b.

Once your group has had some experience with brainstorming, they will find it easier to use on a work-related problem. Here is a practice problem from the shop floor.

For some time your department has been receiving complaints about the dirt and grease spots on your products. These complaints come from two major customers. The problem seems to occur as the products are packaged and shipped from your department. Brainstorm for possible causes of the dirt and grease.

Problem 6-2.

In a brainstorm session, your section has generated a list of possible causes for cracks and tears in trim molding. You have offered to arrange these ideas on a cause and effect diagram. Using the following brainstorm ideas, set up a C and E diagram.

Brainstorm Topics for Problem 6-2

release agent not evenly applied

cure time too short

not enough mix put in mold

mold too hot

too much catalyst

specifications

strips pulled out too hard

mix ratios incorrect

mold dirty

maintenance not adequate

poor mixing

scales not clean

unloading molds

mold too cool

weighing raw materials

preheat varies

mold pitted/scrached

temperature of curing

materials contaminated in storage

loading of molds

temperature of mold

catalyst

specifications too loose

strips twisted while hot

too little catalyst

release agent left out

scales not accurate

What major causes or "bones" will you use on your C and E diagram? Did the brainstorm group cover all the major areas? If they neglected one area, how can this area be covered? Are there any other possible main causes that your group might consider for this problem?

Problem 6-3a.

The assembly of hoses has been criticized because of too many defects. Of 14,993 hose assemblies inspected in one week, a total of 1509, or 10.1 percent, were defective. The inspection report is given below.

Hose Assembly Inspection Report

Defects	1st shift	2nd shift	3rd shift
Too short	30	35	26
Too long	44	44	44
Missing threads	70	69	70
Leaks	330	321	347
Damaged	8	11	5
Other	22	20	13
O.K.	4508	4495	4481

A management team has expressed concern that the three shifts do not have equal supervision and this may be contributing to the problem. Make a Pareto diagram of the three shifts. How will you set up the horizontal and vertical scales? Can you combine the data for the three shifts or should you break it out by shifts? Why or why not?

When you look at the completed Pareto diagram, do you see any differences among the shifts? Will the Pareto diagram(s) help you to convince the management team of what you have found?

Problem 6-3b.

Suppose a management team asks you to dig a little deeper. Develop a Pareto diagram for defects in hose assemblies. What does the finished diagram tell *you*? On the basis of the diagram, what recommendations could you make to the management team?

Problem 6-4.

The Quality Council has asked you to make a flow chart of the process for repairing the metal component AZ9. You will need to record the steps in the repair of the parts, the times for and between steps, and distances parts move. Since you are fairly familiar with this repair process, you decide to track a single part as it goes through the operations. You make some notes over a few days in order to be certain of times to complete operational steps, and times and distances between operations. The list of steps, times, and distances that follow are the result of your observations. Use this list to construct a process flow chart for the repair of part AZ9.

Repair of Metal Component, AZ9

Step	Activity Description	Process	Time (Minutes)	Distance (Feet)
1.	Incoming Acceptance	#001	4	5
2.	Wait after accepting	—	25	—
3.	Move to inspection	—	0.5	8
4.	Inspect	#003	2	—
5.	If repairable, move to cleaning	—	4	300
6.	If not repairable, move to letter writing	—	3	240
7.	Wait before cleaning	—	60	—
8.	Cleaning	#008	120	—
9.	Wait after cleaning	—	20	—

No.	Description	Code		
10.	Move to inspection	—	2	80
11.	Wait before inspection	—	35	—
12.	Inspect	#009	1	4
13.	If repairable, move to acid clean	—	2	110
14.	If not repairable, move to letter writing	—	2	150
15.	Wait before writing letter	—	30	—
16.	Write letter to customer	#011	7	—
17.	Pack for shipping	#012	5	4
18.	Wait before acid clean	—	180	—
19.	Acid clean	#015	180	—
20.	Move to wash	—	3	10
21.	Wash	#016	30	—
22.	Move to electrolytes	—	2	10
23.	Wait before electrolytes	—	5	—
24.	Electrolytic bath	#017	180	—
25.	Move to wash	—	2	10
26.	Wash	#022	30	—
27.	Move to dry	—	1	60
28.	Wait before dry	—	15	—
29.	Dry	#023	40	—
30.	Move to grind	—	3	320
31.	Wait before grind	—	240	—
32.	Grind	#030	12	—
33.	Wait after grind	—	50	—
34.	Move to inspection	—	2	160
35.	Wait before inspection	—	20	—
36.	Inspection	#033	6	—
37.	If acceptable, move to packing	—	2	160
38.	If not acceptable, move to acid clean	—	2	110
39.	Wait before pack	—	120	—
40.	Pack finished product	#050	4	—
41.	Prepare invoice	#052	8	—

Problem 6-5.

A problem-solving team has gathered data on the relationship between the diameters of particles and the amount of a certain chemical when dissolved in water.

Chemical (ppm)	Particle Diameter (mm)
0.60	1.27
1.00	1.15
0.35	1.13
1.00	1.35
0.25	1.07
0.15	1.03
0.20	1.22
0.85	1.17
1.15	1.26
0.75	1.23
0.10	1.05
0.60	1.19
0.65	1.13
0.10	1.10
1.25	1.28
0.40	1.21
0.40	1.05
0.25	1.13
0.50	1.10
0.60	1.06

(a) Plot this data as a scatter diagram.
(b) Use the corner count test to determine whether there is a straight-line relationship between the variables "particle diameter in millimeters" and "amount of chemical in parts per million."
(c) Are there any data points that you think might be the result of an error?

Elements of a Total Quality Management System

NEW TERMS IN MODULE 7
(in order of appearance)

total quality management (TQM)

continuous improvement

vision or mission statement

policy manual

business plan

cross-functional teams

customer driven

internal customers

empowerment

PDCA cycle

Malcolm Baldrige National Quality Award

ISO 9000

International Organization for Standardization (ISO)

QS-9000

In the first six modules of this book the reader has learned how to use some of the best tools for controlling and improving the quality of manufactured goods. But when and where can production associates use these tools most effectively? In this module we examine the concepts of *total quality management (TQM)* and *continuous improvement (CI),* and explain how the SPC and problem-solving tools described in this book may be used by organizations committed to improving the quality of their products to meet their customers' demands.

Traditional management philosophies assigned the responsibility for increasing productivity to managers and the responsibility for maintaining the quality of the products to the quality control department. As managers began to investigate ways to increase productivity in their organizations, they realized that assigning the responsibility for quality, good or bad, to the quality control department resulted in more inspectors, greater costs, and lower productivity. This division of responsibility did not prevent mistakes from occurring. It just kept bad products from reaching the customers. Therefore, the costs of quality went up while productivity went down.

As global competition increased through the 1970s and 1980s, companies found that they could not compete unless the quality of their products was improved. Customers were demanding quality in everything they purchased and often found that they could purchase higher-quality products from abroad.

Many companies realized that to respond to the wants, needs, and expectations of their customers, they needed to restructure their management and operations systems. Each member of the organization needed to understand that the quality of every action can be improved and that all improvements eventually contribute to a better product and a more satisfied customer. This system of improvement is an important part of total quality management.

WHAT IS TQM?

Total quality management is a management system designed to continuously improve all the processes of a company, both manufacturing and organizational, in order to meet the wants, needs, and expectations of its customers. Customers refers not only to the end users of the product but also to the next functional group in the process. The practice of quality control is integrated into all the processes of the organization. In order for this to work, all employees are involved in quality improvement, from those in leadership positions to the production associates. All strategic decisions must be made with the customer in mind.

In a TQM organization, the commitment to quality starts with the executives, who determine the goals and policies of the company. In order for all employees to support the company's quality improvement effort, these goals are publicized through a *vision or mission statement.* This policy statement defines the direction of the company and the basic processes to be followed in achieving the company vision.

To carry out that vision, TQM requires that the employees know and understand the operating procedures for performing, maintaining, and improving the many processes used in the day-to-day operations. The best way to ensure this is to standardize such procedures. TQM organizations publish and maintain a *policy manual* that clearly describes the current manner of operating and how the organization will operate in the future. The *business plan,* part of the policy manual, lists the specific projects to be undertaken to improve company operations and ensures that the organization will constantly move toward its goals and objectives. Because the plan affects all elements of the organization, it is best implemented by cooperative activities among the many departments of the organization. *Cross-functional teams* enable individuals in the organization to better understand the problems of co-workers, and result in improved performance of the whole organization.

The mission statement and the policy manual are part of the TQM documentation system, which reflects the many activities of all parts of the organization (see Figure 7-1). The management documentation system has two functions: it provides a written record of the responsibilities of each

Level I
Mission Statement — What the company has been and what it intends to become
Policy Statement — Manner of operation now and in the future
Business Plan — Plan for attaining goals

Level II
Procedures — Detail policy; what, who, where

Level III
Written Instructions — Expand policy details; what, how, when of specific operations

Level IV
Databases, Documents, Forms — Provide documentary evidence of performance

QUALITY MANAGEMENT SYSTEM DOCUMENTATION

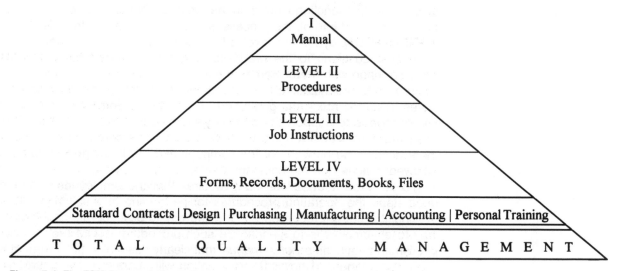

Figure 7-1. The TQM documentation system.

element of the organization and it provides a method for documenting the results of the important activities of each element. The other documents in the system—the detailed procedures, the written instructions, and the forms, databases, and documents—are derived from and reflect the vision of the mission statement and the policy manual.

The business plan contains the key features of a successful TQM effort. These are:

— The importance of establishing a prevention mode of managing process improvement rather than a detection mode.
— The need for training employees in the techniques of SPC and group problem solving.
— The empowering of employees at all levels to improve their processes and the quality of the product.
— The successful activities of cross-functional continuous improvement teams in meeting the wants, needs, and expectations of all customers.

KEYS TO TQM

In a successful TQM organization, everything that the organization does must be *customer driven*. By that we mean that the wants, needs, and expectations of the organization's customers are the primary considerations in determining the actions of all employees. At first, this focus on the customer may seem obvious—if the paying customers are not happy, they won't buy the next time. However, TQM extends the definition of customer to include all types of customers, internal and external. *Internal customers* in any manufacturing or service organization are the persons or group of persons who are next in line in the process under consideration. Internal customers depend upon the results of the actions of the individual or group of individuals supplying them with a product or service. The wants, needs, and expectations of these people dictate what the output of the processes must be. Each group of internal customers, in turn, has customers in the process, continuing downstream until ultimately the process reaches the final, paying customer. The final (external) customer is the one who must be satisfied with the product if the company expects to keep selling the products they are producing. By a ripple effect, the requirements of the final customer ultimately determine the actions of all parts of the organization.

TQM requires that company managers at all levels play a key role in its implementation. TQM managers are leaders instead of directors. They are willing to provide the needed training and opportunity to address continuous improvement opportunities in all areas of their responsibility. TQM stresses the use of the knowledge and skills of every member of the organization. Organizations following a TQM system move decision making down to the lowest level possible.

The person who has the information and the ability to make good decisions is often the associate right on the production floor. Wise managers realize that the knowledge of the systems and processes held by the employees is a tremendous asset. The solutions to problems and improvements in the organization can best be developed by those employees who are most involved with the problem or system. Employees affected by changes made in the system or processes are more likely to support those changes if they have participated in the development of those changes.

Therefore, production associates often are authorized to make decisions that once were strictly the domain of a supervisor or manager. In times past, when something, such as a component from a supplier, would not make a satisfactory assembly, the assembly line could not be stopped until authorized by someone in the management organization. Companies operating with a TQM system have empowered the associates on the assembly line to stop production when the quality level required by the customer cannot be attained. The *empowerment* of employees at all levels working in cross-functional problem-solving teams is a key element in TQM success.

For employee empowerment to be effective, all decisions affecting the processes of the company must be supported by facts. TQM requires that employees use the tools of SPC to monitor and maintain current quality levels and then use the data obtained to make decisions affecting the quality of the products produced. Continuous improvement teams make decisions based on facts and not on personal or gut feelings. The chances of success are much greater when based on facts rather than on opinions.

The move to a TQM system requires a shift from a detection mode to a prevention mode of management. The results of changing to a prevention mode are improved quality and increased productivity. Rather than scrap defective products following an inspection by a quality control inspector, defects are prevented from reaching the final product by adjustments to the process made on the floor. The statistical process control techniques described in this book are intended for monitoring production processes, identifying assignable causes, and solving problems. These are defect-prevention activities that are necessary to ensure that processes maintain their capability and continue to produce the quality required by the customer.

CONTINUOUS IMPROVEMENT

The prevention mode of management is embodied in continuous improvement (CI), the driving force behind the success of TQM. CI involves a clearly defined procedure for attacking and solving problems and developing improvements. This is done through the actions of teams of associates from various parts of the organization working together, with the leadership of managers. Product design engineers, process engineers, materials experts, and purchasing people often can bring specialized knowledge to a production floor problem-solving group.

Continuous improvement is neither spontaneous nor self-directing. Projects for continuous improvement must be planned and scheduled. Many companies have found the best way to maintain their continuous improvement activities is to create a steering committee. The steering committee, which has a rotating membership, consists of employees from all departments and levels of the organization. The steering committee identifies and prioritizes the obstacles to attaining the goals and objectives of the business plan. These obstacles could include any activity, or lack of activity, of the organization. On rare occasions, problems affecting the quality of a product or the productivity of the process involve only a small group or department in an organization. When this occurs, the team accepting the task of finding solutions is made up of employees from only that area. Most often, however, problems affect many areas or functions of the organization and require input from each area to arrive at the solution. Therefore, the steering committee recruits cross-functional teams to formally organize and attack individual problems and find solutions.

Successful cross-functional problem-solving teams follow a formalized approach to analyze problems and find solutions. Many of these approaches are based on the plan, do, check, act (PDCA) cycle. The SPC and problem-solving techniques presented in this book may be used effectively at various phases of the *PDCA cycle*. The following sections describe each phase and which tools may be used.

PLAN

The planning phase of a quality improvement project usually takes the most time and effort. A project that is not thoroughly researched and planned is doomed to fail. At this phase a problem is identified, the problematic processes are analyzed, and potential solutions are proposed. Because this phase requires a thorough examination of an existing process, many of the SPC and problem-solving tools are used. The key to the success of this phase is that everyone learns what is to be done, how it will be done, when it will be done, and by whom it will be done.

When a team assembles to address a particular problem, they must first understand the processes around which the problem occurs in order to identify the cause of the problem. Causes of problems may be located at any point in the process. A problem may be apparent at one point in the process while the cause or causes of the problem may be located at a point far up the process stream. The process flow chart can be used to depict the relationships of all the activities in the process. (See page 168 for a detailed explanation of how to create a process flow chart.) If a flow chart has already been recorded in the company's documents, it is worth the team's time to review the flow chart for accuracy and currentness. By creating the process flow chart, the team gains an intimate understanding of the process and the points at which potential causes of problems may be found. As much information as possible on all the processes involved should be pulled together at this point, so that everyone has a clear understanding of the problem.

After the team has digested the process flow chart, they can begin to formulate a strategy for arriving at a solution. The strategy should be a brief statement of how the team plans to go about obtaining information about the conditions surrounding the problem, how they plan to identify possible causes, locate the causes in the processes, determine and test possible corrective actions, and recommend the best solution to the steering committee. The strategy statement should be reviewed by the steering committee to ensure that the team's proposed actions are in line with the committee's intentions.

With an understanding of the processes and conditions surrounding the problem, the team is ready to conduct a brainstorming session to identify several possible causes of the problem. (See page 150 for a thorough explanation of brainstorming.) All of the potential causes identified in the brainstorming must be investigated. In order to fully understand each potential cause, they should be plotted on a cause and effect diagram to determine the relationship of the cause to the problem, as described on pages 156-162.

Once the potential causes are agreed on by the team, they must decide which of the factors is most likely to be the main cause of the problem. Pareto analysis (162-169) is an effective way to prioritize the main causes of the problem. The team should focus their efforts on the cause rated as the top priority and work to correct or eliminate it. Those causes listed further down on the priority list should be attacked after the main cause has been solved.

At the end of the planning stage, the team has a detailed understanding of the process or processes involved in the problem. They have enough data to understand the customer's needs and they have identified some potential causes of and solutions to the problem. Now that they know the problem, they can work to fix it. A plan of action is then developed to eliminate the cause or implement the solution to the problem.

DO

Once the team has agreed on the first priority cause of the problem and how they plan to eliminate the cause, they should try out the solution in the process to demonstrate its effectiveness. This step may be as long or as short as necessary to fully try out the solution. Most important, the team should ensure that procedures are set up to measure the performance of the process before and after the solution has been implemented. All data should be recorded for later analysis to check for the effectiveness of the solution that was tried.

CHECK

In this phase, the team members, or the production associates, use such SPC tools as control charts, histograms, scatter diagrams, and other techniques to analyze the process performance before and after the solution. Sometimes, the selected solution proves not to be effective or is only partially effective. The team may have to try other solutions on their priority list until the cause of the problem has eliminated. When analysis of the results indicates that the solution has been effective, the team is ready to finish the project.

ACT

In the concluding phase, the team must establish what needs to be done to keep the problem from recurring and report their findings to the steering committee. This report should contain all the information and data collected by the team showing how and why they arrived at their solution. Related problems may arise in the future and another team may find the information contained in the report to be of great value. As a result of the team's report and the decision to revise the operating practices and procedures, revisions are made and published in the required documentation system (see Figure 7-1). All the appropriate employees are trained to implement the new practices and procedures.

The material in this module has covered most of the activities found in a company using a total quality management system of operation. The key elements of TQM can be summarized as:

— Importance of customer satisfaction.
— Activities driven by the company vision and mission statement.
— Managerial leadership.
— Prevention mode of managing.
— Employee training.
— Statistical process control.
— Cross-functional teamwork.
— Continuous improvement.

The value of TQM and CI concepts has been confirmed by their use in the many state and national quality awards and standards. In different ways and to different degrees, both the *Malcolm Baldrige National Quality Award*—and all the state awards derived from the national award—and the international *ISO 9000* series of standards—as well as the other international standards based on ISO 9000—standardize the steps taken in a TQM effort and promote the use of the statistical process control and quality improvement techniques covered in this book.

THE MALCOLM BALDRIGE NATIONAL QUALITY AWARD

The U.S. National Institute of Standards and Technology (NIST) each year presents the Malcolm Baldrige National Quality Award to U.S. companies who exemplify performance excellence. It is intended to promote the integration of TQM concepts into the daily practices of American companies, ensuring performance excellence and improvement through competition. By understanding and following the criteria of the Baldrige Award, companies should be able to satisfy both their customers and their employees while achieving positive business results. The criteria provide companies with a common language and a common way to understand where to apply all of the theories, tools, and approaches that are part of running an effective organization. Another benefit of the Baldrige criteria is that they enable U.S. companies to share information on successful performance strategies and the benefits derived from using those strategies, improving the performance and competitiveness of our domestic market.

The Baldrige Award is given to at most two companies in three categories: manufacturing companies, service companies, and small businesses. Companies applying for participation in the competition for the annual awards are judged in seven areas of operation, which you will notice are similar to the keys of TQM listed previously. These areas are:

— Leadership.
— Strategic planning.
— Customer and market focus.
— Information and analysis.
— Human resource development and management.
— Process management.
— Business results.

Winners of the award have the opportunity, and are expected, to share with others their experiences of developing a company that is worthy of the award. Many states have also established regional awards for quality excellence based on the Baldrige Award. Such awards reflect the increased awareness of the need for continuous improvement of quality in all areas of manufacturing and service in the United States. In fact, many companies who are not even planning to apply for the award have realized the benefit of the Baldrige criteria and are modeling their business processes on them. In the award's first 10 years the criteria have evolved to reflect the advances in the quality improvement field. As the award criteria continue to gain widespread use by manufacturing and service companies, NIST plans to institute new criteria to cover such fields as education and healthcare.

QUALITY MANAGEMENT STANDARDS

While the Baldrige criteria focus on the quality improvement practices of the entire organization, the American National Quality System Standards and the *International Organization for Standardization (ISO)* standards focus specifically on the capabilities of a company to control its internal processes. The two standards, which are in fact identical, are tools a company may use to ensure and demonstrate that customers are receiving what they expect.

The international standards developed as large manufacturers insisted that their suppliers meet rigid quality requirements. As international trade increased, there arose a need for a way to standardize the quality management requirements of manufacturers worldwide. The International Organization for Standardization (ISO), with the participation of representatives from many countries, responded to that need by publishing standards dealing with quality system requirements, the ISO 9000 series. Various countries have published their own version of the ISO 9000 series standards. In the United States, the American National Standard Q-9000 series corresponds to the ISO 9000 series. These standards set the requirements that should be implemented if an organization wants to be identified as practicing total quality management.

The main focus of the ISO 9000 series is that a company documents its procedures and that it follows those documented procedures in actual practice. Each section relates to a specific aspect of satisfying customers. Companies must decide for themselves how to apply the requirements to their processes and which ones apply. When a company believes that its processes adhere to the requirements, they may undergo a certification audit by a sanctioned group. If the auditor agrees that the company has satisfied the requirements, the company receives ISO certification. Such certification proves to the company's customers that it has documented its procedures and is able to follow them. Many large manufacturers who purchase materials and products from other manufacturers now require their suppliers to be certified to one or more of the international standards.

The Big Three U.S. automobile makers—Chrysler, Ford, and General Motors—have created their own standard, the Quality System Requirements *QS-9000,* to ensure that they are being supplied with quality products. QS-9000 expands on the ISO 9000 series to include the specific quality assurance requirements of each of the auto manufacturers. The Big Three require their suppliers to be certified in conformance with the QS-9000 standard. Companies who wish to sell to the auto makers must either improve their business processes accordingly or lose the opportunity to access this huge market to others.

8

Solutions to Practice Problems

MODULE 2: FREQUENCY HISTOGRAMS AND CHECKSHEETS

Problem 2-1a.

The original 25 torque readings listed in Problem 2-1a have been developed into the frequency histogram shown in Figure 8-1.

The shape of the histogram looks normal, but remember that only twenty-five pieces were measured to develop this histogram, so we can get only a rough idea of how normal the process is.

When you place the clamping torque specification limits on the histogram you can see that several of the readings are out of specification on the low side. (See Figure 8-1.)

In fact, you can see on the histogram that there were four torque readings in the 10-11 cell interval and one each in the 8-9 and 6-7 cells, a total of six readings outside the specification. The answer to the question "How does this process compare to the specification?" is, "It does not meet the specification."

Obviously, corrective action is needed. Problem 2-1b describes what was done to correct the situation.

Problem 2-1b.

The frequency histogram shown in Figure 8-2 was developed from the twenty readings taken after corrective action was applied. Compare this histogram to the one in Figure 2-14.

We used the same cell interval for this histogram as for the histogram in Figure 8-1. In this way we could make a direct comparison of the torque readings before and after the corrective action was taken.

As Figure 8-2 shows, the torque readings are now centered on the specification and they are all within the specification limits. The corrective action was effective.

Problem 2-2.

This problem shows what happens when the outputs of two processes are mixed together. As you will recall, one of the rules for making a histogram analysis is to use measurements from only once source—one drill fixture, one machining head, one batch of material, one shift, and so on.

Figure 8-3 shows the histogram developed from the measurements listed in Problem 2-2. Compare this histogram to those in Figures 2-9 and 2-17.

Figure 8-1. Histogram of hose clamp torque data (Problem 2-1a).

FREQUENCY HISTOGRAMS — WORKSHEET

Title _HOSE CLAMP TORQUE — SPEC. 12-24 FT-LBS_

● Tally the data

Midpoint	Interval	Boundaries	Tally	Tally Check	Frequency
6.5	6-7	5.5 / 7.5	I	I	1
8.5	8-9	7.5 / 9.5	I	I	1
10.5	10-11	9.5 / 11.5	IIII	IIII	4
12.5	12-13	11.5 / 13.5	THH III	THH III	8
14.5	14-15	13.5 / 15.5	THH II	THH II	7
16.5	16-17	15.5 / 17.5	III	III	3
18.5	18-19	17.5 / 19.5	I	I	1
20.5	20-21	19.5 / 21.5			
22.5	22-23	21.5 / 23.5			
24.5	24-25	23.5 / 25.5			

● Prepare the graph

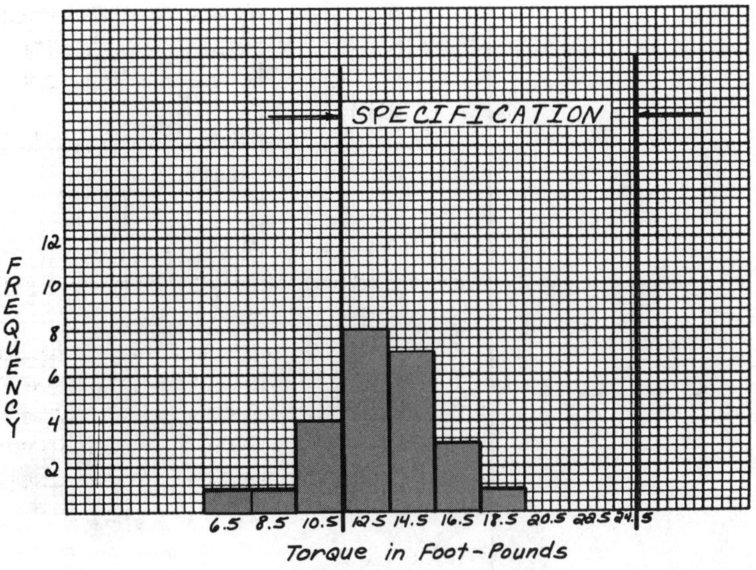

Figure 8-2. Histogram of hose clamp torque data (Problem 2-1b).

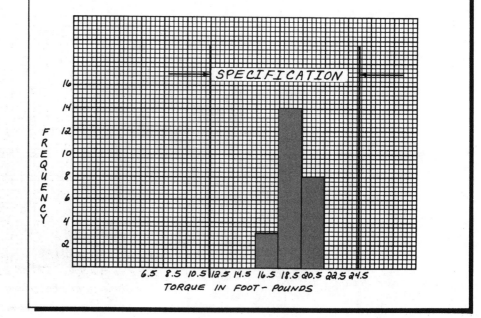

FREQUENCY HISTOGRAMS – WORKSHEET

Title *HOSE CLAMP TORQUE – SPEC. 12-24 FT.-LBS.*

● Tally the data

Midpoint	Interval	Boundaries	Tally	Tally Check	Frequency
6.5	6-7	5.5/7.5			
8.5	8-9	7.5/9.5			
10.5	10-11	9.5/11.5			
12.5	12-13	11.5/13.5			
14.5	14-15	13.5/15.5			
16.5	16-17	15.5/17.5	III	III	3
18.5	18-19	17.5/19.5	⊥⊥⊥ ⊥⊥⊥ IIII	⊥⊥⊥ ⊥⊥⊥ IIII	14
20.5	20-21	19.5/21.5	⊥⊥⊥ III	⊥⊥⊥ III	8
22.5	22-23	21.5/23.5			
24.5	24-25	23.5/25.5			

● Prepare the graph

Figure 8-3. Histogram of hole location data (Problem 2-2).

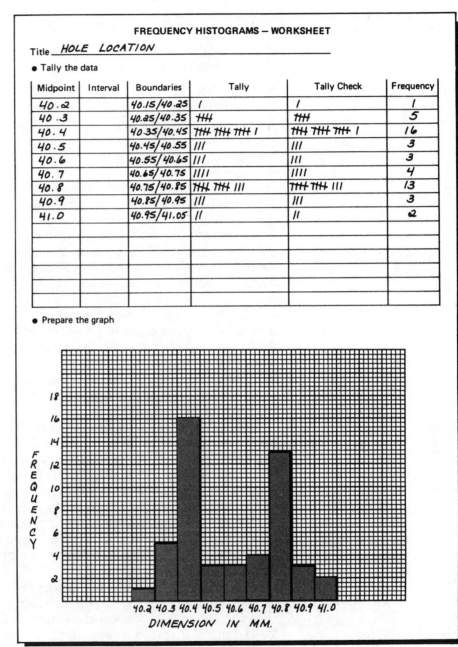

FREQUENCY HISTOGRAMS — WORKSHEET

Title _HOLE LOCATION_

● Tally the data

Midpoint	Interval	Boundaries	Tally	Tally Check	Frequency
40.2		40.15/40.25	I	I	1
40.3		40.25/40.35	⊬⊬	⊬⊬	5
40.4		40.35/40.45	⊬⊬ ⊬⊬ ⊬⊬ I	⊬⊬ ⊬⊬ ⊬⊬ I	16
40.5		40.45/40.55	III	III	3
40.6		40.55/40.65	III	III	3
40.7		40.65/40.75	IIII	IIII	4
40.8		40.75/40.85	⊬⊬ ⊬⊬ III	⊬⊬ ⊬⊬ III	13
40.9		40.85/40.95	III	III	3
41.0		40.95/41.05	II	II	2

● Prepare the graph

Could you tell there was something wrong with the data when you looked at the list of measurements before you made the histogram? In this case it is easy to answer the question, "Is there anything wrong with this data?" The histogram says, "Yes, there is!"

Problem 2-3.

In this problem you are comparing the output of four processes that make the same product. In doing this type of histogram analysis it is best to use the same scale for the frequency and the same number of units in the cell intervals in all the histograms. In this way the comparisons will be easier to make.

If you have made histograms using the data given in the problem, they should look something like those in Figures 8-4 through 8-8.

It is easy to compare the histograms by lining them up in a vertical column in front of you. You will see that the middle of the histograms, which is your best estimate of the process average, is at 58 in Figure 8-4; at 62 in Figure 8-5; between 62 and 66 in Figure 8-6; and at 70 in Figure 8-7. The question "Do you see any differences among the averages of the first four histograms?" should be answered "yes."

The second question in this problem is "Do you see any differences among the spreads of the first four histograms?" The histograms show that the spread of each (the lowest to the highest cell interval) is about the same, even though the measurements are clustered around different averages. You can estimate from these four histograms that the averages of the four processes are different but that the spread around these averages is about the same in each process.

The fifth histogram (Figure 8-8) was developed from a composite of measurements from each of the first four processes. When we made this histogram we broke one of the rules for using histograms—that is, to use data from only one source. We did this to make a point, however. The point is that while frequency histograms are easy to use, they are not as powerful as some other statistical techniques for detecting when something is wrong.

The histogram in Figure 8-8 gives no indication that you are dealing with data from more than one source, such as you could see easily in Figure 8-3 of Problem 2-2. The point to remember is that the histogram cannot always detect differences in processes.

If you were buying parts from a supplier and took a one hundred-piece sample from an incoming shipment, you might have the kind of situation shown in Figure 8-8. You would estimate that your supplier could produce these parts in a spread of approximately .032 inch around an average of .062 inch. But if you knew that the parts came from four separate processes and if you made the histogram analysis as shown in Figures 8-4 through 8-7, then you would estimate something entirely different—that you could adjust process ABCD up a little and process MNOP down a little to reduce the overall spread of the four processes to approximately .024 inch.

Figure 8-4. Histogram of A, B, C, D shaft movement data (Problem 2-3).

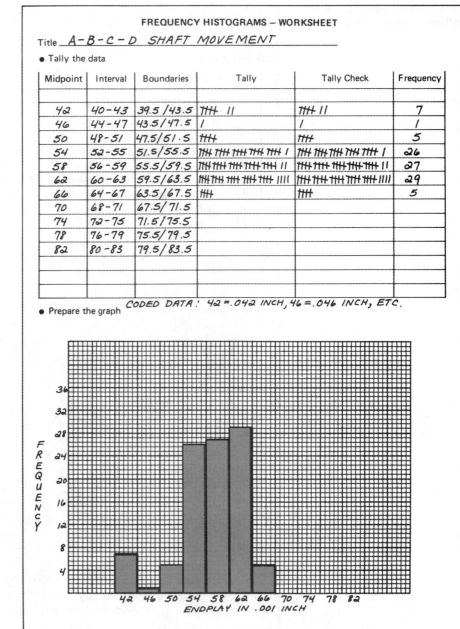

Figure 8-5. Histogram of E, F, G, H shaft movement data (Problem 2-3).

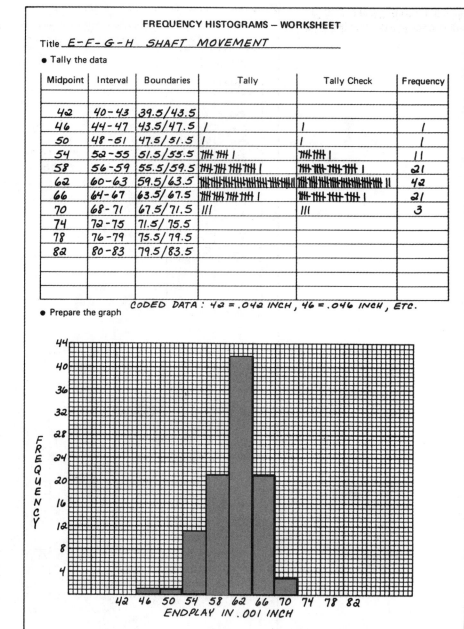

FREQUENCY HISTOGRAMS — WORKSHEET

Title *E-F-G-H SHAFT MOVEMENT*

● Tally the data

Midpoint	Interval	Boundaries	Tally	Tally Check	Frequency
42	40-43	39.5/43.5			
46	44-47	43.5/47.5	I	I	I
50	48-51	47.5/51.5	I	I	I
54	52-55	51.5/55.5	7HT 7HT I	7HT 7HT I	11
58	56-59	55.5/59.5	7HT 7HT 7HT 7HT I	7HT 7HT 7HT 7HT I	21
62	60-63	59.5/63.5	7HT 7HT 7HT 7HT 7HT 7HT 7HT 7HT II	7HT 7HT 7HT 7HT 7HT 7HT 7HT 7HT II	42
66	64-67	63.5/67.5	7HT 7HT 7HT 7HT I	7HT 7HT 7HT 7HT I	21
70	68-71	67.5/71.5	III	III	3
74	72-75	71.5/75.5			
78	76-79	75.5/79.5			
82	80-83	79.5/83.5			

CODED DATA : 42 = .042 INCH, 46 = .046 INCH, ETC.

● Prepare the graph

Figure 8-6. Histogram of I, J, K, L shaft movement data (Problem 2-3).

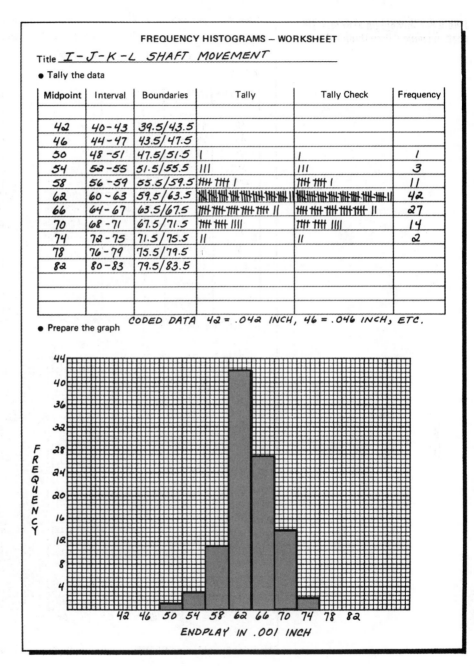

FREQUENCY HISTOGRAMS – WORKSHEET

Title *I – J – K – L SHAFT MOVEMENT*

● Tally the data

Midpoint	Interval	Boundaries	Tally	Tally Check	Frequency
42	40–43	39.5/43.5			
46	44–47	43.5/47.5			
50	48–51	47.5/51.5	I	I	1
54	52–55	51.5/55.5	III	III	3
58	56–59	55.5/59.5	₶₶ ₶₶ I	₶₶ ₶₶ I	11
62	60–63	59.5/63.5	₶₶ ₶₶ ₶₶ ₶₶ ₶₶ ₶₶ ₶₶ II	₶₶ ₶₶ ₶₶ ₶₶ ₶₶ ₶₶ ₶₶ II	42
66	64–67	63.5/67.5	₶₶ ₶₶ ₶₶ ₶₶ ₶₶ II	₶₶ ₶₶ ₶₶ ₶₶ ₶₶ II	27
70	68–71	67.5/71.5	₶₶ ₶₶ IIII	₶₶ ₶₶ IIII	14
74	72–75	71.5/75.5	II	II	2
78	76–79	75.5/79.5			
82	80–83	79.5/83.5			

CODED DATA   42 = .042 INCH, 46 = .046 INCH, ETC.

● Prepare the graph

ENDPLAY IN .001 INCH

Figure 8-7. Histogram of M, N, O, P shaft movement data (Problem 2-3).

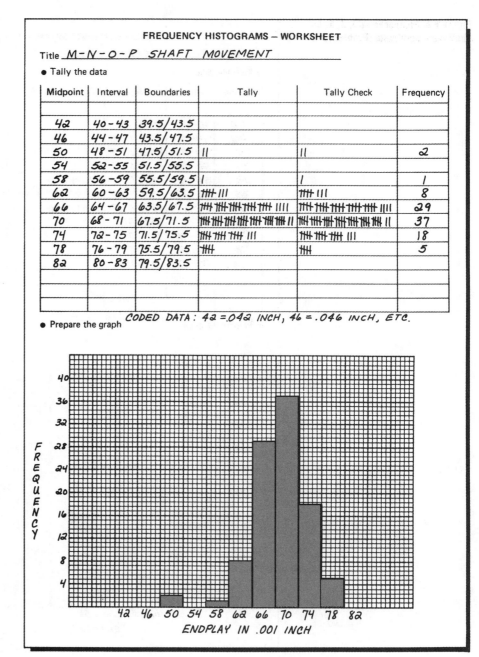

FREQUENCY HISTOGRAMS — WORKSHEET

Title _M－N－O－P SHAFT MOVEMENT_

● Tally the data

Midpoint	Interval	Boundaries	Tally	Tally Check	Frequency
42	40－43	39.5/43.5			
46	44－47	43.5/47.5			
50	48－51	47.5/51.5	II	II	2
54	52－55	51.5/55.5			
58	56－59	55.5/59.5	I	I	1
62	60－63	59.5/63.5	ℍℍ III	ℍℍ III	8
66	64－67	63.5/67.5	ℍℍ ℍℍ ℍℍ ℍℍ ℍℍ IIII	ℍℍ ℍℍ ℍℍ ℍℍ ℍℍ IIII	29
70	68－71	67.5/71.5	ℍℍ ℍℍ ℍℍ ℍℍ ℍℍ ℍℍ ℍℍ II	ℍℍ ℍℍ ℍℍ ℍℍ ℍℍ ℍℍ ℍℍ II	37
74	72－75	71.5/75.5	ℍℍ ℍℍ ℍℍ III	ℍℍ ℍℍ ℍℍ III	18
78	76－79	75.5/79.5	ℍℍ	ℍℍ	5
82	80－83	79.5/83.5			

CODED DATA : 42 =.042 INCH, 46 = .046 INCH, ETC.

● Prepare the graph

Figure 8-8. Histogram of A, E, I, M shaft movement data (Problem 2-3).

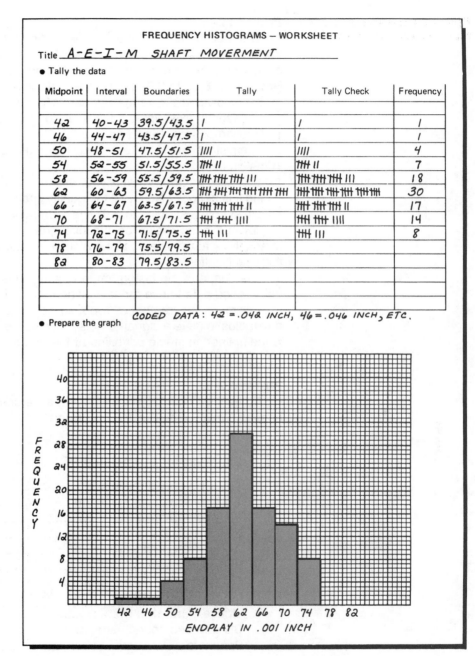

FREQUENCY HISTOGRAMS — WORKSHEET

Title *A-E-I-M SHAFT MOVERMENT*

● Tally the data

Midpoint	Interval	Boundaries	Tally	Tally Check	Frequency
42	40-43	39.5/43.5	I	I	1
46	44-47	43.5/47.5	I	I	1
50	48-51	47.5/51.5	IIII	IIII	4
54	52-55	51.5/55.5	TTH II	TTH II	7
58	56-59	55.5/59.5	TTH TTH TTH III	TTH TTH TTH III	18
62	60-63	59.5/63.5	TTH TTH TTH TTH TTH TTH	TTH TTH TTH TTH TTH TTH	30
66	64-67	63.5/67.5	TTH TTH TTH II	TTH TTH TTH II	17
70	68-71	67.5/71.5	TTH TTH IIII	TTH TTH IIII	14
74	72-75	71.5/75.5	TTH III	TTH III	8
78	76-79	75.5/79.5			
82	80-83	79.5/83.5			

CODED DATA : 42 = .042 INCH, 46 = .046 INCH, ETC.

● Prepare the graph

ENDPLAY IN .001 INCH

Problem 2-4.

The data from the signal-to-noise ratio test shows a range of 18 (36 is the largest value and 18 is the smallest). Ten intervals appear to be a better choice than 18. When we divide the range of 18 by 10, the result is 1.8. Rounding 1.8 up to 2.0 results in ten intervals of 2. If we had rounded down to 1.0 or divided the range by, say, 15, we would have had 18 intervals. The horizontal axis would have been too long and too flat to show the true distribution pattern. (See Figure 2-8.)

The histogram in Figure 8-9 was made using the measurements provided in the problem.

You were asked, "What is your estimate of the quality of the radios made during this period?" Note that the quality characteristic—the decibel level—is specified only as a minimum. A line representing this minimum specification (15db) has been drawn on the histogram. To estimate the quality of the radios, look at the shape of the histogram and see where it is in relation to the specification.

The shape of the histogram in Figure 8-9 is close to a normal curve, so this is good data to use for estimating quality. The entire histogram is above the minimum requirement of 15db, so we can say that we should not expect any radios to have a signal-to-noise ratio below 15db as long as the process is maintained in stable condition at the present level.

Problem 2-5.

A checklist checksheet for buying a personal computer for home business use might look like the following:

Checklist for Purchasing PC

133 MHz speed minimum .... _____
1.6 gig hard drive, minimum ...... _____
VGA color monitor .... _____
IBM compatible .... _____
3.5 inch floppy disk drive .... _____
Back-up tape drive .... _____
Surge protect .... _____
Laser or ink jet printer .... _____
Mouse .... _____
CD-rom and sound card .... _____
Speakers .... _____
Modem .... _____
Brown woodwork station
    on wheels .... _____
Maximum price of $4,000.00 ...... _____

Figure 8-9. Histogram of signal-to-noise ratio data (Problem 2-4).

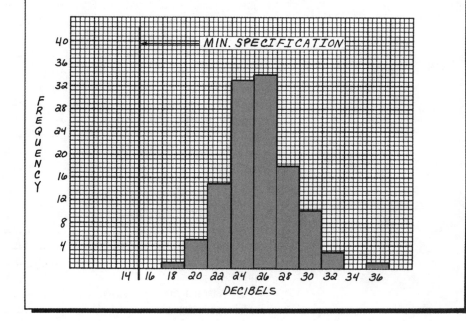

FREQUENCY HISTOGRAMS — WORKSHEET

Title _SIGNAL TO NOISE RATIO – SPEC. 15db MINMUM_

● Tally the data

Midpoint	Interval	Boundaries	Tally	Tally Check	Frequency
14	14-15	13.5/15.5			
16	16-17	15.5/17.5			
18	18-19	17.5/19.5	I	I	1
20	20-21	19.5/21.5	ﬀﬀ	ﬀﬀ	5
22	22-23	21.5/23.5	ﬀﬀ ﬀﬀ ﬀﬀ	ﬀﬀ ﬀﬀ ﬀﬀ	15
24	24-25	23.5/25.5	ﬀﬀ ﬀﬀ ﬀﬀ ﬀﬀ ﬀﬀ ﬀﬀ III	ﬀﬀ ﬀﬀ ﬀﬀ ﬀﬀ ﬀﬀ ﬀﬀ III	33
26	26-27	25.5/27.5	ﬀﬀ ﬀﬀ ﬀﬀ ﬀﬀ ﬀﬀ ﬀﬀ IIII	ﬀﬀ ﬀﬀ ﬀﬀ ﬀﬀ ﬀﬀ ﬀﬀ IIII	34
28	28-29	27.5/29.5	ﬀﬀ ﬀﬀ ﬀﬀ III	ﬀﬀ ﬀﬀ ﬀﬀ III	18
30	30-31	29.5/31.5	ﬀﬀ ﬀﬀ	ﬀﬀ ﬀﬀ	10
32	32-33	31.5/33.5	III	III	3
34	34-35	33.5/35.5			
36	36-37	35.5/37.5	I	I	1

● Prepare the graph

Problem 2-6.

The following is a checksheet for possible defects or problems with a PC.

Defect/Problem Checksheet for PC

Monitor
Dim .... _____
Fuzzy .... _____
Electrical snaps .... _____
Color changes unexpectedly ...... _____
Picture flutters .... _____
Won't work at all .... _____
Other .... _____

Central unit
Won't start .... _____
Shuts down unexpectedly .... _____
Static electricity shuts it down .... _____
Loses data on hard disk .... _____
Loses time and date .... _____
Other .... _____

Mouse
Won't function .... _____
Works intermittently .... _____
Locks up .... _____
Other .... _____

Floppy drive
Won't engage .... _____
Won't copy in .... _____
Won't copy out .... _____
Chews up floppy disk .... _____
Other .... _____

Keyboard
Keys won't function .... _____
Works intermittently .... _____
Locks up .... _____
Types in wrong language .... _____
Other .... _____

Printer
Won't turn on .... _____
Ejects extra page .... _____
Page number in wrong location ... _____
Some characters incorrect .... _____
Paper jams .... _____
Other .... _____

Problem 2-7.

A location checksheet for recording where defects or leaks are occurring in the seal of the front windshield might look like the following. The "Xs" represent the places where we found leaks after looking at 50 windshields.

How did you label your checksheet? In this case, you probably would want to write down such things as date, car model, shift, number of windshields checked, and person doing the data gathering.

Problem 2-7. Location checksheet for leaks in front windshield seal.

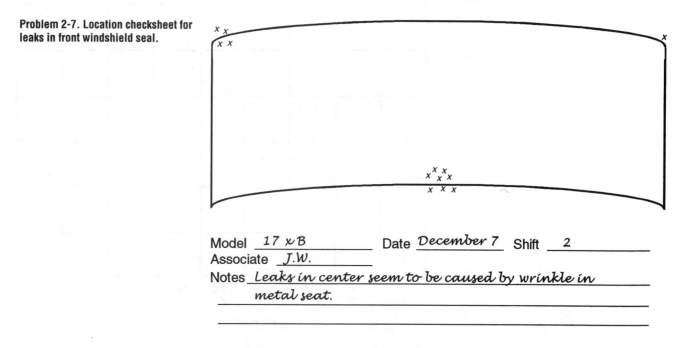

Model   _17 x B_   Date _December 7_ Shift   _2_

Associate _J.W._

Notes _Leaks in center seem to be caused by wrinkle in_

         metal seat.

Problem 2-8.

The intervals you use on your frequency histogram worksheet for oil temperature will depend on the type of stamping press you have in mind. For example, you could run the scale from 91°F to 170°F. Our solution uses this scale for temperature.

Problem 2-9.

This checksheet shows how we set up a simple matrix in order to record the number of unscheduled shutdowns in the six envelope machines for one week. From this checksheet, we could learn which machines perform well and which may need overhaul. We might find major differences between the shifts or none at all. If we also record possible causes for the stoppages,

Problem 2-8. Frequency histogram checksheet for oil temperature of stamping press.

Date _____

Press _____

TEMPERATURE °F

Associate _____

Notes _____

_____

_____

such as paper web breaks, or paper jams, we can proceed to set up an Item Checksheet on which to record types of problems and the number of occurrences of each. Such information will help us prioritize problems and develop measures to prevent future shutdowns, thus facilitating continuous improvement of this process.

Problem 2-9. Matrix checksheet for unscheduled shutdowns

Machine No.	Shift A	Shift B
Associate _____ Date _____		
1		
2		
3		
4		
5		
6		
Notes: _____		

MODULE 3: VARIABLE CHARTS
Problem 3-1.

The measurements used in this problem were taken from metal pins that were turned on a lathe. The pins used in the study were made over a relatively short time period, so we would expect the diameter measurements to be clustered around an average in the shape of a normal curve. This would be true as long as no assignable causes were present in the operation.

You were asked, "Does a frequency histogram of the measurements look normal? Is the operation stable?"

Figure 8-10 shows a histogram of the measurements. This histogram does not match perfectly a normal distribution curve, but as you remember, a sample will not always fit the underlying frequency distribution. (See Figures 2-11, 2-12, and 2-13.) The best we can say about this histogram is that it probably represents a nearly normal underlying frequency distribution.

The second question concerns the stability of the operation and requires an average and range chart to give the answer.

The measurements are listed in five-piece subgroups and are identified according to the time the pins were produced. This information is entered on the average and range chart form. The averages and ranges for each subgroup have been calculated and entered on the chart form.

Figure 8-11 shows the average and range chart developed using the pin diameters given in Problem 3-1. Figure 8-12 shows the calculations needed to obtain the process average ($\overline{\overline{X}}$), the average range ($\overline{R}$), and the control limits.

Figure 8-10. Histogram of pin diameter data (Problem 3-1).

FREQUENCY HISTOGRAMS — WORKSHEET

Title *PIN DIAMETER — SPEC. .250 ± .008*

● Tally the data

Midpoint	Interval	Boundaries	Tally	Tally Check	Frequency
.244		.2435/.2445			
.245		.2445/.2455	I	I	1
.246		.2455/.2465	IIII	IIII	4
.247		.2465/.2475	III	III	3
.248		.2475/.2485	THT IIII	THT IIII	9
.249		.2485/.2495	THT THT THT I	THT THT THT I	16
.250		.2495/.2505	THT THT THT THT IIII	THT THT THT THT IIII	24
.251		.2505/.2515	THT THT THT THT THT II	THT THT THT THT THT II	27
.252		.2515/.2525	THT III	THT III	8
.253		.2525/.2535	III	III	3
.254		.2535/.2545	IIII	IIII	4
.255		.2545/.2555	I	I	1

● Prepare the graph

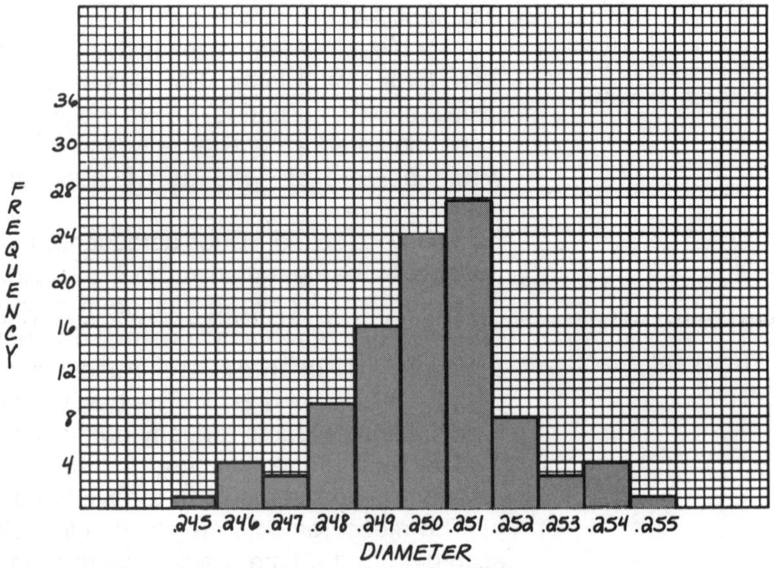

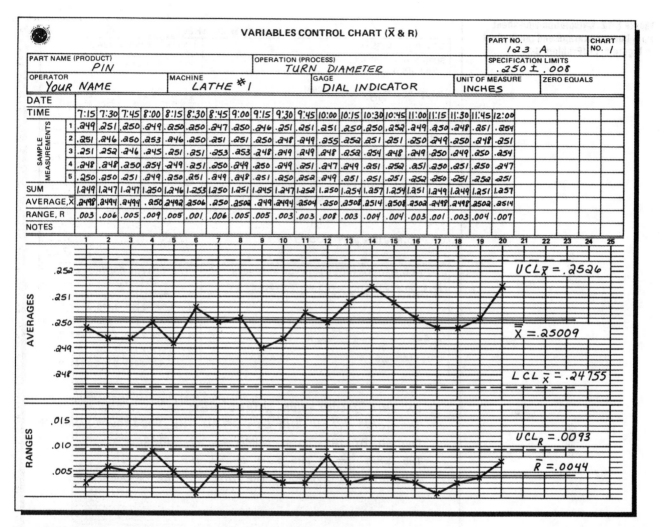

VARIABLES CONTROL CHART (X̄ & R)

	PART NO.		CHART
	123 A		NO. 1

PART NAME (PRODUCT)	OPERATION (PROCESS)	SPECIFICATION LIMITS
PIN	TURN DIAMETER	.250 ± .008

OPERATOR	MACHINE	GAGE	UNIT OF MEASURE	ZERO EQUALS
YOUR NAME	LATHE #1	DIAL INDICATOR	INCHES	

DATE

TIME	7:15	7:30	7:45	8:00	8:15	8:30	8:45	9:00	9:15	9:30	9:45	10:00	10:15	10:30	10:45	11:00	11:15	11:30	11:45	12:00
SAMPLE MEASUREMENTS 1	.249	.251	.250	.249	.250	.250	.247	.250	.246	.251	.251	.251	.250	.250	.252	.249	.250	.248	.251	.254
2	.251	.246	.250	.253	.246	.250	.251	.251	.250	.248	.249	.255	.252	.251	.251	.250	.249	.250	.248	.251
3	.251	.252	.246	.245	.251	.251	.253	.253	.248	.249	.249	.248	.252	.254	.248	.249	.250	.249	.250	.254
4	.248	.248	.250	.254	.249	.251	.250	.249	.250	.249	.250	.247	.249	.251	.252	.251	.250	.251	.250	.247
5	.250	.250	.251	.249	.250	.251	.249	.248	.251	.250	.252	.249	.251	.251	.251	.252	.250	.251	.252	.251
SUM	1.249	1.247	1.247	1.250	1.246	1.253	1.250	1.251	1.245	1.247	1.252	1.250	1.254	1.257	1.254	1.251	1.249	1.249	1.251	1.257
AVERAGE,X̄	.2498	.2494	.2494	.250	.2492	.2506	.250	.2502	.249	.2494	.2504	.250	.2508	.2514	.2508	.2502	.2498	.2498	.2502	.2514
RANGE, R	.003	.006	.005	.009	.005	.001	.006	.005	.005	.003	.003	.008	.003	.004	.004	.003	.001	.003	.004	.007

NOTES

$UCL_{\bar{X}} = .2526$

$\bar{\bar{X}} = .25009$

$LCL_{\bar{X}} = .24755$

$UCL_R = .0093$

$\bar{R} = .0044$

Figure 8-11. Average and range chart of pin diameter data (Problem 3-1).

Figure 8-12. Calculation worksheet from back of average and range chart in Figure 8-11 (Problem 3-1).

CALCULATION WORK SHEET

CONTROL LIMITS

SUBGROUPS INCLUDED _____ *20* _____

$\bar{R} = \frac{\Sigma R}{k} = \frac{088}{20} = .0044$ _____ =

$\bar{\bar{X}} = \frac{\Sigma \bar{X}}{k} = \frac{5.0019}{20} = .25009$ _____ =

OR

$\bar{X}'$ (MIDSPEC. OR STD.) = _____ =

$A_2 \bar{R} = .577 \times .0044 = .00254$ x _____ = _____

$UCL_{\bar{x}} = \bar{\bar{X}} + A_2\bar{R}$ = .25263 =

$LCL_{\bar{x}} = \bar{\bar{X}} - A_2\bar{R}$ = .24755 =

$UCL_R = D_4\bar{R} = 2.114 \times .0044 = .0093$ x. =

LIMITS FOR INDIVIDUALS
COMPARE WITH SPECIFICATION OR TOLERANCE LIMITS

$\bar{\bar{X}}$ =

$\frac{3}{d_2}\bar{R}$ = x = _____

$UL_x = \bar{\bar{X}} + \frac{3}{d_2}\bar{R}$ =

$LL_x = \bar{\bar{X}} - \frac{3}{d_2}\bar{R}$ =

US =

LS = _____

US − LS =

$6\sigma = \frac{6}{d_2}\bar{R}$ =

MODIFIED CONTROL LIMITS FOR AVERAGES

BASED ON SPECIFICATION LIMITS AND PROCESS CAPABILITY. APPLICABLE ONLY IF: US − LS > 6σ.

US = LS =

$A_M\bar{R} =$ x = _____ $A_M\bar{R}$ = = _____

$URL_{\bar{x}} = US - A_M\bar{R}$ = $LRL_{\bar{x}} = LS + A_M\bar{R}$ =

FACTORS FOR CONTROL LIMITS

n	A_2	D_4	d_2	$\frac{3}{d_2}$	A_M
2	1.880	3.268	1.128	2.659	0.779
3	1.023	2.574	1.693	1.772	0.749
4	0.729	2.282	2.059	1.457	0.728
5	0.577	2.114	2.326	1.290	0.713
6	0.483	2.004	2.534	1.184	0.701

NOTES

ON THIS CALCULATION WORKSHEET,
THE TERM $\frac{\Sigma R}{K}$ IS THE SUM OF ALL THE SUBGROUP RANGES (R)
DIVIDED BY THE TOTAL NUMBER OF SUBGROUPS
THE TERM $\frac{\Sigma \bar{X}}{K}$ IS THE SUM OF ALL THE SUBGROUP
AVERAGES ($\bar{X}$) DIVIDED BY THE TOTAL NUMBER OF SUBGROUPS.

The sample averages and ranges are plotted and the control limit lines are drawn on the chart. The first thing to look for is a point or points outside the control limits on either the range chart or the average chart. There are none. You might be inclined to say that the operation is stable, but as you remember, the shape of the histogram for this data did not match the normal curve. Therefore you could not be fully confident that the underlying frequency distribution was normal. Something—possibly an assignable cause—might be distorting the normal distribution curve. You must look more closely at the average and range chart to find evidence for a possible cause of distortion in the frequency histogram of the pin diameters.

A closer look at the chart shows that the range values for sample subgroups 13 through 19 all fall below the average range ($\overline{R}$). This is seven points in a row, and as you remember, seven points in a row above or below the average line on the average or the range chart can be interpreted as a sign that an assignable cause is present. The average and range chart gives some evidence for why the histogram did not match the normal distribution curve.

The histogram cannot detect the presence of assignable causes. It can only show the shape of the distribution of the measurements. The average and range chart detects the presence of assignable causes, but does not tell anything about the shape of the underlying distribution.

Problem 3-2.

This problem asks if a histogram of the measurements looks normal. The second question asks if an assignable cause might be present, and if so, what that cause could be.

In this problem the measurements are around .750 inch. They were taken in groups of four. To make the numbers easier to handle, they were coded by subtracting .750 from each measurement. When a part measured .755, a 5 was recorded. When a part measured .754, a 4 was recorded.

Figure 8-13 includes the histogram for these measurements.

This histogram has a tail off to the left, which indicates that something is distorting the normal distribution of the data.

Figure 8-14 shows the average and range chart developed from these measurements and Figure 8-15 shows the calculations for the control limits. Note that the sample size in this case is four pieces, and remember that the factors used to calculate the control limits are different for each sample size. (See Figure 8-15).

Figure 8-15 shows the calculations for control limits using all 25 subgroups on the chart. The upper control limit for the range (UCL_R) is 7.39, but the range for subgroup 19 is 8. This indicates that an assignable cause was present when this subgroup was taken. This subgroup should be removed from the data. The control limits for the subgroup averages ($\overline{X}$) were calculated on the basis of the 25 original subgroups. As the control chart shows (Figure 8-14), the averages for subgroups 19 and 20 are outside the

Figure 8-13. Histogram of undercut diameter data (Problem 3-2).

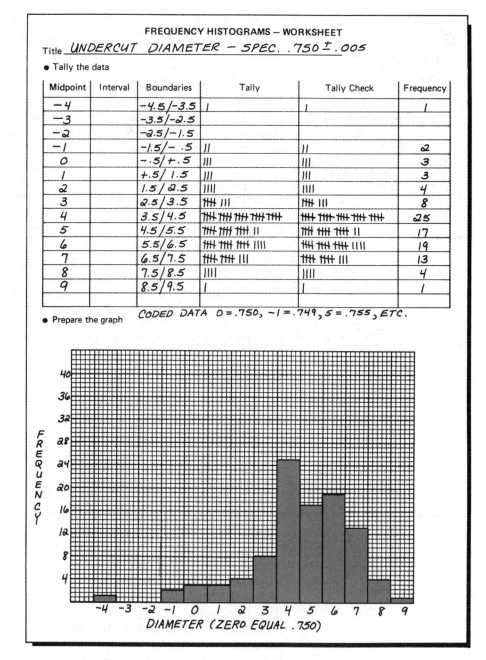

FREQUENCY HISTOGRAMS – WORKSHEET

Title _UNDERCUT DIAMETER – SPEC. .750 ± .005_

● Tally the data

Midpoint	Interval	Boundaries	Tally	Tally Check	Frequency
−4		−4.5/−3.5	I	I	I
−3		−3.5/−2.5			
−2		−2.5/−1.5			
−1		−1.5/− .5	II	II	2
0		− .5/+ .5	III	III	3
1		+ .5/ 1.5	III	III	3
2		1.5 / 2.5	IIII	IIII	4
3		2.5 / 3.5	TTTT III	TTTT III	8
4		3.5 / 4.5	TTTT TTTT TTTT TTTT TTTT	TTTT TTTT TTTT TTTT TTTT	25
5		4.5 / 5.5	TTTT TTTT TTTT II	TTTT TTTT TTTT II	17
6		5.5 / 6.5	TTTT TTTT TTTT IIII	TTTT TTTT TTTT IIII	19
7		6.5 / 7.5	TTTT TTTT III	TTTT TTTT III	13
8		7.5 / 8.5	IIII	IIII	4
9		8.5 / 9.5	I	I	I

CODED DATA 0 = .750, −1 = .749, 5 = .755, ETC.

● Prepare the graph

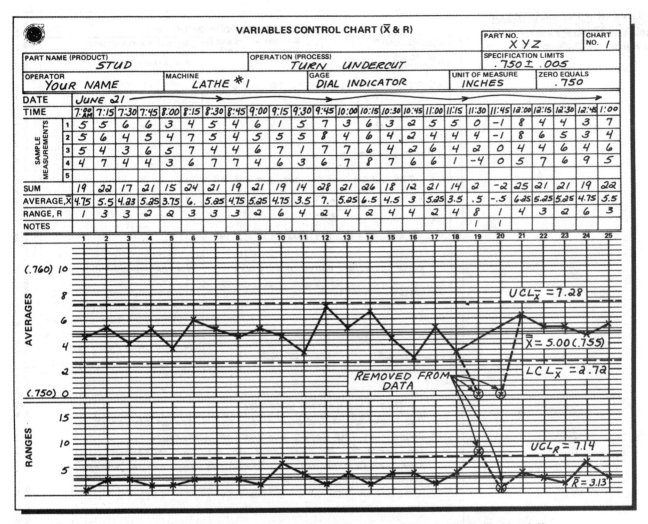

VARIABLES CONTROL CHART (X̄ & R)

PART NO.	CHART NO.
X Y Z	1

PART NAME (PRODUCT)	OPERATION (PROCESS)	SPECIFICATION LIMITS
STUD	TURN UNDERCUT	.750 ± .005

OPERATOR	MACHINE	GAGE	UNIT OF MEASURE	ZERO EQUALS
YOUR NAME	LATHE #1	DIAL INDICATOR	INCHES	.750

DATE JUNE 21

TIME	7:00 AM	7:15	7:30	7:45	8:00	8:15	8:30	8:45	9:00	9:15	9:30	9:45	10:00	10:15	10:30	10:45	11:00	11:15	11:30	11:45	12:00	12:15	12:30	12:45	1:00
1	5	5	6	6	3	4	5	4	6	1	5	7	3	6	3	2	5	5	0	-1	8	4	4	3	7
2	5	6	4	5	4	7	5	4	5	5	5	8	4	6	4	2	4	4	4	-1	8	6	5	3	4
3	5	4	3	6	5	7	4	4	6	7	1	7	7	6	4	2	6	4	2	0	4	4	6	4	6
4	4	7	4	4	3	6	7	7	4	6	3	6	7	8	7	6	6	1	-4	0	5	7	6	9	5
5																									
SUM	19	22	17	21	15	24	21	19	21	19	14	28	21	26	18	12	21	14	2	-2	25	21	21	19	22
AVERAGE, X̄	4.75	5.5	4.23	5.25	3.75	6.	5.25	4.75	5.25	4.75	3.5	7.	5.25	6.5	4.5	3	5.25	3.5	.5	-.5	6.25	5.25	5.25	4.75	5.5
RANGE, R	1	3	3	2	2	3	3	3	2	6	4	2	4	2	4	4	2	4	8	1	4	3	2	6	3
NOTES																			1	1					

Figure 8-14. Average and range chart of undercut diameter data, showing point outside control limits (Problem 3-2).

lower control limit for averages (LCL$_{\bar{x}}$). Subgroups 19 and 20 were removed from the data and new averages and ranges were calculated after they were removed. (See Figure 8-15.)

Figure 8-14 shows the completed control chart with control limits calculated on the basis of 23 subgroups. If you examine this completed chart, you may get some clues to help you identify the assignable cause. The control chart is filled out properly to show the time each subgroup was measured and recorded. Subgroups 19 and 20 were measured and recorded at 11:30 and 11:45. Could it be that the regular operator ate lunch at this time

Figure 8-15. Calculation worksheet from back of average and range chart in Figure 8-14 (Problem 3-2).

CALCULATION WORK SHEET

CONTROL LIMITS	SUBGROUP 19 AND 20 REMOVED FROM DATA. 23	LIMITS FOR INDIVIDUALS COMPARE WITH SPECIFICATION OR TOLERANCE LIMITS

SUBGROUPS INCLUDED ___25___

$\bar{R} = \dfrac{\Sigma R}{k} = \dfrac{81}{25} = 3.24$ $\dfrac{72}{23} = 3.13$

$\bar{\bar{X}} = \dfrac{\Sigma \bar{X}}{k} = \dfrac{115}{25} = 4.6$ $\dfrac{115}{23} = 5.00$

OR

$\bar{X}'$ (MIDSPEC. OR STD.) =   =

$A_2 \bar{R} = .729 \times 3.24 = 2.36$ $.729 \times 3.13 = 2.28$

$UCL_{\bar{x}} = \bar{\bar{X}} + A_2 \bar{R} = 6.96$ $= 7.28$

$LCL_{\bar{x}} = \bar{\bar{X}} - A_2 \bar{R} = 2.24$ $= 2.72$

$UCL_R = D_4 \bar{R} = 2.282 \times 3.24 = 7.39$ $2.282 \times 3.13 = 7.14$

LIMITS FOR INDIVIDUALS column:

$\bar{\bar{X}}$ =

$\dfrac{3}{d_2} \bar{R} =$ x   = _____

$UL_x = \bar{\bar{X}} + \dfrac{3}{d_2}\bar{R}$ =

$LL_x = \bar{\bar{X}} - \dfrac{3}{d_2}\bar{R}$ =

US =

LS =

US − LS =

$6\sigma = \dfrac{6}{d_2}\bar{R}$ =

MODIFIED CONTROL LIMITS FOR AVERAGES

BASED ON SPECIFICATION LIMITS AND PROCESS CAPABILITY. APPLICABLE ONLY IF: US − LS > 6σ.

US =   LS =

$A_M \bar{R} =$ x   = _____ $A_M \bar{R}$ = _____

$URL_{\bar{x}} = US - A_M \bar{R}$ = $LRL_{\bar{x}} = LS + A_M \bar{R}$ =

FACTORS FOR CONTROL LIMITS

n	A_2	D_4	d_2	$\dfrac{3}{d_2}$	A_M
2	1.880	3.268	1.128	2.659	0.779
3	1.023	2.574	1.693	1.772	0.749
4	0.729	2.282	2.059	1.457	0.728
5	0.577	2.114	2.326	1.290	0.713
6	0.483	2.004	2.534	1.184	0.701

NOTES

ON THIS CALCULATION WORKSHEET.
THE TERM $\frac{\Sigma R}{K}$ IS THE SUM OF ALL THE SUBGROUP RANGES (R) DIVIDED BY THE TOTAL NUMBER OF SUBGROUPS.
THE TERM $\frac{\Sigma \bar{X}}{K}$ IS THE SUM OF ALL THE SUBGROUP AVERAGES ($\bar{X}$) DIVIDED BY THE TOTAL NUMBER OF SUBGROUPS.
1. ASSOCIATE RELIEVED FOR LUNCH 11^{30} TO 11^{50} HB

of day and someone else filled in to keep production going? If this was the case (and it was here), it was very helpful to note the change in operators on the control chart. To do this, write a number in the box above subgroup number (19) and below the range value (8) in the row on the chart marked "NOTES." Write the same number on the back of the chart form in the area marked "NOTES" with a short explanation of what happened at that time. In this case it would be something like: "Associate relieved for lunch 11:30 to 11:50." The person who writes the note should sign or initial it.

Problem 3-3.

In Problem 2-3 you examined shaft movement data with frequency histograms. In this problem you are asked to examine the same groups of measurements with a different statistical technique, the average and range chart. The control charts that you developed from the data given in the problem should look like those in Figures 8-16 through 8-25.

Do you see any differences between the averages ($\overline{X}$) on the control charts and the averages on the histograms? The averages shown on the control charts follow the same pattern that you saw in the histogram analysis, but they are not the same values. The reason for this is that the values quoted as averages based on the histograms were found by eyeballing the histograms, but the values quoted as averages based on the control charts were found by calculating the average of the subgroup averages. Also, notice that the averages quoted from the histograms are given in whole numbers, while those quoted from the control charts are given in decimals.

All these averages were obtained from the same data, but the statistical technique used in the control chart gives a more precise answer than the eyeballing used in the histogram. Both methods give *estimates* of the true process average, but the control chart gives more exact estimates.

The control chart for operations A, E, I, and M (Figures 8-24 and 8-25) shows three points out of control on the averages chart. This is a clear enough indication of assignable causes to throw out all the data and collect new data. This chart shows that the average and range chart is far better than the frequency histogram in detecting when something is wrong with the operation or with the data used to make the control chart and histogram.

The histogram in Figure 8-8 gives no indication of anything unusual in the data, but the average and range chart in Figure 8-24 shows very clearly that something is wrong. In this example you know that the data comes from four different operations making the same product, but even if you did not have this information, the control chart would tell you to start looking for assignable causes. The histogram, however, would not have alerted you to this problem.

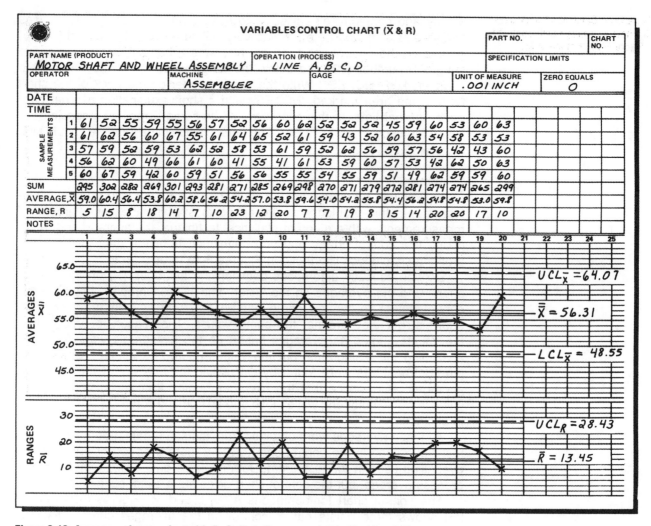

VARIABLES CONTROL CHART (X̄ & R)

| | | PART NO. | | CHART NO. |

PART NAME (PRODUCT)
MOTOR SHAFT AND WHEEL ASSEMBLY

OPERATION (PROCESS)
LINE A, B, C, D

SPECIFICATION LIMITS

OPERATOR

MACHINE
ASSEMBLER

GAGE

UNIT OF MEASURE
.001 INCH

ZERO EQUALS
0

DATE

TIME

SAMPLE MEASUREMENTS	1	61	52	55	59	55	56	57	52	56	60	62	52	52	52	45	59	60	53	60	63					
	2	61	62	56	60	67	55	61	64	65	52	61	59	43	52	60	63	54	58	53	53					
	3	57	59	52	59	53	62	52	58	53	61	59	52	62	56	59	57	56	42	43	60					
	4	56	62	60	49	66	61	60	41	55	41	61	53	59	60	57	53	42	62	50	63					
	5	60	67	59	42	60	59	51	56	56	55	55	54	55	59	51	49	62	59	59	60					

SUM	295	302	282	269	301	293	281	271	285	269	298	270	271	279	272	281	274	274	265	299					
AVERAGE, X̄	59.0	60.4	56.4	53.8	60.2	58.6	56.2	54.2	57.0	53.8	59.6	54.0	54.2	55.8	54.4	56.2	54.8	54.8	53.0	59.8					
RANGE, R	5	15	8	18	14	7	10	23	12	20	7	7	19	8	15	14	20	20	17	10					

NOTES

$UCL_{\bar{X}} = 64.07$

$\bar{\bar{X}} = 56.31$

$LCL_{\bar{X}} = 48.55$

$UCL_R = 28.43$

$\bar{R} = 13.45$

Figure 8-16. Average and range chart of A, B, C, D shaft movement data (Problem 3-3).

Figure 8-17. Calculation worksheet from back of average and range chart in Figure 8-16 (Problem 3-3).

CALCULATION WORK SHEET

CONTROL LIMITS *LINE A, B, C, D*

SUBGROUPS
 INCLUDED _____ _20_ _____   _____

$\bar{R} = \frac{\Sigma R}{k} = \dfrac{269}{20} = 13.45$ _____ =

$\bar{X} = \frac{\Sigma \bar{X}}{k} = \dfrac{1126.2}{20} = 56.31$ _____ =

OR

$\bar{X}'$ (MIDSPEC. OR STD.) = =

$A_2\bar{R} = .577 \times 13.45 = \underline{7.76}$ x = _____

$UCL_{\bar{x}} = \bar{X} + A_2\bar{R}$ = 64.07 =

$LCL_{\bar{x}} = \bar{X} - A_2\bar{R}$ = 48.55 =

$UCL_R = D_4\bar{R} = 2.114 \times 13.45 = 28.43$ x =

LIMITS FOR INDIVIDUALS
COMPARE WITH SPECIFICATION
OR TOLERANCE LIMITS

$\bar{\bar{X}}$ =

$\frac{3}{d_2}\bar{R}$ = x = _____

$UL_x = \bar{\bar{X}} + \frac{3}{d_2}\bar{R}$ =

$LL_x = \bar{\bar{X}} - \frac{3}{d_2}\bar{R}$ =

US =

LS = _____

US − LS =

$6\sigma = \frac{6}{d_2}\bar{R}$ =

MODIFIED CONTROL LIMITS FOR AVERAGES

BASED ON SPECIFICATION LIMITS AND PROCESS CAPABILITY.
APPLICABLE ONLY IF: US − LS > 6σ.

US = LS =

$A_M\bar{R} =$ x = _____ $A_M\bar{R}$ = _____

$URL_{\bar{x}} = US - A_M\bar{R}$ = $LRL_{\bar{x}} = LS + A_M\bar{R}$ =

FACTORS FOR CONTROL LIMITS

n	A_2	D_4	d_2	$\frac{3}{d_2}$	A_M
2	1.880	3.268	1.128	2.659	0.779
3	1.023	2.574	1.693	1.772	0.749
4	0.729	2.282	2.059	1.457	0.728
5	0.577	2.114	2.326	1.290	0.713
6	0.483	2.004	2.534	1.184	0.701

NOTES

VARIABLES CONTROL CHART ($\bar{X}$ & R)

PART NO. | CHART NO.

PART NAME (PRODUCT): MOTOR SHAFT AND WHEEL ASSEMBLY | OPERATION (PROCESS): LINE E, F, G, H | SPECIFICATION LIMITS

OPERATOR | MACHINE: ASSEMBLER | GAGE | UNIT OF MEASURE: .001 INCH | ZERO EQUALS: 0

	1	2	3	4	5	6	7	8	9	10	11	12	13	14	15	16	17	18	19	20
DATE																				
TIME																				
SAMPLE MEASUREMENTS 1	56	63	62	60	62	68	61	63	68	59	56	63	64	63	65	60	57	63	58	55
2	56	56	65	59	51	62	57	55	53	63	56	60	65	63	68	55	62	65	59	62
3	61	60	63	60	62	55	63	60	62	56	60	63	55	67	60	61	67	65	65	59
4	67	55	59	65	52	57	59	65	62	65	56	62	60	58	61	62	65	55	64	55
5	58	46	60	65	58	60	64	66	67	62	62	62	62	60	64	65	62	60	55	57
SUM	298	280	309	309	285	302	304	309	312	305	290	310	306	311	318	303	313	308	301	288
AVERAGE, $\bar{X}$	59.6	56.0	61.8	61.8	57.0	60.4	60.8	61.8	62.4	61.0	58.0	62.0	61.2	62.2	63.6	60.6	62.6	61.6	60.2	57.6
RANGE, R	11	17	6	6	11	13	7	11	15	9	6	3	10	9	8	10	10	10	10	7
NOTES																				

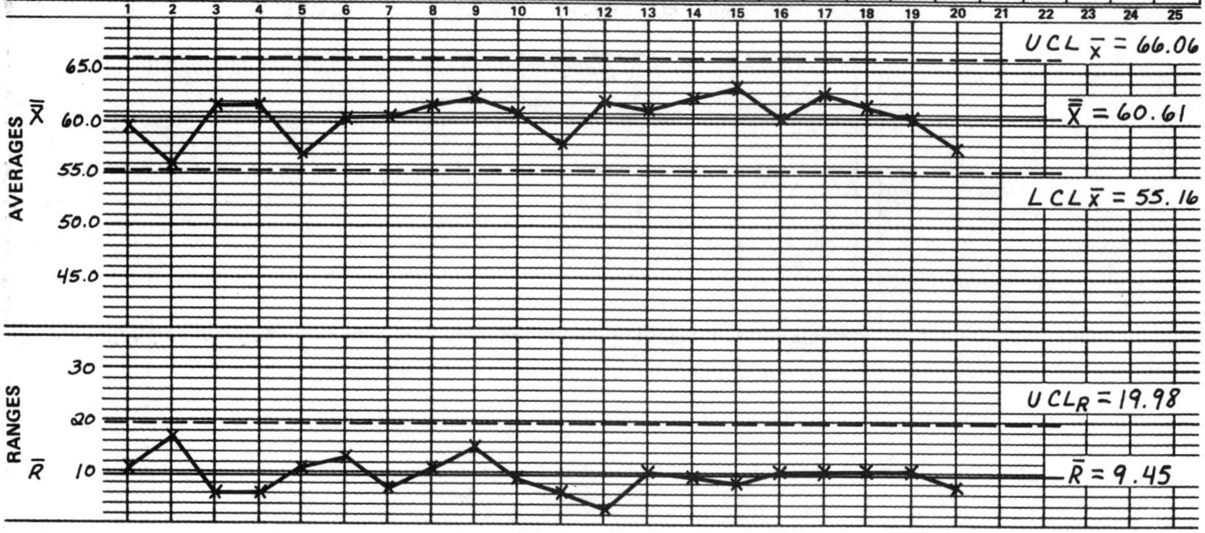

AVERAGES $\bar{X}$
65.0
60.0
55.0
50.0
45.0
$UCL_{\bar{X}} = 66.06$
$\bar{\bar{X}} = 60.61$
$LCL_{\bar{X}} = 55.16$
RANGES $\bar{R}$
30
20
10
$UCL_R = 19.98$
$\bar{R} = 9.45$

Figure 8-18. Average and range chart of E, F, G, H shaft movement data (Problem 3-3).

Figure 8-19. Calculation worksheet from back of average and range chart in Figure 8-18 (Problem 3-3).

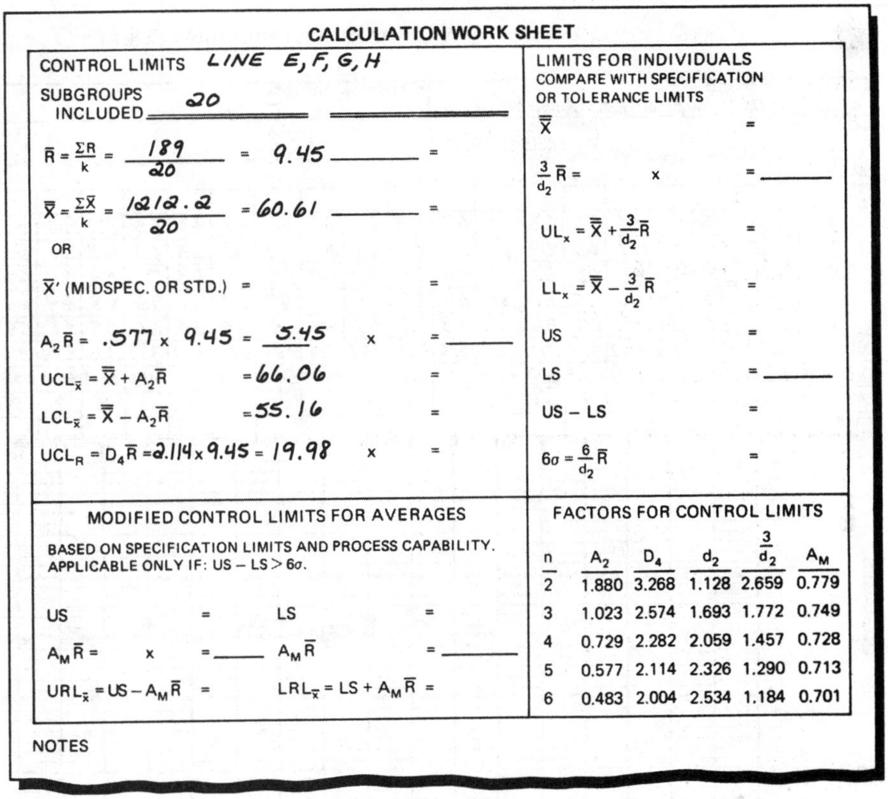

CALCULATION WORK SHEET

CONTROL LIMITS   *LINE E, F, G, H*

SUBGROUPS INCLUDED _____ *20* _____   _____

LIMITS FOR INDIVIDUALS
COMPARE WITH SPECIFICATION OR TOLERANCE LIMITS

$\bar{R} = \frac{\Sigma R}{k} = \frac{189}{20} = 9.45$ _____ =

$\bar{\bar{X}} = \frac{\Sigma \bar{X}}{k} = \frac{1212.2}{20} = 60.61$ _____ =

OR

$\bar{X}'$ (MIDSPEC. OR STD.) = _____ =

$A_2 \bar{R} = .577 \times 9.45 = \underline{5.45}$ x   = _____

$UCL_{\bar{x}} = \bar{\bar{X}} + A_2 \bar{R} = 66.06$ =

$LCL_{\bar{x}} = \bar{\bar{X}} - A_2 \bar{R} = 55.16$ =

$UCL_R = D_4 \bar{R} = 2.114 \times 9.45 = 19.98$ x   =

$\bar{\bar{X}}$ =

$\frac{3}{d_2} \bar{R} =$ x   = _____

$UL_x = \bar{\bar{X}} + \frac{3}{d_2} \bar{R}$ =

$LL_x = \bar{\bar{X}} - \frac{3}{d_2} \bar{R}$ =

US =

LS = _____

US − LS =

$6\sigma = \frac{6}{d_2} \bar{R}$ =

MODIFIED CONTROL LIMITS FOR AVERAGES

BASED ON SPECIFICATION LIMITS AND PROCESS CAPABILITY. APPLICABLE ONLY IF: US − LS > 6σ.

US   =   LS   =

$A_M \bar{R} =$ x   = _____ $A_M \bar{R} =$ = _____

$URL_{\bar{x}} = US - A_M \bar{R} =$ $LRL_{\bar{x}} = LS + A_M \bar{R} =$

FACTORS FOR CONTROL LIMITS

n	A_2	D_4	d_2	$\frac{3}{d_2}$	A_M
2	1.880	3.268	1.128	2.659	0.779
3	1.023	2.574	1.693	1.772	0.749
4	0.729	2.282	2.059	1.457	0.728
5	0.577	2.114	2.326	1.290	0.713
6	0.483	2.004	2.534	1.184	0.701

NOTES

VARIABLES CONTROL CHART ($\bar{X}$ & R)

| PART NO. | | CHART NO. |

| PART NAME (PRODUCT) | OPERATION (PROCESS) | SPECIFICATION LIMITS |
| MOTOR SHAFT AND WHEEL ASSEMBLY | LINE I, J K, L | |

| OPERATOR | MACHINE ASSEMBLER | GAGE | UNIT OF MEASURE .001 INCH | ZERO EQUALS 0 |

DATE

TIME

SAMPLE MEASUREMENTS	1	62	65	68	59	70	63	54	67	63	60	62	67	65	66	65	59	61	67	61	62
	2	62	62	64	61	63	69	61	62	62	66	62	57	65	65	63	62	68	64	60	68
	3	72	59	67	58	68	62	66	56	68	62	60	65	62	63	58	52	63	64	65	60
	4	63	62	60	65	62	61	60	64	69	64	61	67	59	61	72	68	64	62	65	62
	5	51	63	59	64	61	56	65	63	63	69	69	68	69	60	65	65	68	59	52	61

SUM	310	311	318	307	324	311	306	312	325	321	314	324	320	315	323	306	324	316	303	313
AVERAGE, X	62.0	62.2	63.6	61.4	64.8	62.2	61.2	62.4	65.0	64.2	62.8	64.8	64.0	63.0	64.6	61.2	64.8	63.2	60.6	62.6
RANGE, R	21	6	9	7	9	13	12	11	7	9	9	11	10	6	14	16	7	8	13	8

NOTES

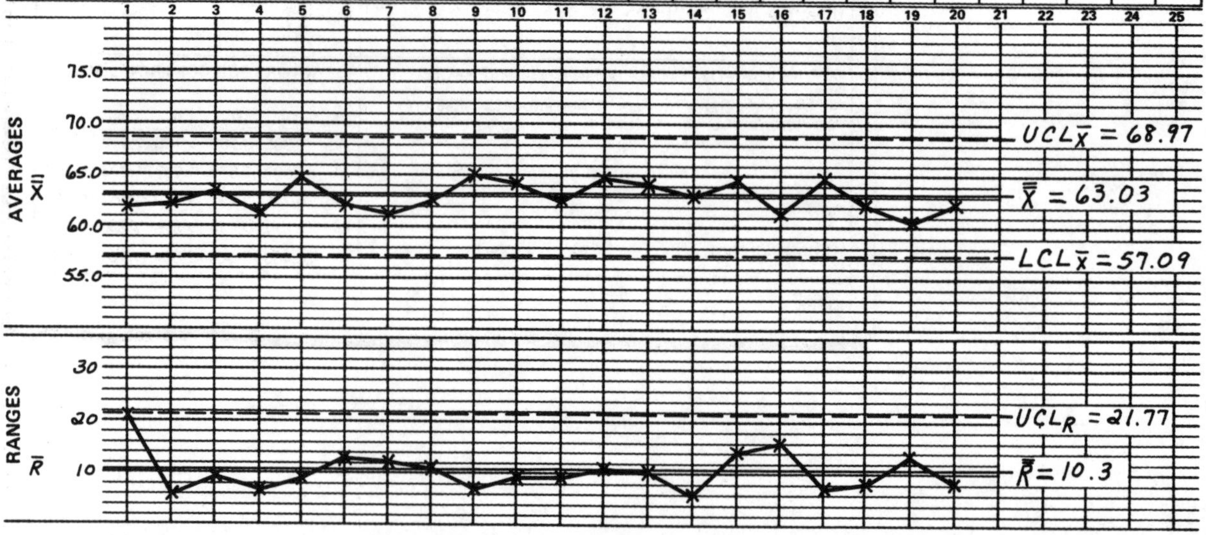

AVERAGES $\bar{X}$

$UCL\bar{x} = 68.97$

$\bar{\bar{X}} = 63.03$

$LCL\bar{x} = 57.09$

RANGES $\bar{R}$

$UCL_R = 21.77$

$\bar{R} = 10.3$

Figure 8-20. Average and range chart of I, J, K, L shaft movement data (Problem 3-3).

Figure 8-21. Calculation worksheet from back of average and range chart in Figure 8-20 (Problem 3-3).

CALCULATION WORK SHEET

CONTROL LIMITS *LINE I, J, K, L*

SUBGROUPS INCLUDED ___ *20* ___

$\bar{R} = \frac{\Sigma R}{k} = \frac{206}{20} = 10.3$ ___ =

$\bar{\bar{X}} = \frac{\Sigma \bar{X}}{k} = \frac{1260.6}{20} = 63.03$ ___ =

OR

$\bar{X}'$ (MIDSPEC. OR STD.) = ___ =

$A_2\bar{R} = .577 \times 10.3 = \underline{5.94}$ x ___ =

$UCL_{\bar{x}} = \bar{\bar{X}} + A_2\bar{R} = 68.97$ =

$LCL_{\bar{x}} = \bar{\bar{X}} - A_2\bar{R} = 57.09$ =

$UCL_R = D_4\bar{R} = 2.114 \times 10.3 = 21.77$ x =

LIMITS FOR INDIVIDUALS
COMPARE WITH SPECIFICATION OR TOLERANCE LIMITS

$\bar{\bar{X}}$ =

$\frac{3}{d_2}\bar{R} =$ x = ___

$UL_x = \bar{\bar{X}} + \frac{3}{d_2}\bar{R}$ =

$LL_x = \bar{\bar{X}} - \frac{3}{d_2}\bar{R}$ =

US =

LS = ___

US − LS =

$6\sigma = \frac{6}{d_2}\bar{R}$ =

MODIFIED CONTROL LIMITS FOR AVERAGES

BASED ON SPECIFICATION LIMITS AND PROCESS CAPABILITY. APPLICABLE ONLY IF: US − LS > 6σ.

US = LS =

$A_M\bar{R} =$ x = ___ $A_M\bar{R}$ = ___

$URL_{\bar{x}} = US - A_M\bar{R}$ = $LRL_{\bar{x}} = LS + A_M\bar{R}$ =

FACTORS FOR CONTROL LIMITS

n	A_2	D_4	d_2	$\frac{3}{d_2}$	A_M
2	1.880	3.268	1.128	2.659	0.779
3	1.023	2.574	1.693	1.772	0.749
4	0.729	2.282	2.059	1.457	0.728
5	0.577	2.114	2.326	1.290	0.713
6	0.483	2.004	2.534	1.184	0.701

NOTES

VARIABLES CONTROL CHART ($\bar{X}$ & R)

PART NO.	CHART NO.

PART NAME (PRODUCT)	OPERATION (PROCESS)	SPECIFICATION LIMITS
MOTOR SHAFT AND WHEEL ASSEMBLY	LINE M, N, O, P	

OPERATOR	MACHINE	GAGE	UNIT OF MEASURE	ZERO EQUALS
	ASSEMBLER		.001 INCH	0

DATE																									
TIME																									
SAMPLE MEASUREMENTS 1	70	65	64	75	60	67	79	65	66	72	70	65	65	65	63	73	70	66	71	70					
2	70	70	68	72	68	63	70	69	69	65	70	78	63	66	66	70	50	68	72	66					
3	50	73	65	75	66	70	65	78	65	70	73	65	70	67	75	79	68	69	69	72					
4	68	70	72	64	69	70	72	69	62	68	70	66	73	71	59	66	69	70	74	69					
5	71	69	73	69	72	78	64	68	67	62	62	66	63	72	64	64	66	73	64	70					
SUM	329	347	342	355	335	348	350	349	329	337	345	340	334	341	327	352	323	346	350	347					
AVERAGE, $\bar{X}$	65.8	69.4	68.4	71.0	67.0	69.6	70.0	69.8	65.8	67.4	69.0	68.0	66.8	68.2	65.4	70.4	64.6	69.2	70.0	69.4					
RANGE, R	21	8	9	11	12	15	15	13	7	10	11	13	10	7	16	15	20	7	10	6					
NOTES																									

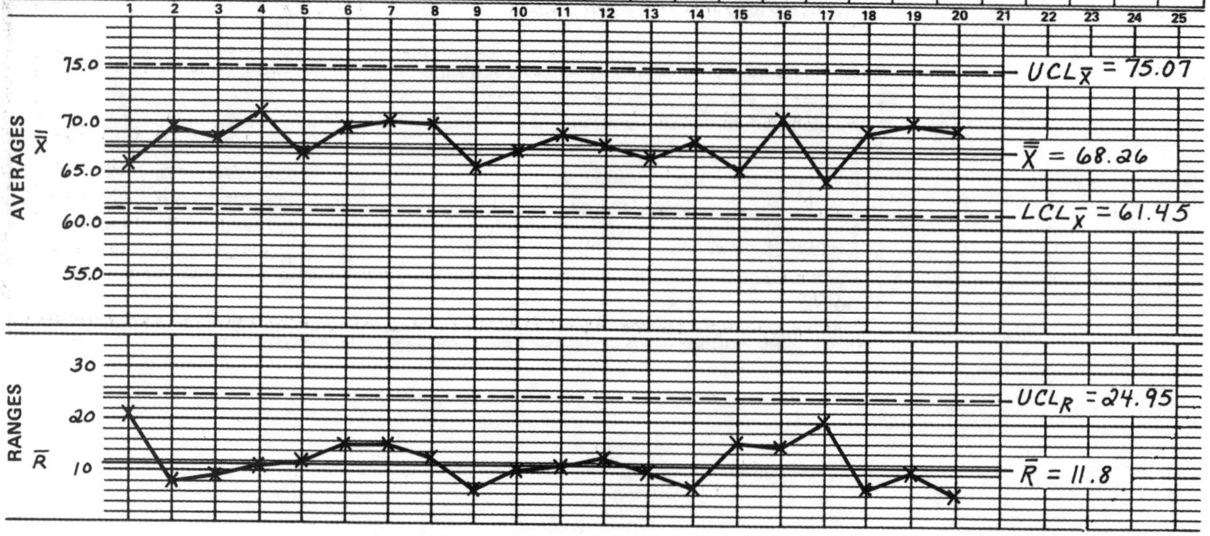
1 2 3 4 5 6 7 8 9 10 11 12 13 14 15 16 17 18 19 20 21 22 23 24 25
AVERAGES $\bar{\bar{X}}$
75.0
70.0
65.0
60.0
55.0
$UCL_{\bar{X}} = 75.07$
$\bar{\bar{X}} = 68.26$
$LCL_{\bar{X}} = 61.45$
RANGES $\bar{R}$
30
20
10
$UCL_R = 24.95$
$\bar{R} = 11.8$

Figure 8-22. Average and range chart of M, N, O, P shaft movement data (Problem 3-3).

Figure 8-23. Calculation worksheet from back of average and range chart in Figure 8-22 (Problem 3-3).

CALCULATION WORK SHEET

CONTROL LIMITS *LINE M, N, O, P*

SUBGROUPS
INCLUDED _____ *20* _____

$\bar{R} = \frac{\Sigma R}{k} = \dfrac{236}{20} = 11.8$ _____ =

$\bar{\bar{X}} = \frac{\Sigma \bar{X}}{k} = \dfrac{1365.2}{20} = 68.26$ _____ =

OR

$\bar{X}'$ (MIDSPEC. OR STD.) =   =

$A_2\bar{R} = .577 \times 11.8 = \underline{6.81}$ x   = _____

$UCL_{\bar{x}} = \bar{\bar{X}} + A_2\bar{R}$ $= 75.07$ =

$LCL_{\bar{x}} = \bar{\bar{X}} - A_2\bar{R}$ $= 61.45$ =

$UCL_R = D_4\bar{R} = 2.114 \times 11.8 = 24.95$ x   =

LIMITS FOR INDIVIDUALS
COMPARE WITH SPECIFICATION
OR TOLERANCE LIMITS

$\bar{\bar{X}}$ =

$\frac{3}{d_2}\bar{R} =$ x   = _____

$UL_x = \bar{\bar{X}} + \frac{3}{d_2}\bar{R}$ =

$LL_x = \bar{\bar{X}} - \frac{3}{d_2}\bar{R}$ =

US   =

LS   = _____

US − LS   =

$6\sigma = \frac{6}{d_2}\bar{R}$ =

MODIFIED CONTROL LIMITS FOR AVERAGES

BASED ON SPECIFICATION LIMITS AND PROCESS CAPABILITY.
APPLICABLE ONLY IF: US − LS > 6σ.

US   =   LS   =

$A_M\bar{R} =$ x   = _____ $A_M\bar{R}$ = _____

$URL_{\bar{x}} = US - A_M\bar{R}$ = $LRL_{\bar{x}} = LS + A_M\bar{R}$ =

FACTORS FOR CONTROL LIMITS

n	A_2	D_4	d_2	$\frac{3}{d_2}$	A_M
2	1.880	3.268	1.128	2.659	0.779
3	1.023	2.574	1.693	1.772	0.749
4	0.729	2.282	2.059	1.457	0.728
5	0.577	2.114	2.326	1.290	0.713
6	0.483	2.004	2.534	1.184	0.701

NOTES

VARIABLES CONTROL CHART (X̄ & R)

PART NO.		CHART NO.

PART NAME (PRODUCT)	OPERATION (PROCESS)		
MOTOR SHAFT AND WHEEL ASSEMBLY	A, E, I, M	SPECIFICATION LIMITS	

OPERATOR	MACHINE	GAGE	UNIT OF MEASURE	ZERO EQUALS
	ASSEMBLER		.001 INCH	O

DATE																									
TIME																									
SAMPLE MEASUREMENTS 1	61	52	55	59	55	56	63	62	60	62	62	65	68	59	70	70	65	64	75	60					
2	61	62	56	60	67	56	56	65	59	51	62	62	64	61	63	70	70	68	72	68					
3	57	59	52	59	53	61	60	63	60	62	72	59	67	58	68	50	73	65	75	66					
4	56	62	60	49	66	67	55	59	65	52	63	62	60	65	62	68	70	72	64	69					
5	60	67	59	42	60	58	46	60	65	58	51	63	59	64	61	71	69	73	69	72					
SUM	295	302	282	269	301	298	280	309	309	285	310	311	318	307	324	329	347	342	355	335					
AVERAGE, X̄	59.0	60.4	56.4	53.8	60.2	59.6	56.0	61.8	61.8	57.0	62.0	62.2	63.6	61.4	64.8	65.8	69.4	68.4	71.0	67.0					
RANGE, R	5	15	8	18	14	11	17	6	6	11	21	6	9	7	9	21	8	9	11	12					
NOTES																									

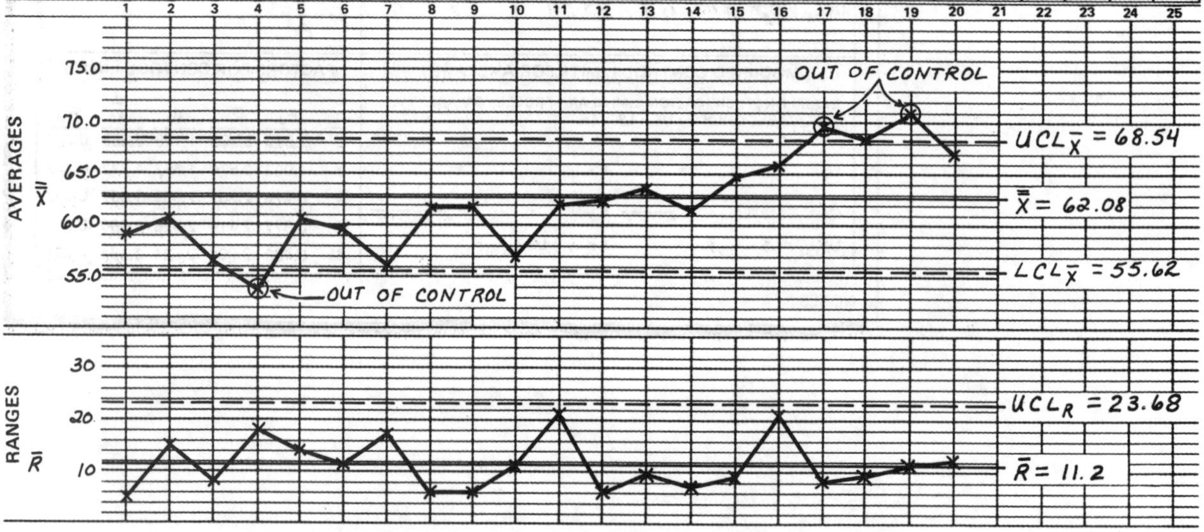

Figure 8-24. Average and range chart of A, E, I M shaft movement data, showing points outside control limits (Problem 3-3).

Figure 8-25. Calculation worksheet from back of average and range chart in Figure 8-24 (Problem 3-3).

CALCULATION WORK SHEET

CONTROL LIMITS A, E, I, M

SUBGROUPS INCLUDED ___ 20 ___

$\bar{R} = \dfrac{\Sigma R}{k} = \dfrac{224}{20} = 11.2$ _____ =

$\bar{\bar{X}} = \dfrac{\Sigma \bar{X}}{k} = \dfrac{1241.6}{20} = 62.08$ _____ =

OR

$\bar{X}'$ (MIDSPEC. OR STD.) =   =

$A_2\bar{R} = .577 \times 11.2 = \underline{6.46}$ x   = _____

$UCL_{\bar{x}} = \bar{\bar{X}} + A_2\bar{R}$ $= 68.54$ =

$LCL_{\bar{x}} = \bar{\bar{X}} - A_2\bar{R}$ $= 55.62$ =

$UCL_R = D_4\bar{R} = 2.114 \times 11.2 = 23.68$ x   =

LIMITS FOR INDIVIDUALS
COMPARE WITH SPECIFICATION OR TOLERANCE LIMITS

$\bar{\bar{X}}$ =

$\dfrac{3}{d_2}\bar{R} =$ x   = _____

$UL_x = \bar{\bar{X}} + \dfrac{3}{d_2}\bar{R}$ =

$LL_x = \bar{\bar{X}} - \dfrac{3}{d_2}\bar{R}$ =

US   =

LS   = _____

US − LS   =

$6\sigma = \dfrac{6}{d_2}\bar{R}$ =

MODIFIED CONTROL LIMITS FOR AVERAGES

BASED ON SPECIFICATION LIMITS AND PROCESS CAPABILITY. APPLICABLE ONLY IF: US − LS > 6σ.

US   =   LS   =

$A_M\bar{R} =$ x   = _____ $A_M\bar{R}$ = _____

$URL_{\bar{x}} = US - A_M\bar{R}$ = $LRL_{\bar{x}} = LS + A_M\bar{R}$ =

FACTORS FOR CONTROL LIMITS

n	A_2	D_4	d_2	$\dfrac{3}{d_2}$	A_M
2	1.880	3.268	1.128	2.659	0.779
3	1.023	2.574	1.693	1.772	0.749
4	0.729	2.282	2.059	1.457	0.728
5	0.577	2.114	2.326	1.290	0.713
6	0.483	2.004	2.534	1.184	0.701

NOTES

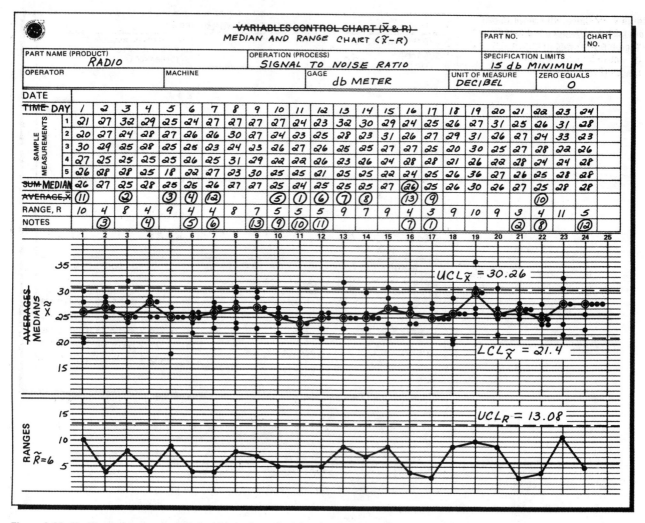

Figure 8-26. Median and range chart of signal-to-noise ratio data, showing determination of median of medians and median range (Problem 3-4).

Problem 3-4.

The median and range chart that you constructed from the decibel readings of the signal-to-noise ratios in Problem 2-4 should look like the chart in Figure 8-26. The calculations for the control limits are shown in Figure 8-27.

In constructing this chart you used five-piece subgroups to obtain 24 medians to plot on the chart. When there are 24 subgroups, the median of medians ($\widetilde{\widetilde{X}}$) is the value of the median between the twelfth and the thirteenth subgroup medians (count up from the smallest median value). Figure 8-26 shows that the value of the median of the twelfth subgroup is 26 and

Figure 8-27. Calculation worksheet from back of median and range chart in Figure 8-26, showing calculations of control limits for medians and ranges (Problem 3-4).

CALCULATION WORK SHEET

CONTROL LIMITS

SUBGROUPS
INCLUDED _____

$\bar{R} = \dfrac{\Sigma R}{k} =$ _____ = _____ =

$\bar{\bar{X}} = \dfrac{\Sigma \bar{X}}{k} =$ _____ = _____ =

OR

$\bar{X}'$ (MIDSPEC. OR STD.) = _____ =

$A_2\bar{R} =$ ____ x ____ = _____ x ____ = _____

$UCL_{\bar{x}} = \bar{\bar{X}} + A_2\bar{R} =$ _____ =

$LCL_{\bar{x}} = \bar{\bar{X}} - A_2\bar{R} =$ _____ =

$UCL_R = D_4\bar{R} =$ ____ x ____ = _____ x ____ =

LIMITS FOR INDIVIDUALS
COMPARE WITH SPECIFICATION OR TOLERANCE LIMITS

$\bar{\bar{X}}$ =

$\dfrac{3}{d_2}\bar{R} =$ ____ x ____ = _____

$UL_x = \bar{\bar{X}} + \dfrac{3}{d_2}\bar{R} =$ _____

$LL_x = \bar{\bar{X}} - \dfrac{3}{d_2}\bar{R} =$ _____

US =

LS· = _____

US − LS =

$6\sigma = \dfrac{6}{d_2}\bar{R} =$ _____

MODIFIED CONTROL LIMITS FOR AVERAGES

BASED ON SPECIFICATION LIMITS AND PROCESS CAPABILITY. APPLICABLE ONLY IF: US − LS > 6σ.

US = _____   LS = _____

$A_M\bar{R} =$ ____ x ____ = _____ $A_M\bar{R} =$ _____ = _____

$URL_{\bar{x}} = US - A_M\bar{R} =$ _____ $LRL_{\bar{x}} = LS + A_M\bar{R} =$ _____

FACTORS FOR CONTROL LIMITS

n	A_2	D_4	d_2	$\dfrac{3}{d_2}$	A_M
2	1.880	3.268	1.128	2.659	0.779
3	1.023	2.574	1.693	1.772	0.749
4	0.729	2.282	2.059	1.457	0.728
5	0.577	2.114	2.326	1.290	0.713
6	0.483	2.004	2.534	1.184	0.701

NOTES

MEDIAN R ($\tilde{R}$) IS 6   (NUMBER 12 RANGE IS 5 AND NUMBER 13 RANGE IS 7)

$UCL_R = \tilde{D}_4$ TIMES $\tilde{R}$ (S)
  = 2.18 TIMES 6
  = 13.08

MEDIAN OF MEDIANS ($\tilde{\tilde{X}}$) IS 26

$UCL_{\tilde{x}} = \tilde{\tilde{X}} + \tilde{A}_2 \tilde{R}$
  = 26 + .71 X 6
  = 26 + 4.26
  = 30.26

$LCL_{\tilde{x}} = \tilde{\tilde{X}} - \tilde{A}_2 \tilde{R}$
  = 26 − 4.26
  = 21.4

the value of the median of the thirteenth subgroup is also 26, so the median of medians is 26.

When you count up from the smallest range value (3), you see that the twelfth value is 5 and the thirteenth is 7. The median range is 6, halfway between these two values. Figure 8-27 shows the control limit calculation for the range. The $\widetilde{D}_4$ factor obtained from Figure 3-23 is 2.18 because the subgroup sample size is 5 pieces. (As you may recall, $\widetilde{D}_4$ and $\widetilde{A}_2$ are special factors for calculating median and range control charts.)

Figure 8-27 also shows calculations for the upper and lower control limits for the subgroup medians, using the $\widetilde{A}_2$ factor obtained from Figure 3-23. The control limits shown on the chart (Figure 8-26) reveal that all range values and all median values lie within the control limits, so you can use this data to establish a median and range chart for future production and to estimate the process average.

The histogram developed in Problem 2-4 shows that the process average probably lies in the cell interval of 26/27. The median and range chart shows that the median of medians ($\widetilde{\widetilde{X}}$) is 26, so you can see that the two methods of analyzing the process average are in agreement.

MODULE 4: ATTRIBUTE CHARTS
Problem 4-1.

The inspection results listed in this problem show the number of defectives (not defects) in a 48-piece sample. This data can be used to construct a percent defective chart. The chart you construct should look like the one in Figure 8-28.

Figure 8-29 shows the calculations for the average percent defective ($\bar{p}$) and the upper and lower control limits.

The question is whether the dirt and grease spots are a problem for management or for the people on the production floor. The average percent defective ($\bar{p}$ is very high (52.1%), and many managers and production floor workers assume that when it is that high, somebody on the production floor must be doing something wrong. The control chart, however, shows that all sample averages are inside the control limits. This statistical analysis technique says that the high percentage of dirt and grease spots is built into the system. The workers on the production floor cannot make a significant lasting improvement without making system changes that require the approval and action of management.

Problem 4-2.

You must construct six c-charts to answer the question, "Which machines need attention by the setup person on the production floor?" These c-charts should look like those shown in Figures 8-30, 8-32, 8-34, 8-36, 8-38, and 8-40. The control limit calculations for those charts are shown in Figures 8-31, 8-33, 8-35, 8-37, 8-39, and 8-41.

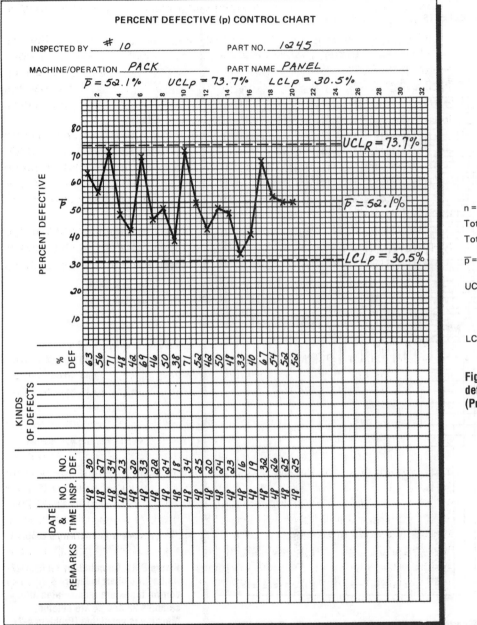

PERCENT DEFECTIVE (p) CONTROL CHART

INSPECTED BY _# 10_   PART NO. _1245_

MACHINE/OPERATION _PACK_   PART NAME _PANEL_

$\bar{p} = 52.1\%$ $UCL_p = 73.7\%$ $LCL_p = 30.5\%$

$n = 48$

Total defective = 500

Total inspected = 960

$\bar{p} = \frac{500}{960} \times 100\% = 52.1\%$

$UCL_p = 52.1 + 3 \sqrt{\dfrac{52.1\,(100 - 52.1)}{48}}$

$\quad = 52.1 + 21.6$

$\quad = 73.7\%$

$LCL_p = 52.1 - 21.6$

$\quad = 30.5$

Figure 8-29. Calculations for percent defective chart in Figure 8-28 (Problem 4-1).

Figure 8-28. Percent defective chart of dirt and grease on panels at packing operation (Problem 4-1).

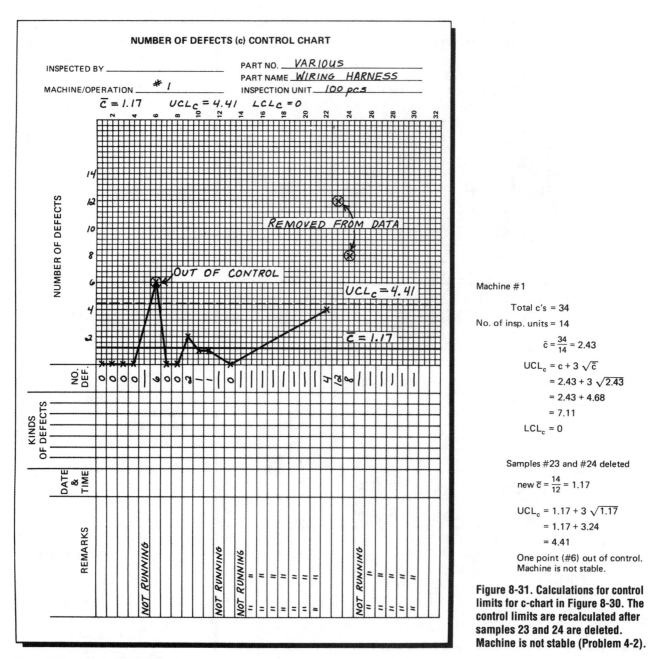

NUMBER OF DEFECTS (c) CONTROL CHART

INSPECTED BY _____

MACHINE/OPERATION ___ *# 1* ___

PART NO. *VARIOUS*

PART NAME *WIRING HARNESS*

INSPECTION UNIT *100 pcs*

$\bar{c} = 1.17$ $UCL_c = 4.41$ $LCL_c = 0$

Machine #1

Total c's = 34

No. of insp. units = 14

$$\bar{c} = \frac{34}{14} = 2.43$$

$$UCL_c = c + 3\sqrt{\bar{c}}$$

$$= 2.43 + 3\sqrt{2.43}$$

$$= 2.43 + 4.68$$

$$= 7.11$$

$$LCL_c = 0$$

Samples #23 and #24 deleted

$$\text{new } \bar{c} = \frac{14}{12} = 1.17$$

$$UCL_c = 1.17 + 3\sqrt{1.17}$$

$$= 1.17 + 3.24$$

$$= 4.41$$

One point (#6) out of control. Machine is not stable.

Figure 8-31. Calculations for control limits for c-chart in Figure 8-30. The control limits are recalculated after samples 23 and 24 are deleted. Machine is not stable (Problem 4-2).

Figure 8-30. c-chart of wiring harness machine #1 output, showing points removed from the data (Problem 4-2).

When you review the control charts, you can answer the question. Machine number 1 (Figure 8-30) was running only fourteen times when the auditor came around to inspect the 100 pieces. The first calculation of control limits showed that two points (samples 23 and 24) were outside the control limits. When these were thrown out and new control limits were calculated, sample 6 was outside the new control limit. You can conclude that the output of this machine is too unstable to establish a control chart. The assignable causes must be found and eliminated. This machine needs the attention of the setup person on the production floor.

Machine number 2 (Figure 8-32) showed two points out of control (samples 12 and 21) when the control limits were first calculated. When these two samples were removed and the control limits were recalculated, two more points were out of control. This machine is operating at a very low average number of defects per inspection unit, but the control chart indicates that it is not stable and needs attention. The next step should be to increase the number of pieces in an inspection unit from 100 to, say, 200. A control chart made on the basis of a larger inspection unit may tell a different story.

Machine number 3 (Figure 8-34) is operating at a much higher average number of defects per inspection unit ($\bar{c} = 3.24$) than the other machines, but the control chart shows that all the points lie inside the control limits. This machine is stable, but at a high reject rate. The setup person on the production floor cannot do anything to improve the quality. The variation is built into the process, and management must take action to improve this machine.

Machine number 4 (Figure 8-36) is shown to be unstable. Sample 5 was removed from the calculations and the control limits were recalculated. Samples 15 and 25 are now outside the control limit. This machine needs the attention of the floor setup person to find and eliminate the assignable causes.

Machine number 5 (Figure 8-38) is one of the worst machines. Three points are out of control on the first calculation of control limits. If the assignable causes can be eliminated, this machine gives evidence of being the best performer in the group; when the out-of-control points are removed, the average number of defects ($\bar{c}$) is very low.

Machine number 6 (Figure 8-40) is a stable machine. All points are inside the control limits. It does not need the attention of the setup person on the production floor.

Before you constructed the control charts for this problem could you have detected that the machines that did *not* need attention would be numbers 3 and 6? Quite often managers and production floor persons will look for assignable causes on the basis of the numbers reported by audit inspectors. Without a control chart, however, it is difficult to tell if the defects reported are due to assignable causes or to chance causes.

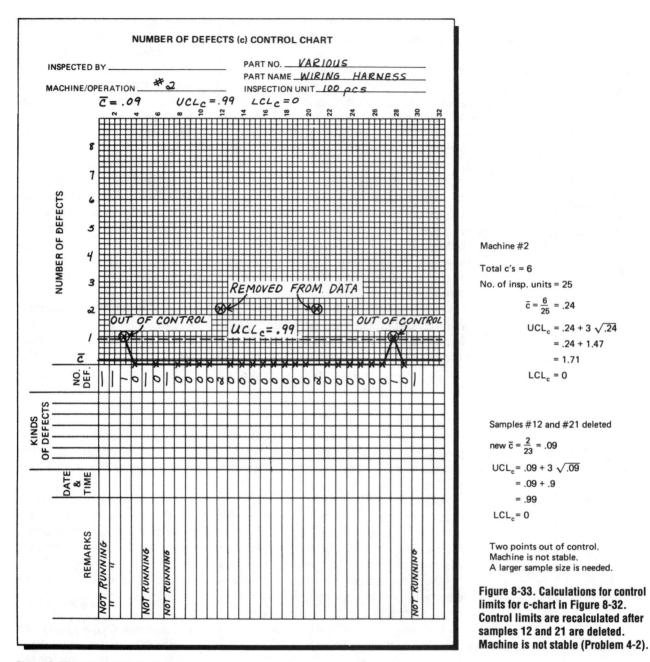

NUMBER OF DEFECTS (c) CONTROL CHART

INSPECTED BY _____

MACHINE/OPERATION _____ #2 _____

PART NO. _VARIOUS_

PART NAME _WIRING HARNESS_

INSPECTION UNIT _100 pcs_

$\bar{c} = .09$ $UCL_c = .99$ $LCL_c = 0$

NUMBER OF DEFECTS

REMOVED FROM DATA

OUT OF CONTROL $UCL_c = .99$ OUT OF CONTROL

NO. DEF.

KINDS OF DEFECTS

DATE & TIME

REMARKS   NOT RUNNING   NOT RUNNING   NOT RUNNING   NOT RUNNING

Machine #2

Total c's = 6
No. of insp. units = 25

$$\bar{c} = \frac{6}{25} = .24$$

$$UCL_c = .24 + 3\sqrt{.24}$$
$$= .24 + 1.47$$
$$= 1.71$$
$$LCL_c = 0$$

Samples #12 and #21 deleted

new $\bar{c} = \frac{2}{23} = .09$

$$UCL_c = .09 + 3\sqrt{.09}$$
$$= .09 + .9$$
$$= .99$$
$$LCL_c = 0$$

Two points out of control.
Machine is not stable.
A larger sample size is needed.

Figure 8-33. Calculations for control limits for c-chart in Figure 8-32. Control limits are recalculated after samples 12 and 21 are deleted. Machine is not stable (Problem 4-2).

Figure 8-32. c-chart of wiring harness machine #2 output, showing points removed from the data and points still outside control limits (Problem 4-2).

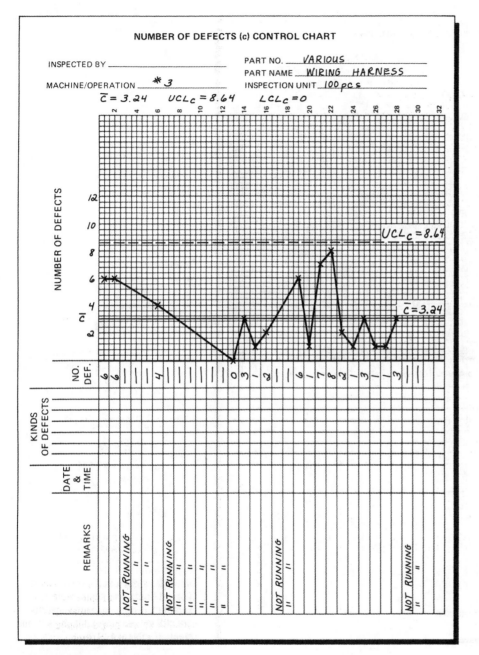

NUMBER OF DEFECTS (c) CONTROL CHART

INSPECTED BY _____

MACHINE/OPERATION ____ *# 3*

PART NO. ____ *VARIOUS*

PART NAME ____ *WIRING HARNESS*

INSPECTION UNIT ____ *100 pcs*

$\bar{c} = 3.24$ $UCL_c = 8.64$ $LCL_c = 0$

$UCL_c = 8.64$

$\bar{c} = 3.24$

Figure 8-34. c-chart of wiring harness machine #3 output, showing all points inside control limits (Problem 4-2).

Machine #3

Total c's = 55

No. of insp. units = 17

$\bar{c} = \dfrac{55}{17} = 3.24$

$UCL_c = 3.24 + 3\sqrt{3.24}$

$= 3.24 + 5.4$

$= 8.64$

$LCL_c = 0$

All points are within the control limits. Machine is stable but at a high reject rate. A management solvable problem.

Figure 8-35. Calculations for control limits for c-chart in Figure 8-34. Machine is stable, but at a high reject rate (Problem 4-2).

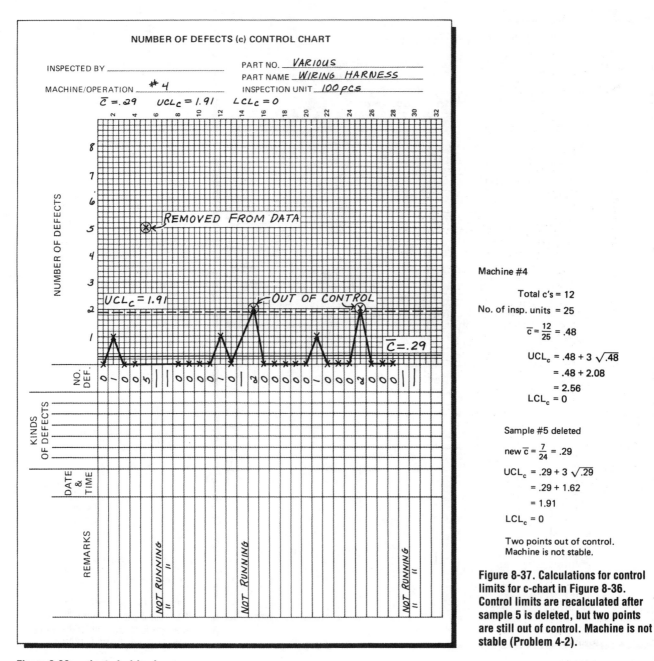

Figure 8-36. c-chart of wiring harness machine #4 output, showing point removed from the data and two points still outside control limits (Problem 4-2).

Machine #4

$$\text{Total c's} = 12$$
$$\text{No. of insp. units} = 25$$
$$\bar{c} = \frac{12}{25} = .48$$
$$UCL_c = .48 + 3\sqrt{.48}$$
$$= .48 + 2.08$$
$$= 2.56$$
$$LCL_c = 0$$

Sample #5 deleted
$$\text{new } \bar{c} = \frac{7}{24} = .29$$
$$UCL_c = .29 + 3\sqrt{.29}$$
$$= .29 + 1.62$$
$$= 1.91$$
$$LCL_c = 0$$

Two points out of control. Machine is not stable.

Figure 8-37. Calculations for control limits for c-chart in Figure 8-36. Control limits are recalculated after sample 5 is deleted, but two points are still out of control. Machine is not stable (Problem 4-2).

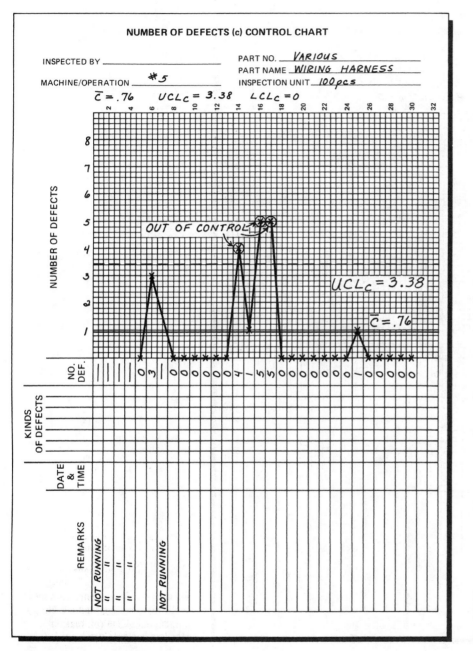

NUMBER OF DEFECTS (c) CONTROL CHART

INSPECTED BY _____

MACHINE/OPERATION _____ #5 _____

PART NO. _VARIOUS_

PART NAME _WIRING HARNESS_

INSPECTION UNIT _100 pcs_

$\bar{c} = .76$ $UCL_c = 3.38$ $LCL_c = 0$

$UCL_c = 3.38$

$\bar{c} = .76$

OUT OF CONTROL

Figure 8-38. c-chart for wiring harness machine #5 output, showing three points outside control limits (Problem 4-2).

Machine #5

Total c's = 19

No. of insp. units = 25

$$\bar{c} = \frac{19}{25} = .76$$

$$UCL_c = .76 + 3\sqrt{.76}$$

$$= .76 + 2.62$$

$$= 3.38$$

$$LCL_c = 0$$

Three points out of control.
Machine is not stable.

Figure 8-39. Calculations for control limits for c-chart in Figure 8-38. Three points are out of control. Machine is not stable (Problem 4-2).

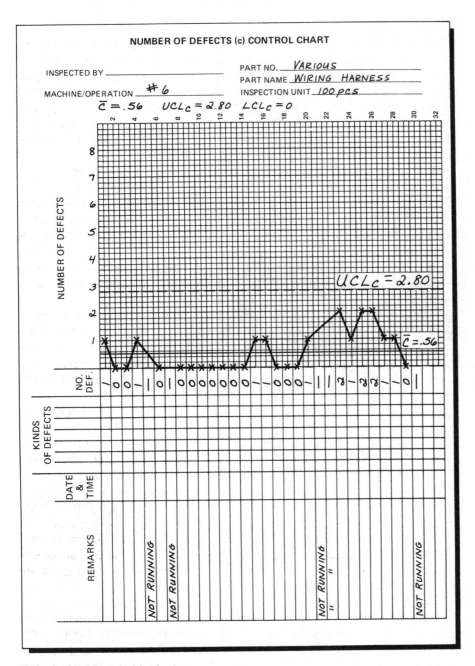

NUMBER OF DEFECTS (c) CONTROL CHART

INSPECTED BY _____

MACHINE/OPERATION ___#6___

PART NO. _VARIOUS_

PART NAME _WIRING HARNESS_

INSPECTION UNIT _100 pcs_

$\bar{c} = .56$ $UCL_c = 2.80$ $LCL_c = 0$

$UCL_c = 2.80$

$\bar{c} = .56$

NUMBER OF DEFECTS

NO. DEF. | 1 | 0 | 0 | 1 | 1 | 0 | 1 | 0 | 0 | 0 | 0 | 0 | 0 | 0 | 0 | 1 | 1 | 0 | 0 | 0 | 1 | 1 | 2 | 1 | 2 | 2 | 1 | 1 | 0 | 1

KINDS OF DEFECTS

DATE & TIME

REMARKS: NOT RUNNING   NOT RUNNING   NOT RUNNING "   NOT RUNNING

Machine #6

Total c's = 14

No. of insp. units = 25

$\bar{c} = \frac{14}{25} = .56$

$UCL_c = .56 + 3\sqrt{.56}$

$= .56 + 2.24$

$= 2.80$

$LCL_c = 0$

All points are within the control limits. Machine is stable.

Figure 8-41. Calculations for control limits for c-chart in Figure 8-40. No points are outside control limits. Machine is stable (Problem 4-2).

Figure 8-40. c-chart of wiring harness machine #6 output, showing all points inside control limits (Problem 4-2).

Problem 4-3.

When using inspection data on hand to analyze quality problems, it's important to make clear what the data represent. These data show the number of defective units in each of the five defect categories. You cannot tell from these records how many units in each sample were defective. Neither can you tell how many defects of each kind were in each sample because when the audit inspector sees a scratch on a part, that part is recorded as defective because of scratches. Even if the part had more than one scratch, it is recorded as one defective.

The inspection results presented in this problem must be used to construct separate percent defective charts for each category of defect.

The p-chart for "scratches" is shown in Figure 8-42 and the calculations for the control limits are shown in Figure 8-43. The process average percent defective ($\bar{p}$) is 13.2%. A sample size of 100 at this percent defective results in an upper control limit (UCL$_p$) of 23.35% and a lower control limit (LCL$_p$) of 3.05%. (See Figure 8-43.) All the sample percent defectives are inside the control limits, so you can say that the $\bar{p}$ of 13.2% is stable for this production system.

The second defect category is "wrinkles." The p-chart is shown in Figure 8-44 and the calculations for the control limits are shown in Figure 8-45. The process average percent defective ($\bar{p}$) is 8.1%. The upper control limit (UCL$_p$) is 16.29% and the lower control limit (LCL$_p$) is zero. All points are inside the control limits, so this category can be considered statistically stable.

The third defect category is "bent." The p-chart is shown in Figure 8-46 and the calculations for the control limits are shown in Figure 8-47. The process average percent defective ($\bar{p}$) is 4.25%. The upper control limit (UCL$_p$) is 10.3% and the lower control limit is zero. This chart shows that the category is in control because no points lie outside the control limit.

The fourth defect category is "cracks." The p-chart is shown in Figure 8-48 and the calculations for the control limits are shown in Figure 8-49. The process average percent defective ($\bar{p}$) is 1.9%. The upper control limit (UCL$_p$) is 6.0% and the lower control limit is zero. Note that the percent defective scale has been expanded on this chart. When the $\bar{p}$ is small it is a good idea to expand the percent defective scale to make the chart more readable. All sample percentages are inside the control limits, so you can say that this defect category is stable at an average of 1.9%.

The fifth defect category is "wrong part." The p-chart is shown in Figure 8-50 and the calculations for the control limits are shown in Figure 8-51. The process average percent defective ($\bar{p}$) is very low, .25%, and most of the sample percent defectives are zero. This control chart shows a point (sample 6) outside the upper control limit, which is 1.75%. When a control chart has a very low process average percent defective, it is not unusual to see a point or two outside the upper control limit, even though the process is actually stable.

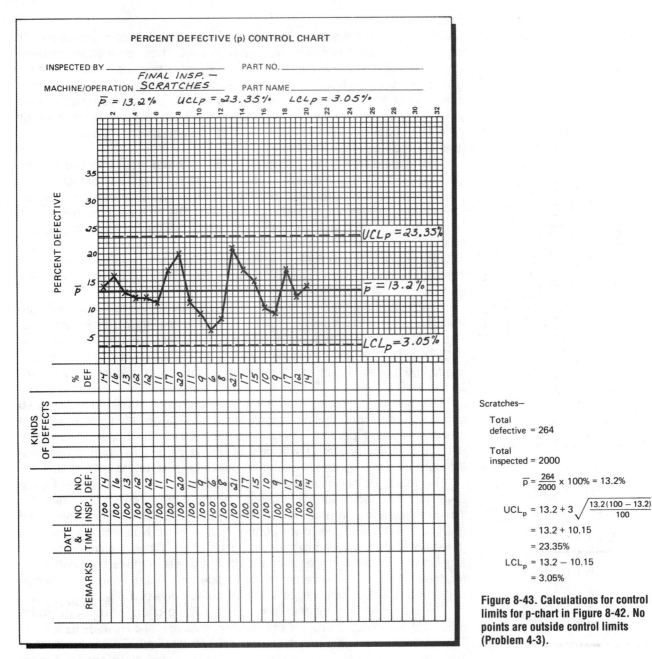

Figure 8-42. Percent defective chart of final inspection records, showing percent defective for scratches. (Problem 4-3).

Scratches—

Total defective = 264

Total inspected = 2000

$$\bar{p} = \frac{264}{2000} \times 100\% = 13.2\%$$

$$UCL_p = 13.2 + 3\sqrt{\frac{13.2(100-13.2)}{100}}$$

$$= 13.2 + 10.15$$

$$= 23.35\%$$

$$LCL_p = 13.2 - 10.15$$

$$= 3.05\%$$

Figure 8-43. Calculations for control limits for p-chart in Figure 8-42. No points are outside control limits (Problem 4-3).

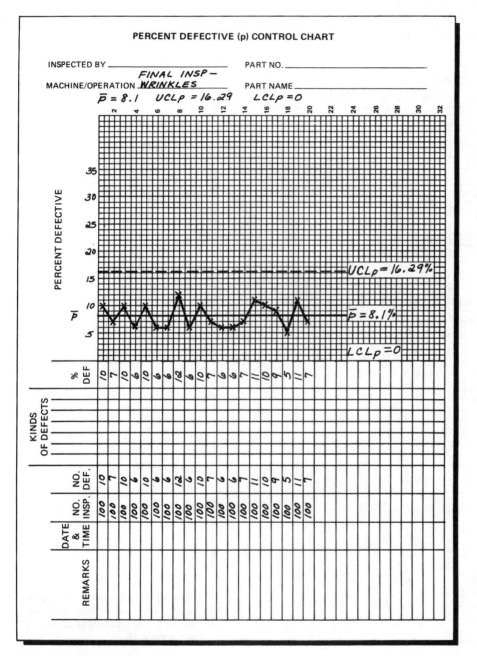

Figure 8-44. Percent defective chart of final inspection records for wrinkles (Problem 4-3).

Wrinkles—

Total defective = 162

Total inspected = 2000

$$\bar{p} = \frac{162}{2000} \times 100\% = 8.1\%$$

$$UCL_p = 8.1 + 3\sqrt{\frac{8.1(100-8.1)}{100}}$$

$$= 8.1 + 8.19$$

$$= 16.29$$

$$LCL_p = 8.1 - 8.19$$

$$= -.09$$

$$= 0$$

Figure 8-45. Calculations for control limits for p-chart in Figure 8-44. No points are outside control limits (Problem 4-3).

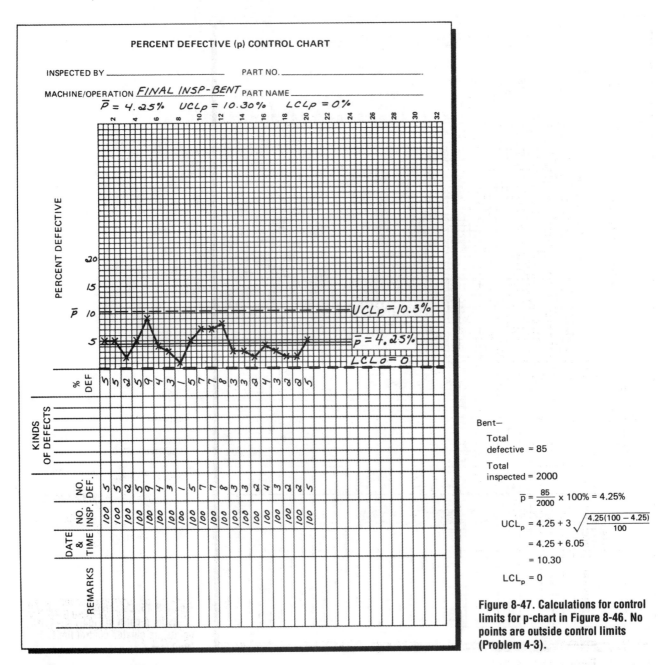

PERCENT DEFECTIVE (p) CONTROL CHART

INSPECTED BY _____   PART NO. _____.

MACHINE/OPERATION *FINAL INSP-BENT* PART NAME _____

$\bar{P}$ = 4.25%   UCLp = 10.30%   LCLp = 0%

Bent—

Total
defective = 85

Total
inspected = 2000

$$\bar{p} = \frac{85}{2000} \times 100\% = 4.25\%$$

$$UCL_p = 4.25 + 3\sqrt{\frac{4.25(100 - 4.25)}{100}}$$

$$= 4.25 + 6.05$$

$$= 10.30$$

$$LCL_p = 0$$

Figure 8-47. Calculations for control limits for p-chart in Figure 8-46. No points are outside control limits (Problem 4-3).

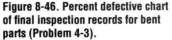

Figure 8-46. Percent defective chart of final inspection records for bent parts (Problem 4-3).

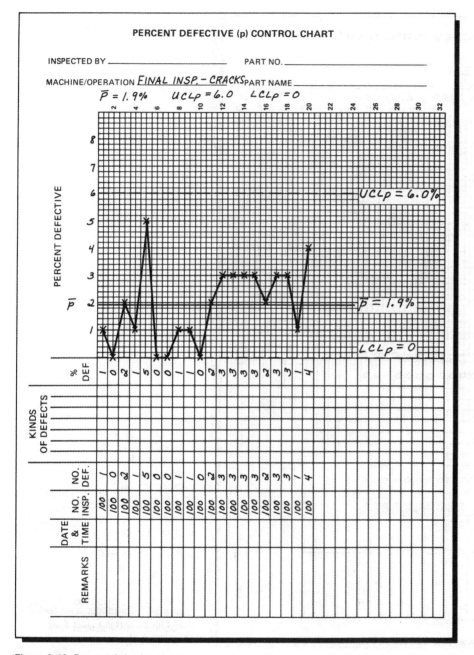

Figure 8-48. Percent defective chart of final inspection records for cracks (Problem 4-3).

Cracks—

Total defective = 38

Total inspected = 2000

$$\bar{p} = \frac{38}{2000} \times 100\% = 1.9\%$$

$$UCL_p = 1.9 + 3\sqrt{\frac{1.9(100-1.9)}{100}}$$

$$= 1.9 + 4.10$$

$$= 6.0$$

$$LCL_p = 0$$

Figure 8-49. Calculations for control limits for p-chart in Figure 8-48. No points are outside control limits (Problem 4-3).

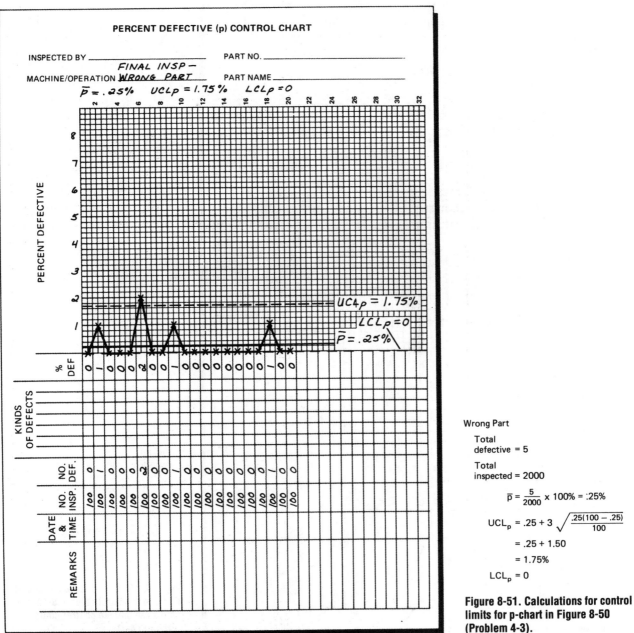

PERCENT DEFECTIVE (p) CONTROL CHART

INSPECTED BY _____   PART NO. _____

MACHINE/OPERATION <u>*WRONG PART*</u>   PART NAME _____

FINAL INSP —

$\bar{P} = .25\%$ $UCL_p = 1.75\%$ $LCL_p = 0$

$UCL_p = 1.75\%$
$LCL_p = 0$
$\bar{P} = .25\%$

Wrong Part

Total defective = 5

Total inspected = 2000

$$\bar{p} = \frac{5}{2000} \times 100\% = .25\%$$

$$UCL_p = .25 + 3 \sqrt{\frac{.25(100 - .25)}{100}}$$

$$= .25 + 1.50$$

$$= 1.75\%$$

$$LCL_p = 0$$

Figure 8-51. Calculations for control limits for p-chart in Figure 8-50 (Problem 4-3).

Figure 8-50. Percent defective chart of final inspection records for wrong part, showing apparent out-of-control point at sample #6 (Problem 4-3).

As you can see, in a sample size of 100 units, each defective unit represents one percent of the sample. Therefore, points on the control chart will fall only on whole-number lines; that is, 0, 1, 2, 3, etc. percent defective. When the upper control limit is 1.75%, two defectives in the sample will plot as out of control, signaling the presence of an assignable cause. In fact there may be no assignable cause, for reasons that we do not discuss in this book. All you need to know is that when you're using attribute charts with very low reject rates, you should proceed with caution when sample points fall just outside the control limit.

If you and your co-workers made an investigation like the one described in this problem, what recommendations would you suggest for improving quality? On the basis of the control chart analysis you just completed, you would report to management that the defects in your products are due to chance causes in the manufacturing process. Basic changes must be made in the manufacturing system to bring about significant improvement in quality.

MODULE 5: MACHINE AND PROCESS CAPABILITY
Problem 5-1.

The average and range chart in Figure 8-11 shows that the pin diameters are in control, but a probability plot must be made to judge the normality of the underlying distribution. (See Figure 8-52.) The plot points fit a straight line well. The straight line of best fit crosses the top of the probability chart (the $+3\sigma$ line) at about .2558. It crosses the bottom of the chart (the -3σ line) at about .2444. The difference between these two values, .0114, is an estimate of the expected process spread (6σ).

Lines representing the specification limits (.242 and .258) have been drawn on the probability chart. The line of best fit crosses the top and the bottom lines of the chart before it meets the specification limit lines. This is graphic evidence that the process is capable of meeting the specification.

Figure 8-53 is the calculation worksheet for the average and range chart shown in Figure 8-11, but here the calculations for "limits for individuals" have been completed. These calculations give an estimated upper limit for individuals (UL_x) of .25577 and an estimated lower limit for individuals (LL_x) of .24441. The calculated estimates of the process spread (6σ) is .0113. These calculated estimates all agree well with the graphic estimates from the probability plot chart.

The machine capability index (C_{pk}) has been calculated in the lower portion of Figure 8-53. The true capability index is the smaller of two values determined by relating the process average ($\overline{\overline{X}}$) and the process standard deviation (σ) to the upper specification limit (USL) and the lower specification limit (LSL). In this problem the two index values are 1.39 and 1.42. The estimated true machine capability index is 1.39, the smaller of the two values.

Figure 8-52. Probability plot of pin diameter data, showing relationship of the line of best fit to plot points and specification limits (Problem 5-1).

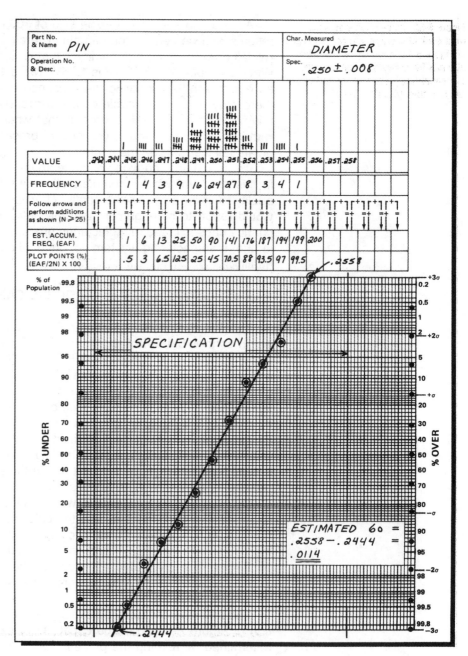

Figure 8-53. Calculation worksheet from back of average and range chart in Figure 8-11, showing calculations of limits for individuals, upper right, and capability index and capability ratio, bottom (Problem 5-1).

CALCULATION WORK SHEET

CONTROL LIMITS

SUBGROUPS INCLUDED ____20____

$\bar{R} = \frac{\Sigma R}{k} = \frac{.088}{20} = .0044$ _____ =

$\bar{\bar{X}} = \frac{\Sigma \bar{X}}{k} = \frac{5.0018}{20} = .25009$ _____

OR

$\bar{X}'$ (MIDSPEC. OR STD.) = _____ =

$A_2\bar{R} = .577 \times .0044 = .00254$ ____ x ____ = _____

$UCL_{\bar{x}} = \bar{\bar{X}} + A_2\bar{R} = .25263$ =

$LCL_{\bar{x}} = \bar{\bar{X}} - A_2\bar{R} = .24755$ =

$UCL_R = D_4\bar{R} = 2.114 \times .0044 = .0093$ x =

LIMITS FOR INDIVIDUALS
COMPARE WITH SPECIFICATION OR TOLERANCE LIMITS

$\bar{\bar{X}}$ = .25009

$\frac{3}{d_2}\bar{R} = 1.290 \times .0044 = .00568$

$UL_x = \bar{\bar{X}} + \frac{3}{d_2}\bar{R}$ = .25577

$LL_x = \bar{\bar{X}} - \frac{3}{d_2}\bar{R}$ = .24441

US = .258

LS = .242

US − LS = .016

$6\sigma = \frac{6}{d_2}\bar{R}$ = .0113

MODIFIED CONTROL LIMITS FOR AVERAGES

BASED ON SPECIFICATION LIMITS AND PROCESS CAPABILITY. APPLICABLE ONLY IF: US − LS > 6σ.

US = _____ LS = _____

$A_M\bar{R}$ = ____ x ____ = _____ $A_M\bar{R}$ = _____

$URL_{\bar{x}} = US - A_M\bar{R}$ = _____ $LRL_{\bar{x}} = LS + A_M\bar{R}$ =

FACTORS FOR CONTROL LIMITS

n	A_2	D_4	d_2	$\frac{3}{d_2}$	A_M
2	1.880	3.268	1.128	2.659	0.779
3	1.023	2.574	1.693	1.772	0.749
4	0.729	2.282	2.059	1.457	0.728
5	0.577	2.114	2.326	1.290	0.713
6	0.483	2.004	2.534	1.184	0.701

NOTES

$$C_{PK} = \frac{USL - \bar{\bar{X}}}{3\sigma} \text{ OR } \frac{\bar{\bar{X}} - LSL}{3\sigma}$$

$$= \frac{.258 - .25009}{.00568} = 1.39 \leftarrow \text{SMALLER OF THE TWO}$$

OR

$$\approx \frac{.25009 - .242}{.00568} = 1.42$$

$$C_{PK} = 1.39$$

$$CR = \frac{6\sigma}{TOTAL\ TOLERANCE} \times 100\% = \frac{.0113}{.016} \times 100\% =$$

$$CR = 70.6\%$$

The machine capability ratio (CR) has also been calculated in Figure 8-53. The capability ratio is the ratio of the estimated process spread (6σ) to the total tolerance and is expressed as a percentage. The estimated process spread is .0113 and the total tolerance of the pin diameter is .016. The capability ratio (CR) is calculated to be 70.6%.

Problem 5-2.

This problem asks if the data shown on the average and range chart in Figure 8-14 can be used to estimate machine capability. To answer this question you must construct a probability plot of the data. (See Figure 8-54.)

In constructing the probability plot in Figure 8-54 the measurements from subgroup samples 19 and 20 were thrown out, just as they were in Problem 3-2. When this was done, the remaining data fit a straight line. This indicates that the data is distributed normally, and the values from the average and range chart can be used to estimate the machine capability.

The upper specification limit line has been drawn on the probability plot chart. The line of best fit crosses this upper specification limit line at the "50% over" horizontal line. Therefore you can estimate that 50% of the output of this machine will be over the specification.

Figure 8-55 is the calculation worksheet on the back of the average and range chart in Figure 8-14. The calculations of "limits for individuals" show that the upper limit for individuals (UL_x) is .7596 and the lower limit for individuals (LL_x) is .7504. The estimated process spread (6σ) is .0091. All these figures compare favorably with the estimates shown in Figure 8-54.

Figure 8-55 shows the calculation of the capability index (C_{pk}). The smaller of the two calculated values is zero, and any value less than one indicates that a process is not capable. Therefore this machine is considered "not capable" as currently set up.

The capability ratio calculation (see Figure 8-55) indicates that the machine has a capability ratio (CR) of 91%. As discussed in Module 5, this method of evaluating machine or process capability requires some additional explanation. In this case we would say, "The machine used less than 100% of the allowed tolerance of .010. It could be 'capable' if the process average ($\overline{\overline{X}}$) were centered on the specification."

Did you notice something interesting in this problem? The associate who relieved the regular associate during lunch and who was responsible for the out-of-control points (samples 19 and 20 in Figure 8-14) was actually producing parts in specification because he knew more about the job. When the regular associate received better instructions and training, he was able to run the lathe at the same level as the relief associate, and the situation of fifty percent out of specification was eliminated. Quality improvements are often just this simple.

Problem 5-3.

The capability of the groups of data presented in Problem 2-3 has been estimated by constructing a probability plot for each group of data and by calculating the limits for individuals and the estimated process spread for each group of data. The capability index and capability ratio have been calculated for each group of data.

The data for process A, B, C, D is analyzed in Figure 8-56 and Figure 8-57. The average and range chart in Figure 8-16 shows that all points are

Figure 8-54. Probability plot of undercut diameter, showing relationship of the line of best fit to plot points and specification limits (Problem 5-2).

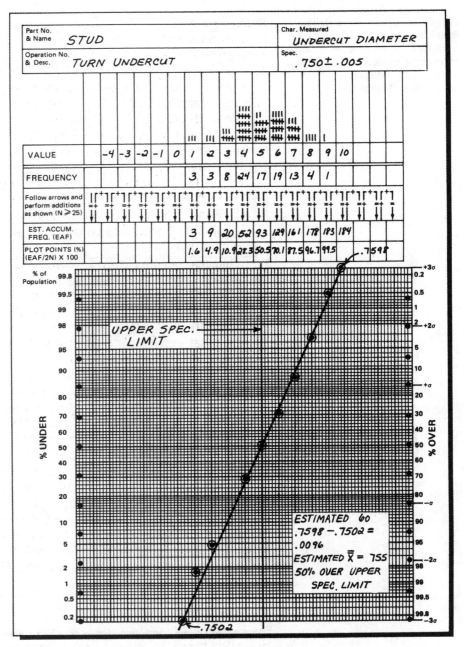

Figure 8-55. Calculation worksheet from back of average and range chart in Figure 8-14, showing calculations of limits for individuals, upper right, and capability index and capability ratio, bottom (Problem 5-2).

CALCULATION WORK SHEET

CONTROL LIMITS

SUBGROUPS INCLUDED _____ 23

$\bar{R} = \dfrac{\Sigma R}{k} =$ _____ $= \dfrac{72}{23} = 3.13$

$\bar{\bar{X}} = \dfrac{\Sigma \bar{X}}{k} =$ _____ $= \dfrac{115}{23} = 5.00$

OR

$\bar{X}'$ (MIDSPEC. OR STD.) $=$ _____ $=$

$A_2\bar{R} =$ _____ $\times$ _____ $= .729 \times 3.13 = \underline{2.28}$

$UCL_{\bar{x}} = \bar{\bar{X}} + A_2\bar{R} =$ _____ $= 7.28$

$LCL_{\bar{x}} = \bar{\bar{X}} - A_2\bar{R} =$ _____ $= 2.72$

$UCL_R = D_4\bar{R} =$ _____ $\times$ _____ $= 2.282 \times 3.13 = 7.14$

LIMITS FOR INDIVIDUALS
COMPARE WITH SPECIFICATION OR TOLERANCE LIMITS

$\bar{\bar{X}}$ 5.00 EQUALS $= .755$

$\dfrac{3}{d_2}\bar{R} = 1.457 \times .00313 = \underline{.0046}$

$UL_x = \bar{\bar{X}} + \dfrac{3}{d_2}\bar{R}$ $= .7596$

$LL_x = \bar{\bar{X}} - \dfrac{3}{d_2}\bar{R}$ $= .7504$

US $= .755$

LS $= \underline{.745}$

US − LS $= .010$

$6\sigma = \dfrac{6}{d_2}\bar{R}$ $= .0091$

MODIFIED CONTROL LIMITS FOR AVERAGES

BASED ON SPECIFICATION LIMITS AND PROCESS CAPABILITY. APPLICABLE ONLY IF: US − LS > 6σ.

US $=$ _____ LS $=$ _____

$A_M\bar{R} =$ _____ $\times$ _____ $=$ _____ $A_M\bar{R} =$ _____ $=$ _____

$URL_{\bar{x}} = US - A_M\bar{R} =$ _____ $LRL_{\bar{x}} = LS + A_M\bar{R} =$ _____

FACTORS FOR CONTROL LIMITS

n	A_2	D_4	d_2	$\dfrac{3}{d_2}$	A_M
2	1.880	3.268	1.128	2.659	0.779
3	1.023	2.574	1.693	1.772	0.749
4	0.729	2.282	2.059	1.457	0.728
5	0.577	2.114	2.326	1.290	0.713
6	0.483	2.004	2.534	1.184	0.701

NOTES

$$C_{PK} = \frac{USL - \bar{\bar{X}}}{3\sigma} \text{ OR } \frac{\bar{\bar{X}} - LSL}{3\sigma}$$

$$= \frac{.755 - .755}{.0046} = 0 \longleftarrow \text{LESS THAN ONE "NOT CAPABLE"}$$

$$= \frac{.755 - .745}{.0046} = 2.17$$

$$CR = \frac{6\sigma}{\text{TOTAL TOLERANCE}} \times 100\%$$

$$= \frac{.0091}{.010} \times 100\% = 91\%$$

MACHINE USES LESS THAN 100% OF THE TOLERANCE. COULD BE CAPABLE IF THE PROCESS AVERAGE ($\bar{\bar{X}}$) WERE CENTERED ON THE SPECIFICATION.

inside the control limits so a probability plot analysis is made to estimate how normally the data is distributed. Although the plot points tend to tail off at the lower end of the chart (see Figure 8-56), a line of best fit has been drawn on the plot points. When drawing a line of best fit on plot points like these, give more weight to the points at the center of the chart than to those at the edges.

The specification limit lines have been drawn on the probability plot chart. The line of best fit crosses the lower specification limit near the ".2% under" line. This means that you can expect about .2% of the parts from this process to fall below the lower specification.

The estimated process spread (6σ) is shown to be 34 (or .034 inch); the lowest value (-3σ) is 39 and the highest value ($+3\sigma$) is 73.

Figure 8-57 is the calculation worksheet on the back of Figure 8-16. Here the "limits for individuals" calculations show that the upper limit for individuals (UL_x) is 73.66 and the lower limit for individuals (LL_x) is 38.96. The process spread (6σ) is calculated to be 34.7. This value agrees well with the values determined graphically in Figure 8-56.

The capability index (C_{pk}) is calculated in Figure 8-57, and the smaller value is .94. Because this value is less than 1.0, the process is "not capable."

The capability ratio (CR), which is calculated in Figure 8-57, is shown to be 86.75%. The process is "capable if the process average is adjusted to center on the specification."

The data for process E, F, G, H is analyzed in Figure 8-58 and Figure 8-59. The average and range chart in Figure 8-18 shows that all points lie inside the control limits. The probability plot shows that the estimated process spread (6σ) is 23, with a low value of 49 and a high value of 72. All plot points and the line of best fit lie inside the specification limits. (See Figure 8-58.)

Figure 8-59 shows that the upper limit for individuals is 72.8, the lower limit for individuals is 48.42, and the estimated process spread is 24.4. These values agree well with those in Figure 8-58.

In Figure 8-59 the capability index (C_{pk}) is shown to be 1.59 and the capability ratio is shown to be 61%. Therefore the process is "capable."

The data for process I, J, K, L is analyzed in Figure 8-60 and Figure 8-61. The average and range chart in Figure 8-20 shows that all points are inside the control limits. The probability plot shows that the estimated process spread (6σ) is 28, with a low value of 49 and a high value of 77. All the plot points and the line of best fit are inside the specification limits. (See Figure 8-60.)

Figure 8-61 shows that the upper limit for individuals is 76.32, the lower limit for individuals is 49.74, and the estimated process spread is 26.57. These values agree fairly well with those in Figure 8-60.

In Figure 8-61 the capability index (C_{pk}) is shown to be 1.28 and the capability ratio (CR) is shown to be 66.4%. Therefore this process is "capable."

The data for process M, N, O, P is analyzed in Figure 8-62 and Figure 8-63. The average and range chart in Figure 8-22 shows that all points are

Figure 8-56. Probability plot of shaft movement data for process A, B, C, D showing relationship of the line of best fit to plot points and specification limits (Problem 5-3).

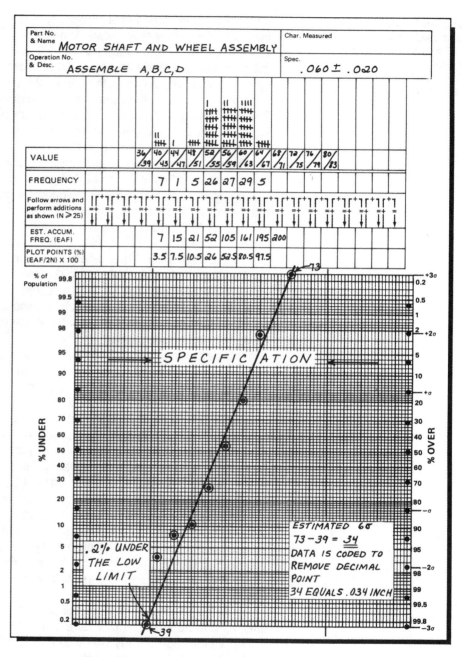

Figure 8-57. Calculation worksheet from back of average and range chart in Figure 8-16, showing calculations of limits for individuals, upper right, and capability index and capability ratio, bottom (Problem 5-3).

PROB 5-3   CALCULATION WORK SHEET

CONTROL LIMITS LINE A, B, C, D	LIMITS FOR INDIVIDUALS COMPARE WITH SPECIFICATION OR TOLERANCE LIMITS

SUBGROUPS INCLUDED _____ 20 _____

$\bar{R} = \frac{\Sigma R}{k} = \frac{269}{20} = 13.45$ _____ =

$\bar{\bar{X}} = \frac{\Sigma \bar{X}}{k} = \frac{1126.2}{20} = 56.31$ _____ =

OR

$\bar{X}'$ (MIDSPEC. OR STD.) =

$A_2 \bar{R} = .577 \times 13.45 = \underline{7.76}$ × _____ = _____

$UCL_{\bar{x}} = \bar{\bar{X}} + A_2 \bar{R} = 64.07$ =

$LCL_{\bar{x}} = \bar{\bar{X}} - A_2 \bar{R} = 48.55$ =

$UCL_R = D_4 \bar{R} = 2.114 \times 13.45 = 28.43$ × =

$\bar{\bar{X}} = 56.31$

$\frac{3}{d_2} \bar{R} = 1.290 \times 13.45 = \underline{17.35}$

$UL_x = \bar{\bar{X}} + \frac{3}{d_2} \bar{R} = 73.66$

$LL_x = \bar{\bar{X}} - \frac{3}{d_2} \bar{R} = 38.96$

US $= 80$

LS $= 40$

US − LS $= 40$

$6\sigma = \frac{6}{d_2} \bar{R} = 34.7$

MODIFIED CONTROL LIMITS FOR AVERAGES	FACTORS FOR CONTROL LIMITS

BASED ON SPECIFICATION LIMITS AND PROCESS CAPABILITY. APPLICABLE ONLY IF: US − LS > 6σ.

US = _____   LS = _____

$A_M \bar{R} =$ × = _____ $A_M \bar{R} =$ = _____

$URL_{\bar{x}} = US - A_M \bar{R} =$ $LRL_{\bar{x}} = LS + A_M \bar{R} =$

n	A_2	D_4	d_2	$\frac{3}{d_2}$	A_M
2	1.880	3.268	1.128	2.659	0.779
3	1.023	2.574	1.693	1.772	0.749
4	0.729	2.282	2.059	1.457	0.728
5	0.577	2.114	2.326	1.290	0.713
6	0.483	2.004	2.534	1.184	0.701

NOTES

$$C_{PK} = \frac{USL - \bar{\bar{X}}}{3\sigma} \text{ OR } \frac{\bar{\bar{X}} - LSL}{3\sigma}$$

$$= \frac{80 - 56.31}{17.35} = 1.37 \quad \text{"NOT CAPABLE"}$$

$$= \frac{\bar{\bar{X}} - LSL}{3\sigma} = \frac{56.31 - 40}{17.35} = .94 \leftarrow \text{LESS THAN ONE}$$

$$CR = \frac{6\sigma}{\text{TOTAL TOLERANCE}} \times 100\%$$

$$= \frac{34.7}{40} \times 100 = 86.75\% \quad \text{"CAPABLE IF PROCESS AVERAGE IS ADJUSTED".}$$

Figure 8-58. Probability plot of shaft movement data for process E, F, G, H, showing relationship of the line of best fit to plot points and specification limits (Problem 5-3).

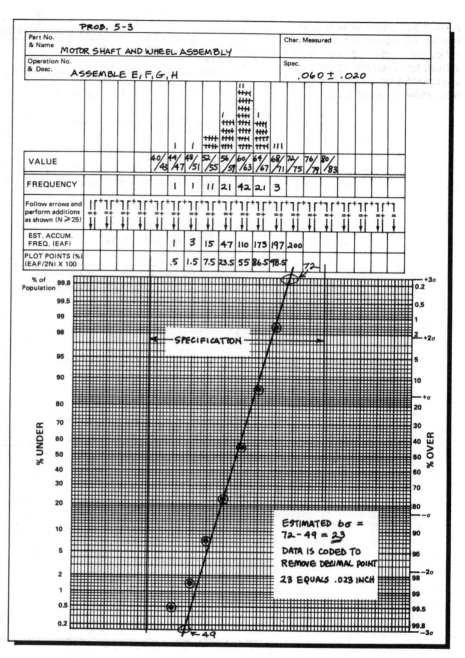

Figure 8-59. Calculation worksheet from back of average and range chart in Figure 8-18, showing calculations of limits for individuals, upper right, and capability index and capability ratio, bottom (Problem 5-3).

PROB 5-3   **CALCULATION WORK SHEET**

CONTROL LIMITS LINE E, F, G, H

SUBGROUPS INCLUDED _____ 20 _____ _____

$\bar{R} = \frac{\Sigma R}{k} = \frac{189}{20} = 9.45$ _____ =

$\bar{\bar{X}} = \frac{\Sigma \bar{X}}{k} = \frac{1212.2}{20} = 60.61$ _____ =

OR

$\bar{X}'$ (MIDSPEC. OR STD.) = _____ =

$A_2\bar{R} = .577 \times 9.45 = \underline{5.45}$ _____ x _____ = _____

$UCL_{\bar{x}} = \bar{\bar{X}} + A_2\bar{R} = 66.06$ _____ =

$LCL_{\bar{x}} = \bar{\bar{X}} - A_2\bar{R} = 55.16$ _____ =

$UCL_R = D_4\bar{R} = 2.114 \times 9.45 = 19.98$ _____ x _____ =

LIMITS FOR INDIVIDUALS
COMPARE WITH SPECIFICATION OR TOLERANCE LIMITS

$\bar{\bar{X}}$ = 60.61

$\frac{3}{d_2}\bar{R} = 1.290 \times 9.45$ = $\underline{12.19}$

$UL_x = \bar{\bar{X}} + \frac{3}{d_2}\bar{R}$ = 72.80

$LL_x = \bar{\bar{X}} - \frac{3}{d_2}\bar{R}$ = 48.42

US = 80

LS = $\underline{40}$

US − LS = 40

$6\sigma = \frac{6}{d_2}\bar{R}$ = 24.4

MODIFIED CONTROL LIMITS FOR AVERAGES	FACTORS FOR CONTROL LIMITS				

BASED ON SPECIFICATION LIMITS AND PROCESS CAPABILITY. APPLICABLE ONLY IF: US − LS > 6σ.

US _____ = LS _____ =

$A_M\bar{R} = $ _____ x _____ = _____ $A_M\bar{R}$ _____ = _____

$URL_{\bar{x}} = US - A_M\bar{R}$ = _____ $LRL_{\bar{x}} = LS + A_M\bar{R}$ =

n	A_2	D_4	d_2	$\frac{3}{d_2}$	A_M
2	1.880	3.268	1.128	2.659	0.779
3	1.023	2.574	1.693	1.772	0.749
4	0.729	2.282	2.059	1.457	0.728
5	0.577	2.114	2.326	1.290	0.713
6	0.483	2.004	2.534	1.184	0.701

NOTES

$$C_{PK} = \frac{USL - \bar{\bar{X}}}{3\sigma} \text{ OR } \frac{\bar{\bar{X}} - LSL}{3\sigma}$$

$$= \frac{80 - 60.61}{12.19} = \underline{1.59} \text{ "CAPABLE"}$$

$$= \frac{\bar{\bar{X}} - LSL}{3\sigma} = \frac{60.61 - 40}{12.19} = 1.69$$

$$CR = \frac{6\sigma}{TOTAL\ TOLERANCE} \times 100\% =$$

$$= \frac{24.4}{40} \times 100\% = 61\% \text{ "CAPABLE"}$$

Figure 8-60. Probability plot of shaft movement data for process I, J, K, L, showing relationship of the line of best fit to plot points and specification limits (Problem 5-3).

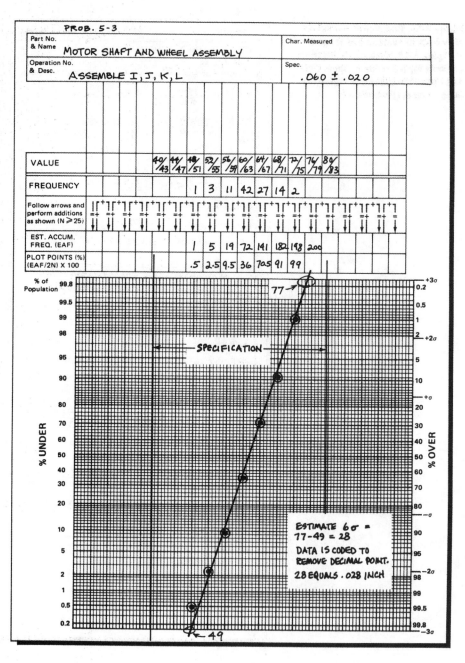

Figure 8-61. Calculation worksheet from back of average and range chart in Figure 8-20, showing calculations of limits for individuals, upper right, and capability index and capability ratio, bottom (Problem 5-3).

PROB 5-3   CALCULATION WORK SHEET

CONTROL LIMITS LINE I, J, K, L

SUBGROUPS
INCLUDED _____ 20 _____   _____

$\bar{R} = \frac{\Sigma R}{k} = \frac{206}{20} = 10.3$ _____ =

$\bar{\bar{X}} = \frac{\Sigma \bar{X}}{k} = \frac{12606}{20} = 63.03$ _____ =

OR

$\bar{X}'$ (MIDSPEC. OR STD.) =   =

$A_2\bar{R} = .577 \times 10.3 = \underline{5.94}$ x   = _____

$UCL_{\bar{x}} = \bar{\bar{X}} + A_2\bar{R} = 68.97$ =

$LCL_{\bar{x}} = \bar{\bar{X}} - A_2\bar{R} = 57.09$ =

$UCL_R = D_4\bar{R} = 2.114 \times 10.3 = 21.77$ x   =

LIMITS FOR INDIVIDUALS
COMPARE WITH SPECIFICATION
OR TOLERANCE LIMITS

$\bar{\bar{X}}$ = 63.03

$\frac{3}{d_2}\bar{R} = 1.290 \times 10.3 = \underline{13.29}$

$UL_x = \bar{\bar{X}} + \frac{3}{d_2}\bar{R}$ = 76.32

$LL_x = \bar{\bar{X}} - \frac{3}{d_2}\bar{R}$ = 49.74

US   = 80

LS   = 40

US − LS   = 40

$6\sigma = \frac{6}{d_2}\bar{R}$ = 26.57

MODIFIED CONTROL LIMITS FOR AVERAGES

BASED ON SPECIFICATION LIMITS AND PROCESS CAPABILITY.
APPLICABLE ONLY IF: US − LS > 6σ.

US   =   LS   =

$A_M\bar{R} =$ x   = _____ $A_M\bar{R}$ = _____

$URL_{\bar{x}} = US - A_M\bar{R} =$ $LRL_{\bar{x}} = LS + A_M\bar{R} =$

FACTORS FOR CONTROL LIMITS

n	A_2	D_4	d_2	$\frac{3}{d_2}$	A_M
2	1.880	3.268	1.128	2.659	0.779
3	1.023	2.574	1.693	1.772	0.749
4	0.729	2.282	2.059	1.457	0.728
5	0.577	2.114	2.326	1.290	0.713
6	0.483	2.004	2.534	1.184	0.701

NOTES

$$C_{PK} = \frac{USL - \bar{\bar{X}}}{3\sigma} \quad OR \quad \frac{\bar{\bar{X}} - LSL}{3\sigma}$$

$$= \frac{80 - 63.03}{13.29} = 1.28 \quad \text{"CAPABLE"}$$

$$= \frac{\bar{\bar{X}} - LSL}{3\sigma} = \frac{63.03 - 40}{13.29} = 1.73$$

$$CR = \frac{6\sigma}{TOTAL\ TOLERANCE} \times 100\% = \frac{26.57}{40} \times 100\% = 66.4\%$$

$$\text{"CAPABLE"}$$

Figure 8-62. Probability plot of shaft movement data for process M, N, O, P, showing relationship of the line of best fit to plot points and specification limits (Problem 5-3).

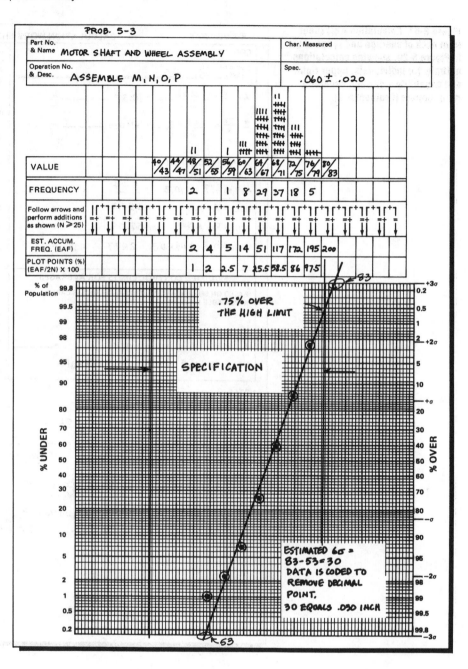

Figure 8-63. Calculation worksheet from back of average and range chart in Figure 8-22, showing calculations of limits for individuals, upper right, and capability index and capability ratio, bottom (Problem 5-3).

PROB 5-3   **CALCULATION WORK SHEET**

CONTROL LIMITS   *LINE M, N, O, P*

SUBGROUPS
INCLUDED _____20_____   _____

$\bar{R} = \frac{\Sigma R}{k} = \frac{236}{20} = 11.8$ _____ =

$\bar{\bar{X}} = \frac{\Sigma \bar{X}}{k} = \frac{1365.2}{20} = 68.26$ _____ =

OR

$\bar{X}'$ (MIDSPEC. OR STD.) = _____ =

$A_2\bar{R} = .577 \times 11.8 = 6.81$ x _____ = _____

$UCL_{\bar{x}} = \bar{\bar{X}} + A_2\bar{R} = 75.07$ =

$LCL_{\bar{x}} = \bar{\bar{X}} - A_2\bar{R} = 61.45$ =

$UCL_R = D_4\bar{R} = 2.114 \times 11.8 = 24.95$ x =

LIMITS FOR INDIVIDUALS
COMPARE WITH SPECIFICATION
OR TOLERANCE LIMITS

$\bar{\bar{X}}$ = 68.26

$\frac{3}{d_2}\bar{R} = 1.290 \times 11.8$ = 15.22

$UL_x = \bar{\bar{X}} + \frac{3}{d_2}\bar{R}$ = 83.48

$LL_x = \bar{\bar{X}} - \frac{3}{d_2}\bar{R}$ = 53.04

US   = 80

LS   = 40

US − LS   = 40

$6\sigma = \frac{6}{d_2}\bar{R}$ = 30.44

MODIFIED CONTROL LIMITS FOR AVERAGES

BASED ON SPECIFICATION LIMITS AND PROCESS CAPABILITY.
APPLICABLE ONLY IF: US − LS > 6σ.

US   =   LS   =

$A_M\bar{R} =$ x   = _____ $A_M\bar{R}$ = _____

$URL_{\bar{x}} = US - A_M\bar{R}$ = $LRL_{\bar{x}} = LS + A_M\bar{R}$ =

FACTORS FOR CONTROL LIMITS

n	A_2	D_4	d_2	$\frac{3}{d_2}$	A_M
2	1.880	3.268	1.128	2.659	0.779
3	1.023	2.574	1.693	1.772	0.749
4	0.729	2.282	2.059	1.457	0.728
5	0.577	2.114	2.326	1.290	0.713
6	0.483	2.004	2.534	1.184	0.701

NOTES

$$C_{PK} = \frac{USL - \bar{\bar{X}}}{3\sigma} \quad OR \quad \frac{\bar{\bar{X}} - LSL}{3\sigma}$$

$$= \frac{80 - 68.26}{15.22} = .77 \longleftarrow \quad \text{"\underline{NOT} CAPABLE"} \atop \text{LESS THAN ONE}$$

$$= \frac{68.26 - 40}{15.22} = 1.86$$

$$CR = \frac{6\sigma}{TOTAL\ TOLERANCE} \times 100\% =$$

$$= \frac{30.44}{40} = 76.1\% \quad \text{"CAPABLE IF PROCESS} \atop \text{AVERAGE IS ADJUSTED"}$$

inside the control limits. The probability plot shows that the estimated process spread (6σ) is 30, with a low value of 53 and a high value of 83. The line of best fit crosses the upper specification limit line at the ".75% over" line, so you can estimate that .75% of the products from this process will be above the upper specification limit.

Figure 8-63 shows that the upper limit for individuals is 83.48, the lower limit for individuals is 53.04, and the estimated process spread is 30.44. These values agree well with those in Figure 8-62.

The capability index (C_{pk}) is shown to be .77 and the capability ratio (CR) is shown to be 76.1%. This process is "not capable as currently set up" but is "capable if the process is adjusted to center on the specification."

The data group A, E, I, M is a mixture of data from the four processes. A capability study of this data would be meaningless as well as unreliable, because the average and range chart in Figure 8-24 shows so many points out of control that the data cannot be used to estimate capabilities.

To summarize this problem, the process average estimated from the probability plots is the value at which the line of best fit crosses the "50% over" line.

The estimated process averages obtained from the probability plots are very close to the process average values estimated from the average and range charts and the histograms. The estimates based on calculations from the average and range charts are most precise when the probability plot points fit a straight line of best fit. When the probability plot points do not fit well with the line of best fit, you should give more weight to the probability plot and histogram in making an estimate of the process average.

Problem 5-4.

The data from Problem 2-4 (signal-to-noise ratio) is used to make a process capability analysis for this problem.

An average and range chart was constructed from this data. (See Figure 8-64.) The calculation worksheet for this chart is shown in Figure 8-65. As shown in Figure 8-64, the subgroup average for sample 19 was outside the upper control limit. The data for this point was thrown out and new control limits were calculated. All remaining points are inside the control limits.

A probability plot was developed from this data. (See Figure 8-66.) The plot points fit very well with the line of best fit, so the calculations for limits for individuals and for estimating the process spread are valid. These calculations are shown in Figure 8-65.

This product has only a minimum specification (15db). The lower limit for individuals is calculated to be 17.68, which indicates that the process is capable of producing all parts above 15 decibels signal-to-noise ratio.

The estimated process average is very close to the median of medians obtained in Problem 3-4 (25.87 versus 26).

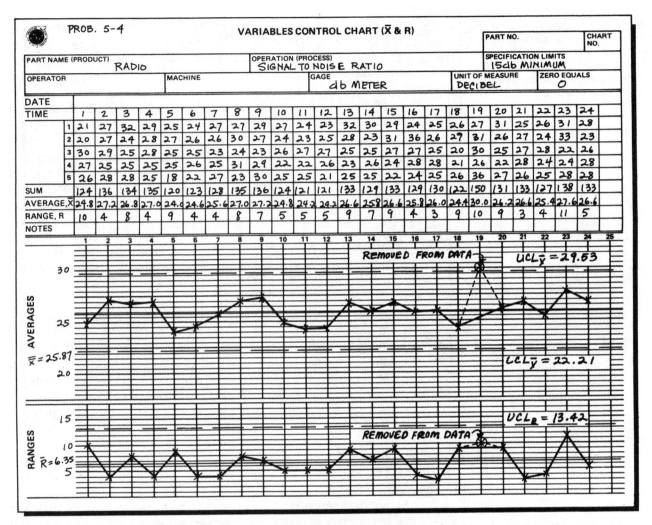

Figure 8-64. Average and range chart of signal-to-noise ratio data, showing a point at sample #19 out of control (Problem 5-4).

The process average can also be estimated with a frequency histogram. Examination of Figure 8-9 shows that the process average is about 26, but the histogram is not as precise as the average and range chart for making such estimates. The capability index (C_{pk}) for this process is 1.33, so this process is capable. When only a minimum specification limit is set the capability index is found with the calculation involving only the lower specification limit. (See Figure 8-65.) When only a maximum limit is specified, only the calculation involving the upper specification limit is used.

Figure 8-65. Calculation worksheet from back of average and range chart in Figure 8-64, showing calculations of control limits, upper left, limits for individuals, upper right, capability index, bottom (Problem 5-4).

PROB 5-4   **CALCULATION WORK SHEET**

CONTROL LIMITS

SUBGROUPS INCLUDED $\underline{\quad 24 \quad}$ $\underline{\quad 23 \quad}$

$\bar{R} = \dfrac{\Sigma R}{k} = \dfrac{156}{24} = 6.5$ $\dfrac{146}{23} = 6.35$

$\bar{\bar{X}} = \dfrac{\Sigma \bar{X}}{k} = \dfrac{625}{24} = 26.04$ $\dfrac{595}{23} = 25.87$

OR

$\bar{X}'$ (MIDSPEC. OR STD.) =   =

$A_2\bar{R} = .577 \times 6.5 = \underline{3.75}$ $.577 \times 6.35 = \underline{3.66}$

$UCL_{\bar{x}} = \bar{\bar{X}} + A_2\bar{R} = 29.79$ $= 29.53$

$LCL_{\bar{x}} = \bar{\bar{X}} - A_2\bar{R} = 22.29$ $= 22.21$

$UCL_R = D_4\bar{R} = 2.114 \times 6.5 = 13.74$ $2.114 \times 6.35 = 13.42$

LIMITS FOR INDIVIDUALS
COMPARE WITH SPECIFICATION OR TOLERANCE LIMITS

$\bar{\bar{X}}$ $= 25.87$

$\dfrac{3}{d_2}\bar{R} = 1.290 \times 6.35 = \underline{8.19}$

$UL_x = \bar{\bar{X}} + \dfrac{3}{d_2}\bar{R}$ $= 34.06$

$LL_x = \bar{\bar{X}} - \dfrac{3}{d_2}\bar{R}$ $= 17.68$

US $= NONE$

LS $= \underline{15}$

US − LS   =

$6\sigma = \dfrac{6}{d_2}\bar{R}$ $= 16.38$

MODIFIED CONTROL LIMITS FOR AVERAGES

BASED ON SPECIFICATION LIMITS AND PROCESS CAPABILITY. APPLICABLE ONLY IF: US − LS > 6σ.

US   =   LS   =

$A_M\bar{R} = $ x $= \underline{\quad}$ $A_M\bar{R} = $ $= \underline{\quad}$

$URL_{\bar{x}} = US - A_M\bar{R} = $ $LRL_{\bar{x}} = LS + A_M\bar{R} = $

FACTORS FOR CONTROL LIMITS

n	A_2	D_4	d_2	$\dfrac{3}{d_2}$	A_M
2	1.880	3.268	1.128	2.659	0.779
3	1.023	2.574	1.693	1.772	0.749
4	0.729	2.282	2.059	1.457	0.728
5	0.577	2.114	2.326	1.290	0.713
6	0.483	2.004	2.534	1.184	0.701

NOTES

$$C_{PK} = \frac{\bar{\bar{X}} - LSL}{3\sigma}$$

$$= \frac{25.87 - 15}{8.19}$$

$$= 1.33$$

THE PROCESS IS <u>CAPABLE</u>.

THE SPECIFICATION IS 15db MINIMUM WITH NO MAXIMUM REQUIREMENT. THE C_{PK} IS CALCULATED USING ONLY THE LOWER SPECIFICATION LIMIT (LSL).

Figure 8-66. Probability plot of signal-to-noise ratio data, showing relationship of the line of best fit to plot points and minimum specification limit (Problem 5-4).

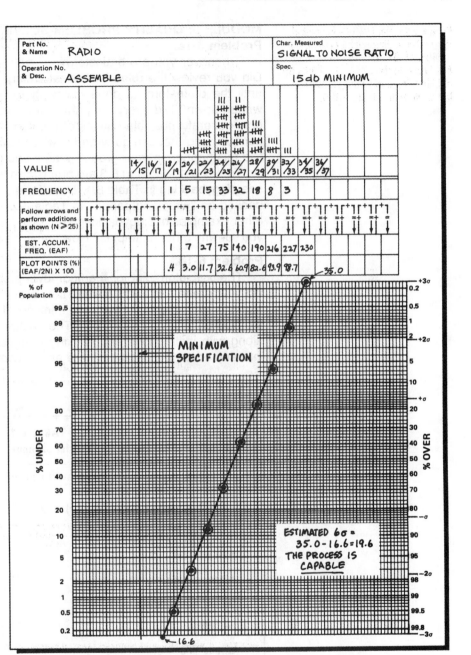

MODULE 6: QUALITY PROBLEM-SOLVING TOOLS
Problem 6-1a.

Whenever you are brainstorming, make sure you check several things. Did you review the rules for brainstorming, such as holding all evaluations until the brainstorm is done? Was there a recorder? Were all the ideas written down? Did everyone participate? Remember, brainstorming doesn't only generate possible causes of problem. It helps build people. The most serious thing that can go wrong is when someone in the group is put down. Did this happen in your group? Was it squared away?

Tables 8-1, 8-2, and 8-3 are brainstorm lists for the fun projects. You can see piggybacking in Table 8-1, Uses for old books: "wall covering" is piggybacked on "wrapping paper." In Table 8-2, Uses for a large red bandanna, other examples of piggybacking are "sling," "bandage," and "tourniquet." Do you see any other examples? How many ideas did your group come up with?

Problem 6-1b.

The brainstorm list for the floor-level problem will depend on what product your group had in mind when they brainstormed. When we did our brainstorm (see Table 8-4), we were thinking of a small product that comes to the packers on a conveyor belt. The packers place it manually into a carton along with instructions and packing materials. We have not put the ideas into any order, but list them here as we wrote them down originally.

TABLE 8-1
Brainstorm, uses for old books (Problem 6-1a).

USES FOR OLD BOOKS

wrapping paper (arts and crafts)	rifle range backstop
wall covering	bird cage lining
fuel sources	novelty
place to hide key	booster chair
props (for construction)	gift
recycling	give to public library
garage sale	prop up leg on coffee table
container	landfill
give to Peace Corps	clothing
paper airplanes	cockroach food

TABLE 8-2
Brainstorm, uses for a large red bandanna (Problem 6-1a.)

USES FOR A LARGE (2 FOOT BY 2 FOOT) RED BANDANNA

fight a bull	tie/scarf
penalty flag for sports	shawl
cleaning rag	diaper
distress flag	pot holder
bandanna	base for baseball game
child's blanket	filter
tablecloth	umbrella
bath towel	sling
polish your shoes	canopy
dye it blue/white and use as a flag	burn it as kindling
bandage	patch
tourniquet	target for gun/arrow
chalkboard eraser	gag
parachute for a cat	window shade
put out a fire	

TABLE 8-3
Brainstorm, uses for old tires (Problem 6-1a).

USES FOR OLD TIRES

recycle—raw material	obstacle course
tire swing	cut up and hook together for mats
sandals	bumpers on cars
planter	playground equipment
erosion control	doghouse
dock bumper	garden border
footholes (football team)	sled in winter
target—ball throwing	hula hoops
insulation	chair
tire races	shoes and boots
recap	buoys, floating apparatus
raft	flooring
bumpers on race course	tower building

TABLE 8-4
Brainstorm, dirt and grease spots (Problem 6-1b).

DIRT AND GREASE SPOTS

packers have dirty hands	grease on packing table
machine drips oil	conveyor has dirt on it
packing material has dirt in it	dirty gloves
product picks up grease on conveyor	box sealer drips oil and grease
fan blows paper dust	product was already dirty when packers got it
product hits greasy bearings	audit inspectors got dirt on it
product not clean before packing	instructions fall on floor and get dirty
we use others' grubby dollies	product falls on floor and gets dirt on it
dirt on packing table	lunch crumbs because packers eat at packing table

---

Problem 6-2.

Figure 8-67 is a cause and effect diagram for cracks and tears in trim molding. How does it compare with the one you developed?

This diagram has four main bones: material, method, machine, and associate. Your diagram should include at least these four.

Keep two things in mind as you study this C and E diagram. First, note that the "associate" bone has no ideas on it. Somehow the brainstorm group missed this area altogether. The group should do another brainstorm—a second pass—to fill in this bone. If the group is new and still lacks confidence in the problem-solving process, they might want to put "associate" on hold while they work on other aspects of the problem. Later, when the group has gained confidence, they can go back and examine "associate."

Second, the cause and effect diagram is a working diagram for a group to use as it tries to see how various ideas relate to each other. There's plenty of room for discussion on how exactly to organize the ideas. Some ideas will fit under more than one main bone. "Scales," for example, appears under both "machine" and "method." If all the heating of the trim mold mix takes place in the mold, "preheat varies" would belong under "mold." The group as a whole should have the final say in the construction of the diagram.

"Environment" is another main area that the brainstorm group could have considered for this problem. Other problems might require other special bones in addition to the five major ones.

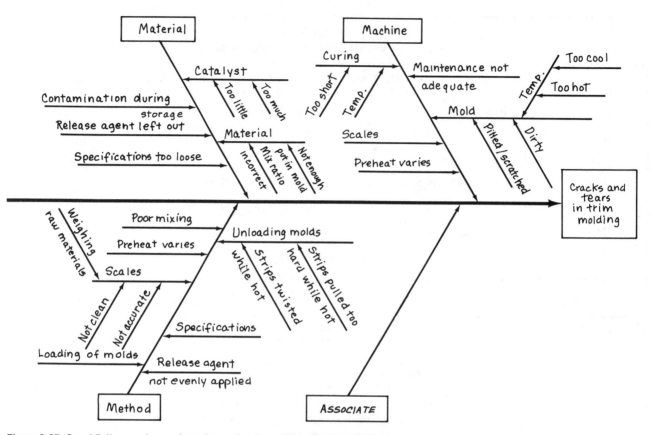

Figure 8-67. C and E diagram for cracks and tears in trim molding (Problem 6-2).

Problem 6-3a.

In this problem the reason for making a Pareto diagram for the three shifts is to see whether unequal supervision contributes to the large number of defective hoses or whether something else is causing the problem. There are two ways to construct the diagram. Either you could combine all types of defects for each shift and then prepare a Pareto diagram of the three shifts or you could prepare three Pareto diagrams, one for each shift, and organize each diagram by types of defects. Which should you do? It will depend on what you find when you look at your data, in this case the audit inspection report.

The first thing to look for in the audit inspection report is whether each shift shows the same rate of defects. Count up the number of defects for each shift. Next, calculate the total inspected for each shift. (See Table 8-5.) Note that the third shift is listed first because it has the most defects.

Now determine the percentage of defects for each shift. Your Pareto diagram should look like Figure 8-68.

TABLE 8-5
Worksheet for Pareto diagram by shifts, Figure 8-68 (Problem 6-3a).

SHIFT	FREQUENCY	CUMULATIVE FREQUENCY	CUMULATIVE PERCENTAGE	NUMBER INSPECTED	PERCENT DEFECTS
third	505[1]	505	33.5	4986[2]	10.13[3]
first	504	1009	66.9	5012	10.06
second	500	1509	100.0	4995	10.01

Calculations:

(1) $26 + 44 + 70 + 347 + 5 + 13 = 505$

(2) $505 + 4481 = 4986$

(3) $(505/4986) \times 100\% = 10.13\%$

Figure 8-68. Pareto diagram by shifts (Problem 6-3a).

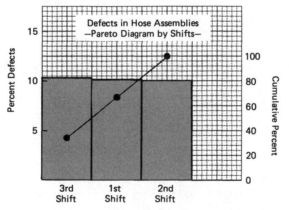

In interpreting the Pareto diagram in Figure 8-68 you can see that all three shifts are producing about the same percentage of defects. On the basis of this diagram you have not found any evidence that unequal supervision is contributing to the problem of defects.

There is something else, however, to compare among the three shifts. All three shifts have the same rate of defects, but they may be producing different kinds of defects. Suppose that when you looked at the inspection report, you found that the first shift produced a lot of hoses that were too short, the second shift produced a large number of hoses with leaks, and the third shift produced large numbers of hoses that were damaged and were missing threads. In that case you should make a Pareto diagram by defects, one for each shift.

TABLE 8-6
Worksheet for Pareto diagram by defects, Figure 8-69 (Problem 6-3b).

DEFECT	FREQUENCY	CUMULATIVE FREQUENCY	CUMULATIVE PERCENTAGE
Leaks	998	998	66.1
Missing threads	209	1207	80.0
Too long	132	1339	88.7
Too short	91	1430	94.8
Damaged	24	1454	96.4
Other	55	1509	100.0

Figure 8-69. Pareto diagram by defects (Problem 6-3b).

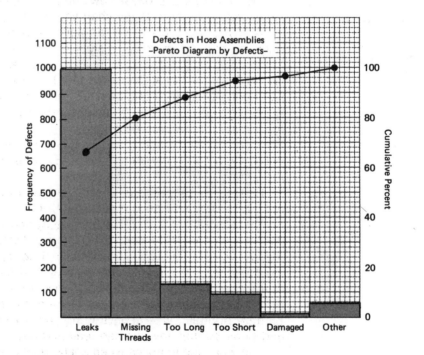

The audit inspection report for this problem shows the same pattern of defects for each of the three shifts. We didn't draw separate diagrams for each shift because we can see that the pattern is the same. Since the numbers and types of defects are common to all three shifts and the percentages are about the same, unequal supervision is not a cause of the defects.

Problem 6-3b.

In Problem 6-3a we have shown that the patterns of defects and the percentages of defects are the same for all three shifts. Therefore we can combine the data for types of defects by shifts when we construct the Pareto diagram. Figure 8-69 shows the Pareto diagram for defects in the hose assemblies. The most frequent defect is leaks, which account for nearly two-thirds of all the defects (see Table 8-6).

Using this diagram, you have strong grounds for recommending to management that they concentrate on solving the problem of leaks in order to reduce the number of defects.

It might strengthen your case if you make Pareto diagrams for defects by shifts. These will show management that leaks are the most serious problem for all three shifts.

Problem 6-4.

Figure 8-70 is a process flow chart for Repair of Metal Component AZ9. How does it compare to the chart you drew?

At first glance, this flow chart appears long and complicated. But this is often the case when we begin studying a process. We can be very surprised at the complexity a flow chart reveals. In order to understand the flow chart for the Repair of Metal Component AZ9, we need to talk about how the chart has been constructed and then what it tells us about the process.

In drawing the chart, we selected the symbol for each step and wrote the number of that step inside the symbol. Next we wrote the description of the step and the company's process number (if any) above the symbol. We noted the time for the step and any distance the part traveled underneath the symbol.

Notice that Step 4 is an inspection: the AZ9 part is either reparable or not. Once this decision is made, the AZ9 moves. The move steps we have numbered as Step 5 and Step 6. The symbols following Step 5 show the flow of the process if the AZ9 is reparable. Likewise the symbols after Step 6 show what happens if the AZ9 cannot be repaired. Be sure to note that the numbering sequence following Step 5 skips to Step 7 and the number of the step following Step 6 skips to 15. Steps 12 and 36 also result from an inspection and involve breaks in the numbering of the steps.

It is important, when constructing your flow chart, that the chart is neat and clear, so that any one can read and understand it easily.

The first thing to notice when analyzing the flow chart for Repair of Metal Component AZ9 is how much time is wasted by delays between operations. To get a good idea of how much time is being wasted, you can calculate the total amount of time for the process and the total time spent waiting. When you compare these times as a ratio, you can easily see the magnitude of this waste. These delays should be one of the first places you and the quality council target for improvement. Begin to ask questions about the delays, such as: Why are there such long waits before operations like "acid

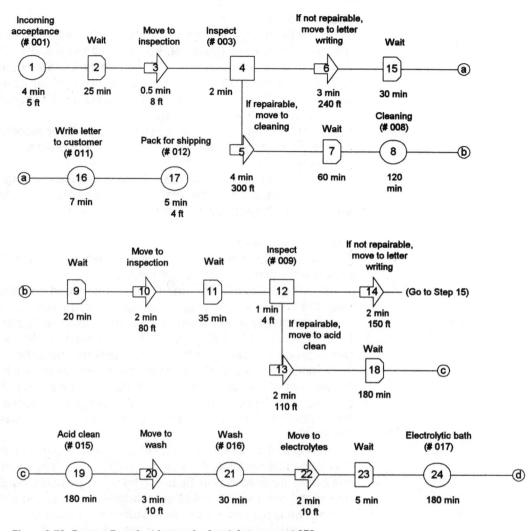

Figure 8-70. Process flow chart for repair of metal component AZ9

clean" (process #015) and "grind" (process #030)? Can improvements in set-up for these operations help reduce the delays? Could changes in batch sizes help? What other improvements can you suggest?

We can use the flow chart in a second round of analysis later if further improvements are required. Now we can select an individual operation, such as Step 32, "grind," for analysis and chart each of its steps. If we include the delays preceding and following this operation, we may be able to make some significant improvements to our overall process.

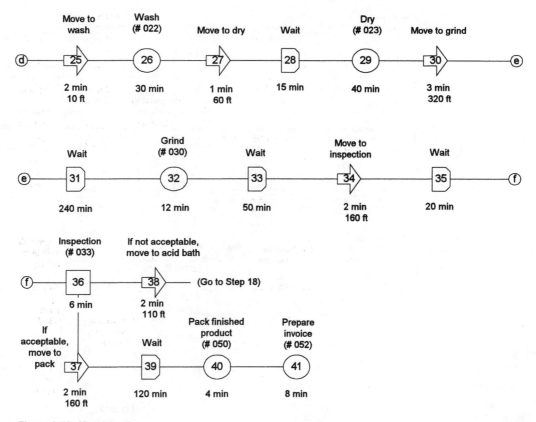

Figure 8-70. (Continued)

Problem 6-5.

(a) Figure 8-71 is the scatter diagram of the data. The diagram shows the plotted variables and the two median lines.

(b) The results of our counts are:

Quarter	Count
Count from right	+6
Count from top	+5
Count from left	+3
Count from bottom	+3
TOTAL	+17

As we move a ruler vertically in from the right side of the diagram, we meet 6 points in the upper right quarter to the right of the vertical median line. The very next point we meet is still to the right of the vertical median but is below the horizontal median line and in a different quarter. Therefore, we stop counting at six. The count for this corner is +6.

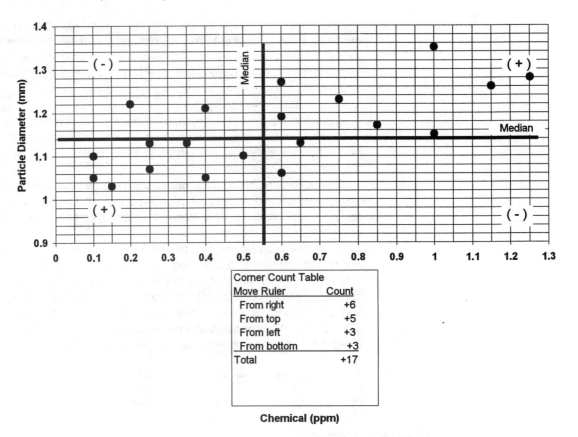

Figure 8-71. Scatter diagram of relationship between diameter of particles and chemical dissolved in water.

When we move the ruler down from the top toward the horizontal median line, we meet 5 points in the upper right quarter. The sixth point is also above the horizontal line but to the left of the vertical median line. So, we do not count it. Our count stops at +5. You will notice that we have already counted 4 of these points when we moved the ruler in from the right. This is not unusual when doing the corner count test.

Counting from the left, we have 3 points. The fourth point lies above the horizontal median line, and we don't count it. Coming up from the bottom, we find 3 points before meeting the fourth point, which lies to the right of the vertical median line.

The results of the four corner counts are all plus counts, and the total of the counts, after dropping the plus signs, is 17. This is higher than the statistician's value of 11. We can conclude therefore that there really is a straight-line relationship.

(c) In this problem, no points stand out as possible errors. But sometimes this is not the case. Supposing we had found a point at 1.2 *ppm* of the chemical and 1.0 *mm* particle diameter. This could be a signal that there is a mistake, either in the particle diameter or in the amount of chemical. Somehow this data point doesn't seem to fit the other data. Such discrepancies can mean a mistake has been made in recording the data. Or it could signal some other problem that would require further study.

Glossary of Terms

A_2—A special factor used to calculate control limits for the averages on the average and range chart.

$\widetilde{A}_2$—A special factor used to calculate control limits for the medians on a median and range chart. $\widetilde{A}_2$ is not the same as A_2, which is used for average and range charts.

assignable causes or special causes—Causes that the production associate can do something about; detectable because they are not always active in the process. We can see assignable causes because they have a stronger effect on the process than chance causes.

attribute chart—A type of chart in which characteristics are not measured in numbers but are considered acceptable or not acceptable, good or bad. The p-chart is an example of an attribute chart.

attribute or counting data—Data that come from nonmeasurable characteristics which can be counted.

attributes—Nonmeasurable characteristics. They are either present or they are not.

average ($\overline{X}$)—The result of dividing the total or sum of a group of measurements by the number of things measured. Average is another term for "mean."

average and range chart—The most commonly used variable chart, also called $\overline{X}$-R ("X bar R") chart.

average range ($\overline{R}$)—The mean or the average value of a group of ranges on an average and range chart. It is used to calculate control limits for both averages and ranges on the average and range chart.

bell-shaped curve—See "normal distribution curve."

boundaries—A line between one interval and the next in the frequency histogram.

brainstorming—A group problem-solving method to bring out many ideas in a short time.

business plan—The part of the policy manual that lists specific projects to be undertaken to improve company oerations.

$\overline{c}$ **(average number of defects for the process)**—Equals the total of defects divided by the number of inspection units. $\overline{c}$ is the average number of defects for the process.

c-chart—A type of attribute control chart that helps monitor the number or count of defects part by part, or by inspection units, in a production run.

capability index (C_p and C_{pk})—The number that expresses the capability of a process or machine. (See "machine capability" and "process capability.") To find this index number, compare the process spread to the specification spread and express it in terms of the standard deviation. The C_p index does not take into account where the process is centered with respect to the tolerance of the part.

capability ratio—The ratio of the machine or process spread (6σ) to the specification tolerance, expressed as a percentage.

cause and effect (C and E) diagram—A diagram that shows in picture or graph form how causes relate to the stated effect or to one another. Also known as a fishbone diagram.

chance causes or system causes—Causes that the production associate can usually do nothing about because they are built into the process. Chance causes are continuously active in the process.

checksheet—A form for collecting data in an organized way so that the data are easy to analyze.

chronic problem—A type of problem that happens over and over again.

connector—A flow chart symbol that indicates a continuation of the process.

continuous improvement—An operating philosophy that works to make every process in an organization better.

control chart—A special type of graph showing the results of periodic small inspections over time, like a movie of the process. A control chart tells when to correct or adjust a process and when to leave it alone.

control limits—Boundaries on a control chart within which the points plotted can vary without the need for correction or adjustment. Control limits are based on past performance and show what can be expected from a process as long as nothing changes.

corner count test—A simple test to determine whether or not a straight-line relationship exists between the two variables on a scatter diagram.

cross-functional teams—Problem-solving groups of associates from among the departments of the organization working cooperatively.

cumulative frequencies—Frequencies added successively on a Pareto diagram.

cumulative percentages—Cumulative frequencies on a Pareto diagram converted to percentages.

customer driven quality—When the wants, needs, and expectations of the customer are the primary considerations in determining all actions of the employees.

d_2—A special factor used with the average range ($\overline{R}$) to determine the standard deviation (σ).

D_4—A special factor used to calculate the upper control limits for ranges on an average and range chart.

$\widetilde{D}_4$—A special factor used to calculate the upper control limits for the ranges on a median and range chart. $\widetilde{D}_4$ is not the same as D_4, which is used for average and range charts.

decision—A flow chart symbol indicating a place in the process being charted where an alternative action may be taken.

delay—A flow chart symbol indicating that there is "waiting" before being able to go on to the next step in a process or component.

dependent variable—The variable that results from, or depends upon, another variable.

empowerment—Giving employees or associates the authority to make decisions relating to their job or work task.

estimated accumulated frequency (EAF)—The accumulated frequency of measurements in a frequency distribution; used to determine the plot points on a probability chart.

estimated process average—1) The value shown at the point where the line of best fit crosses the horizontal 50% line on the probability plot chart; 2) The value $\overline{\overline{X}}$ on the average and range chart.

fishbone diagram—Also known as the cause and effect diagram.

floor solvable problem—A problem in which an assignable cause is present. Often a production associate can find the assignable cause and correct it.

flow chart—See "process flow chart"

fraction defective p-chart—A p-chart that uses fractions instead of percentages. This p-chart shows how many parts are defective compared to the total in the sample. The fractions are usually shown in decimal form.

frequency distribution—The pattern formed by a group of measurements of the same kind of units when the measurements are arranged according to how many times each one occurs.

frequency histogram or histogram—A "snapshot" of a process in block or bar graph form, showing the spread of the measurements in a group of parts and the frequency of each measurement.

in control—A condition in which the points plotted on a control chart vary, but stay inside the control limits. When a process is in control, no assignable causes appear to be at work.

individual and range (X-R) chart—A type of variable control chart based on individual measurements rather than averages or medians of small samples. An X-R chart is helpful in monitoring the manufacture of products made in batches where measurements from the process follow the bell-shaped (normal) curve.

inherent variation—The natural variation in a process, due to chance causes.

inspection—A step in a process flow chart where someone checks or verifies that the task or component meets the requirements.

inspection unit—May consist of one part, such as a batch of rubber, or a group of parts, such as an automobile transmission or electrical system.

internal customer—The next functional group in the process of an organization.

International Organization for Standardization (ISO)—The organization that publishes and administers a series of international standards for the manufacture and distribution of goods and services.

interval or class interval—A division on a frequency histogram marked off by boundaries, and all possible measurements that can fall between those two boundaries.

ISO 9000—An international standard for quality systems management.

line of best fit—A straight line drawn on a probability plot as close as possible to all the data points.

lower control limit (LCL)—The lower boundary above which points plotted on a control chart can vary without the need for correction or adjustment.

lower control limit for averages (LCL$_{\bar{x}}$)—The lower boundary on an average control chart, above which the plotted points can vary without need for correction.

lower limit for individuals (LL$_x$)—The estimated smallest individual part to be produced by the operation. This should not be confused with the lower control limit (LCL$_{\bar{x}}$) for averages.

lower specification limit (LSL)—The smallest acceptable part produced by a process or operation.

machine capability—The short-term ability of a machine to make a part to the specified dimension. Usually measured by comparing the specified dimension to the spread (6σ) of the dimension being produced by that machine.

Malcom Baldrige National Quality Award—An award presented annually to companies in the United States competing in three categories. Winners exemplify performance excellence.

management team solvable problem—A problem in which chance or system causes are at work. To be corrected, it requires basic changes in the process. A management team is primarily responsible for the solution.

mean ($\bar{X}$)—Another term for average.

median—The middle of a group of measurements counting from the smallest to the largest. On the scatter diagram, the median is the line where half the points are on one side and half are on the other.

median and range ($\tilde{X}$-R) chart—A type of variable control chart that uses medians and ranges to determine whether a process needs to be corrected or should be left alone. It is best used in operations that follow the bell-shaped curve and that the associate can easily adjust.

median of medians ($\tilde{\tilde{X}}$)—The middle median of a group of medians, counting from the smallest to the largest; used to calculate control limits for medians.

median of ranges ($\tilde{R}$)—The middle range of a group of ranges on a median and range ($\tilde{X}$-R) control chart, counting from the smallest to the largest; used to calculate control limits for medians and ranges.

midpoint—The point of an interval which is an equal distance between the boundaries of an interval. The midpoint is found by dividing the width of the interval in half and adding this value to the lower boundary.

move—A step in a process flow chart where material, parts, or components travel from one point in the process to another.

n$\overline{p}$ (average number defective for the process)—The number of defective parts in all samples divided by the number of samples taken.

np-chart—A type of attribute control chart that helps monitor the number of defective pieces in a production run.

normal distribution curve—A type of curve in which the measurements tend to cluster around the middle. Because this curve is shaped like a bell, it is sometimes called the bell-shaped curve.

normal probability paper—A special kind of graph paper used to record the probability plot.

operation—A step in a process flow chart where the work is done to complete a task.

out of control—A condition in which the points plotted on a control chart go outside the control limits. This condition indicates that an assignable cause is at work, disrupting the process.

overall mean ($\overline{\overline{X}}$)—The mean or average value of a group of averages from an average and range chart; used to calculate control limits for averages on the average and range chart.

$\overline{p}$ (average percent defective for the process)—On a percent defective p-chart, equals the total number of defectives divided by the total number of parts inspected, then multiplied by 100%. $\overline{p}$ is expressed as a percentage.

$\overline{p}$ (average fraction or proportion defective for the process)—On a fraction defective p-chart, equals the total number of defectives divided by the total number of parts inspected. $\overline{p}$ is expressed as a decimal fraction or proportion.

p-chart—A type of attribute control chart that helps to monitor or control the percent or fraction defective pieces in a production run.

PDCA cycle—Represents PLAN, DO, CHECK, ACT; the basic model for continuous improvement.

Pareto (pa-RAY-toe) analysis—Helps set priorities on which problems to solve first by sorting out the few really important problems from the more numerous but less important ones. Pareto analysis is useful for dealing with chronic problems.

Pareto diagram—A special type of bar graph that records the most frequent problem as the first bar, the next most frequent problem as the next bar, and so on. The Pareto diagram is the picture or graph part of Pareto analysis.

percent defective p-chart—A special type of attribute control chart. This p-chart shows the percentages of units that are defective or do not conform to specifications.

piggybacking—An activity in the brainstorming process by which people build on one another's ideas. It can be used as a prodding technique for brainstorming.

plot points—The points on the probability graph obtained from the frequency distribution of the measurements.

policy manual—A published manual that describes the current manner of operating and how the organization will operate in the future.

probability plot—A method for estimating how well the measurements used to make the average and range chart fit a normal curve. This method also estimates the shape of the distribution.

process capability—The long-term ability of a process or machine to make a part to the specified dimension. Usually measured by comparing the spread (6σ) of the dimension to the specified dimension.

process cause and effect diagram—A type of C and E diagram that follows the product through some or all of the manufacturing or assembly processes.

process flow chart—A diagram that depicts the steps of a particular job or task in sequence. It helps to track the flow of work, parts, or materials through the process of producing a product.

process spread—The width of the curve formed by the frequency distribution. When compared to the specifications, the process spread tells whether the process can make parts within the specifications. Also written as 6σ.

proportion defective p-chart—See "fraction defective p-chart."

Quality System Requirements (QS-9000)—The quality management system standard published by U.S. automobile makers.

R—The symbol for range.

$\overline{R}$—The symbol for average range.

range—The difference between the smallest and the largest of a group of measurements.

sample—Several, but not all, of the possible measurements in a group of one kind of item.

scatter diagram—A graph that shows how two variables may be related.

sigma (σ)—Symbol for standard deviation.

sporadic problem—A type of problem that happens only once in a while.

$\sqrt{}$ (square root)—Symbol for the square root, a special calculation that mathematicians have worked out.

stable process—A situation in which the variations in the product are due to chance causes alone. The product varies in a predictable manner.

standard deviation—A special calculation that describes how closely the measurements cluster around the middle of a normal curve. This number can be used to describe the process spread.

storage—A step in a process flow chart where something, work or materials, etc., is held before going to the next step.

straight-line relationship—A situation where a change in one variable on a scatter diagram results in a change in the other variable. When plotted, you get a straight line.

total quality management (TQM)—A management philosophy that utilizes employee empower-

ment and continuous improvement to meet the wants, needs, and expectations of the customer.

underlying frequency distribution—The pattern created by taking all possible items in a group of the same kind of items and arranging them in a frequency histogram. This pattern will always be the same because it includes all the items.

upper control limit (UCL)—The upper boundary below which points plotted on a control chart can vary without the need for change or correction.

upper control limit for averages UCL$_{\overline{x}}$)—The upper boundary on an average control chart, below which the plotted points can vary without need for correction.

upper limit for individuals (UL$_x$)—The estimated largest individual part to be produced by the operation. This should not be confused with the upper control limit UCL$_{\overline{x}}$) for averages.

upper specification limit (USL)—The largest acceptable part produced by a process or operation.

variable data—Data that come from things that can be measured. The measurements will vary from one piece to the next.

variable chart—A type of chart on which things or characteristics are plotted that are measured in numbers. The average and range ($\overline{X}$-R) chart is an example.

vision or mission statement—A statement that defines the direction of a company and establishes the basic processes to be followed in achieving the vision.

$\overline{X}$—The symbol for average on the average and range chart, pronounced "X bar."

$\overline{\overline{X}}$—The symbol for the average of averages of measurements on the average and range chart. Also called "overall mean."

$\overline{X}$-R chart—A type of variable control chart that uses averages and ranges to show whether the process needs to be adjusted or should be left alone.

Recommended Readings and Resources

1. Brassard, Michael, *The Memory Jogger Plus+*. GOAL/QPC, 13 Branch Street, Methuen, MA 01844.

2. Feigenbaum, A. V. *Total Quality Control*. McGraw-Hill Book Company, 1961.

3. Grant, Eugene L. and Leavenworth, Richard S. *Statistical Quality Control*. McGraw-Hill Book Company, 5th edition, 1980.

4. Imai, Masaaki, *Kaizen*. Random House, 1986.

5. Ishikawa, Kaoru. *Guide to Quality Control*. Quality Resources, 1984.

6. Ishikawa, Kaoru. *What is Total Quality Control? The Japanese Way*. (Translated by Lu, David J.) Prentice Hall, 1985.

7. Juran, J. M. and Gryna, Frank M. *Quality Planning and Analysis*. McGraw-Hill Book Company, 1980.

8. Kume, Hitoshi, *Statistical Methods for Quality Control,* The Association for Overseas Technical Scholarship, Tokyo, 1985.

9. Olmstead, Paul S., and Tukey, John W. "A Corner Test for Association", *Annals of Mathematical Statistics,* Vol. 18, Dec. 1947, pp. 495-513.

10. Ott, Ellis R. *Process Quality Control*. McGraw-Hill Book Company, 1975.

11. Shewhart, Walter A. *Economic Control of Quality of a Manufactured Product*. D. Van Nostrand Company, Inc. Originally published in 1931. Republished in 1980 by the American Society for Quality Control. This is the original book on quality control.

12. Scholtes, Peter R. et al., *The Team Handbook,* Joiner Associates Inc., Madison, WI, 1988.

13. Walton, Mary. *The Deming Management Method*. Dodd, Mead & Company, 1986.

Appendix:
Factors and Formulas

This appendix contains the factors and formulas for calculating control limits for all the control charts described in this book.

Factors and formulas for average and range charts

Sample Size, n	A_2	D_4
2	1.880	3.268
3	1.023	2.574
4	0.729	2.282
5	0.577	2.114
6	0.483	2.004

Upper control limit for averages ($\overline{X}$):
$$UCL_{\overline{X}} = \overline{\overline{X}} + (A_2 \text{ times } \overline{R})$$

Lower control limit for averages ($\overline{X}$)
$$LCL_{\overline{X}} = \overline{\overline{X}} - (A_2 \text{ times } \overline{R})$$

Upper control limit for ranges (R)
$$UCL_R = D_4 \text{ times } \overline{R}$$

Lower control limit for ranges is zero for samples of six or less.

Factors and formulas for median and range charts

Sample Size, n	$\widetilde{A}_2$	$\widetilde{D}_4$
2	2.22	3.87
3	1.26	2.75
4	0.83	2.38
5	0.71	2.18

Upper control limit for medians ($\widetilde{X}$):
$$UCL_{\widetilde{X}} = \widetilde{\widetilde{X}} + (\widetilde{A}_2 \text{ times } \widetilde{R})$$

Lower control limit for medians ($\widetilde{X}$)
$$LCL_{\widetilde{X}} = \widetilde{\widetilde{X}} + (\widetilde{A}_2 \text{ times } \widetilde{R})$$

Upper control limit for ranges (R):
$$UCL_R = \widetilde{D}_4 \text{ times } \widetilde{R}$$

Lower control limit for ranges is zero for samples of six or less.

Factors and formulas for individual and range charts

Sample Size, n	Factor for individuals	D_4
1	2.66	3.268

Upper control limit for individuals (X):
$$UCL_X = \overline{\overline{X}} + (2.66 \text{ times } \overline{R})$$

Lower control limit for individuals (X):
$$LCL_X = \overline{\overline{X}} - (2.66 \text{ times } \overline{R})$$

Upper control limit for ranges (R):
$$UCL_R = D_4 \text{ times } \overline{R}$$

Lower control limit for ranges is zero.

Formulas for p-charts

Upper control limit for p (percent defective):
$$UCL_p = \overline{p} + 3\sqrt{\frac{\overline{p} \times (100\% - \overline{p})}{n}}$$

Lower control limit for p (percent defective):
$$LCL_p = \overline{p} - 3\sqrt{\frac{\overline{p} \times (100\% - \overline{p})}{n}}$$

Upper control limit for p (fraction defective):
$$UCL_p = \overline{p} + 3\sqrt{\frac{\overline{p} \times (1 - \overline{p})}{n}}$$

Lower control limit for p (fraction defective):
$$LCL_p = \overline{p} - 3\sqrt{\frac{\overline{p} \times (1 - \overline{p})}{n}}$$

Formulas for np-charts

Upper control limit for np (number defective):

$$UCL_{np} = n\bar{p} + 3\sqrt{n\bar{p} \times (1 - n\bar{p}/n)}$$

Lower control limit for np (number defective):

$$LCL_{np} = n\bar{p} - 3\sqrt{n\bar{p} \times (1 - n\bar{p}/n)}$$

Formulas for c-charts

Upper control limit for c (count of defects):
$$UCL_c = \bar{c} + 3\sqrt{\bar{c}}$$

Lower control limit for c (count of defects):
$$LCL_c = \bar{c} - 3\sqrt{\bar{c}}$$

Factors and formulas for making capability estimates

Sample Size, n	d_2
2	1.128
3	1.693
4	2.059
5	2.326
6	2.534

Upper limit for individuals:
$$UL_X = \bar{\bar{X}} + 3\bar{R}/d_2$$

Lower limit for individuals:
$$LL_X = \bar{\bar{X}} - 3\bar{R}/d_2$$

Formula for process spread (machine capability):
$$6\sigma = 6\bar{R}/d_2$$

Formula for capability index:
$$C_p = \text{part tolerance}/6\sigma$$
$$C_{pk} = \text{smaller of } (USL - \bar{\bar{X}})/3\sigma \text{ or}$$
$$(\bar{\bar{X}} - LSL)/3\sigma$$

Formula for capability ratio:
$$CR = 6\sigma/\text{part tolerance times } 100\%$$

Index

Other Productivity, Inc. publications that will help you achieve your quality improvement goals.

DOE Simplified
Mark J. Anderson and Patrick J. Whitcomb
ISBN 1-56327-225-3 / Forthcoming

SPC Simplified
Robert T. Amsden, Howard E. Butler, and Davida M. Amsden
ISBN 0-527-76340-3 / 304 pages / $24.95 / Item QRSPC

The Basics of FMEA
Robin E. McDermott, Raymond J. Mikulak, and Michael R. Beauregard
ISBN 0-527-76320-9 / 76 pages / $9.95 / Item QRFMEA

Mistake-Proofing for Operators: The ZQC System
Created by The Productivity Development Team
ISBN 1-56327-127-3 / 96 pages / $25.00 / Item ZQCOP

Target Costing and Value Engineering
Robin Cooper and Regine Slagmulder
ISBN 1-56327-172-9 / 400 pages / $50.00 / Item COSTB1

Quality Function Deployment: Integrating Customer Requirements into Product Design
Yoji Akao (ed.)
ISBN 0-915299-41-0 / 387 pages / $85.00 / Item QFD

Process Discipline
Norman M. Edelson and Carole L. Bennett
ISBN 0-527-76345-4 / 224 pages / $34.95 / Item PDISC

Fast Track to Waste-Free Manufacturing: Straight Talk from a Plant Manager
John W. Davis
ISBN 1-56327-212-1 / 425 pages / $45.00 / Item WFM

Productivity, Inc., Dept. BK, P.O. Box 13390, Portland, OR 97213-0390
Telephone: 1-800-394-6868   Fax: 1-800-394-6286